MW01232573

Berachos
of Praise

MOSAICA PRESS

Berachos
of Praise

Birchos Re'iyah, Shevach, V'Hodaah

RABBI YEHOSHUA FREILICH

Published by Mosaica Press, Inc.
www.mosaicapress.com
info@mosaicapress.com

Special thanks to

Rabbi and Mrs. Hillel Mandel

*for their generosity in making
this project and the publication
of this sefer possible*

לזכר עולם ולעילוי נשמת

In memory of our beloved parents

Yiddu and Judith Mandel

Who, despite having endured the atrocities of the Holocaust and the loss of their extended families, succeeded in building a beautiful family of children, grandchildren, and great-grandchilren who embody the values of Torah, *yiras Shamayim*, and mitzvos

<table>
<tr><td align="center">

אבינו

יהודה בן ר' משה מאנדעל ז"ל

הוריו: ר' משה בן ר' צבי מאנדעל הי"ד

ובלומה בת ר' יעקב שפיצער הי"ד

מהמשפחות המיוחסות בעיר האלמין, הונגריה

אחיו ואחיותיו:

שרה רבקה הי"ד

מנדל (מנדי) הי"ד

חנה הי"ד

יוסף אהרן ז"ל

אסתר ליבא הי"ד

רחל הי"ד

שיינדל בילא הי"ד

יעקב הי"ד

גולדא (גולדי) הי"ד

</td><td align="center">

אמנו

יוטע קרענצא בת ר' הלל הכהן ע"ה

הוריה: ר' הלל בן הרב יצחק יוסף (רבה הראשון של סאמש-אויוואר/גרלה, הונגריה) הכהן הי"ד

ומרים בת הרב אברהם שלמה אליאש (רבה השני של סאמש-אויוואר/ גרלה, הונגריה) הי"ד

אחיה ואחיותיה:

פערל הי"ד

ר' יצחק יוסף ז"ל

רבקה הי"ד

ריקעל הי"ד

חנה הי"ד

אברהם שלמה הי"ד

שרה הי"ד

</td></tr>
</table>

HILLEL AND ADINA MANDEL AND FAMILY
YEHOSHUA AND MIRIAM FREILICH AND FAMILY

In honor of our dear father

Rabbi Shlomo Freilich, *shlita*

Who continues to be a beacon of spiritual light for his children,
grandchildren, great-grandchildren, and great-great-grandchildren
and to all the thousands upon whom he was *mashpia* during the over
sixty years of *rabbanus*

In memory of our dear mother

Rebbetzin Esther Freilich (Radin), *a"h*

An outstanding woman who exemplified a true *ishah tzanuah*,
baalas middos, v'chachamah par excellence
A model of *tefillah* and *shirah*, as well as an outstanding example
of "*kevius*" to all her children, grandchildren, great-grandchildren,
great-great-grandchildren, and all those that knew her

RABBI YEHOSHUA AND MIRIAM FREILICH
RABBI NOACH AND RENA ORLOWEK
RABBI AKIVA AND YOSEPHA FREILICH

"אמר ר' יהודה האי מאן דבעי למהוי חסידא לקיים מילי
דמיטב ואמרי לה מילי דברכות" [בבא קמא ל.]

ביראת כבוד לאבא וסבא היקר וברגשי גיל ושמחה
באים אנו אותך לברך בברכת הנהנין ובברכת השבח,
לרגל הופעת הספר

"ברכות ראיה שבח והודאה"

Berachos of Praise

הספר יוצא לאור לאחר שנים של עמל ויגיעה, פרי בשל , אשר
ניכר בו הנטיעה וההשקיה בלימוד הסוגיות וליבון ההלכות
בדיבוק חברים ושימוש תלמידי חכמים, לאסוקי שמעתתא
אליבא דהלכתא בהל' ברכות המצויות ושאינן מצויות.
רואים אנו בספר זה את תמצית משנתך החינוכית, להנחיל
לנו ולתלמידיך הדור הבא קטנים וגדולים כאחד, לראות תמיד
את טוב ה' בחיי היום יום ובזמנים מיוחדים, אם בדברי מאכל
בברכות הנהנין, אם בנפלאות הבורא יתברך בברכות השבח,
ובכל דבר ודבר בעולם הזה, וכפי ששגור תמיד בפיך הפסוק
"מה רבו מעשך ה' כולם בחכמה עשית" (תהילים קד').
ברכותינו מעומק הלב שתזכה יחד עם אמא שתחי' העומדת
לצידך תמיד בכל פעליך, לראות בנים ובני בנים עוסקים בתורה
ובמצוות, לרוות נחת מכל הבנים והבנות, הנכדים והנכדות,
מתוך בריאות איתנה והרחבת הדעת.

באהבה רבה

יהודה וגיטי פרייליך, פסח ושירה בורק, אלי ויעל
פרייליך, אשר והדסה קידורוף, אלעזר וחוה פרייליך,
משה וטובי פרייליך, והנכדים

הרב ישראל גנס
רח' פנים מאירות 2
קרית מטרסדורף, ירושלים 94423
02-5371782   02-5378927

בס"ד .... *..........*

ראיתי את הקונטרס *......* .... בעניני ברכות הראיה
ושם כתב *......* ר' יהושע פריילך שליט"א, ויש בו תועלת לכלל, כי
הלכות *......* רחוקות אצל הרבה אנשים, *......* ... .
.... את *......* בעוד קונטרסים מועילים לטובת הכלל.

ראיתי את הקונטרס "חידושי הלכות" בעניני ברכות
הראיה אשר כתב הרה"ג ר' יהושע פריילך שליט"א,
ויש בו תועלת לכלל, כי הלכות אלו רחוקות אצל הרבה
אנשים, ולפיכך יש ברכה בו. יהא רעוא שיוסיף תת
תנובה בעוד קונטרסים מועילים לטובת הכלל.

Rabbi Zev Leff

Rabbi of Moshav Matityahu
Rosh HaYeshiva—Yeshiva Gedola Matityahu

בס״ד

הרב זאב לף

מרא דאתרא מושב מתתיהו
ראש הישיבה—ישיבה גדולה מתתיהו

D.N. Modiin 71917   Tel: 08—976—1138 'טל   Fax: 08—976—5326 'פקס   ד.נ. מודיעין 71917

י״ח כסלו תשע״ז
December 18, 2016

Dear Friends,

I have read portions of the manuscript "Birchos Re'iyah and Birchos Shevach Vehoda'ah" by my dear friend and colleague Rabbi Yehoshua Freilich Shlita.

Rabbi Freilich presents a compendium of the halachos of all the various brochos that are made on various sights and experiences. His presentation is impressively detailed and comprehensive, yet organized, lucid and interesting.

Differing halachic opinions are presented where applicable, and all the material is documented as to the sources in the extensive footnotes.

Although I cannot vouch for the halachic veracity of every detail of the presentation—enough information is provided enabling one to intelligently ask his personal Rov for the operable halacha in his specific case.

I commend Rabbi Freilich for a truly magnificent presentation, that will greatly benefit the community with a deep awareness of this area of halacha. I pray that Hashem Yisborach grant Rabbi Freilich and his family life, health, and the wherewithal to continue to merit the community in his many and varied ways.

Sincerely,
With Torah blessings

Rabbi Zev Leff

בס"ד

המכון ע"ש הרב אברהם נחמן וגולדה מרים שוורץ

RABBI A.N. AND G.M. SCHWARTZ INSTITUTE

3737 Clarks Lane, Baltimore, M.D.   רח׳ קצנלבוגן 60, הר נוף, ירושלים

Rabbi **Ephraim Poliakoff,** Rosh Hakollel   הרב **אפרים פוליאקוב,** ראש הכולל

Rabbi Yehoshua Freilich שליט"א is a noted educator in ירושלים and has decided to broaden his role and to become and educator for all of כלל ישראל.

This ספר on the laws of ברכות is a monumental undertaking, representing thorough scholarly research starting from Talmudic sources through the various stages of Halachik exegesis, concluding with the most modern literature on each topic.

The organization and clarity with which each topic is presented is beautiful and engaging, creating an educational paradise for the learned as well as the uninitiated.

I humbly bless Rabbi Freilich שליט"א for his efforts.

תזכה שיפוצו מעינותיך חוצה וישתו רבים לרוות צמאם מהמים שדלית להם

Rabbi Poliakoff

הרב ישעיהו רוטנברג
רב ביהכנ״ס הגר״א בית וגן
ור״מ בישיבת קול יעקב
מח״ס מנחת פרי
רחוב הרב עוזיאל 82 ירושלים
טלפון 02-6423860

בס״ד ניסן תשע״ח

מכתב ברכה

הנה ידידי הרב יהושע פריילִיך שליט״א מפה בית וגן, הביא לפני תכריך
כתבים ספר נכבד בחידושי תורה והלכה בענייני ברכות הראיה, השבח והודאה.
אשר ביודעו ומכירו שכבר יגע ועמל בהלכות אלו זמן רב וברר וליבן הלכות אלו
מפי ספרים וסופרים, וגם דן עמי בכמה בכמה וכמה הלכות, והדברים ערוכים בטוב טעם
ודעת דבר דבור על אופניו.

ובטוחניֵ שכל צורב שיהגה בספר זה יפיק ממנו תועלת ועי״ז יתקלס
ויתפאר שמו יתברך בעולם.

ברכתי שיזכה להפיץ מעיינותיו כהנה וכהנה להגדיל תורה ולהאדירה מתוך
בריות גופא ונהורא מעליא, לאורך ימים טובים ושנים.

הכו״ח לכבוד התורה ועמליה

ישעיהו רוטנברג

מכתב ברכה

כב' ידידי יקירי הר"ר יהושע, הי"ו,

עוסק בחינוך המון שנים ברוב הצלחה ועומד כעת להוציא חיבור
על עניני ברכות בס"ד, על כמה מהענינים שוחחנו יחד, וחזקה
על חבר שלא יוציא מתח"י דבר שאינו מתוקן, ורז"ל הרי אמרו,
האי מאן דבעי למהוי חסידא לקיים מילי דברכות, וברכתי להר"ר
יהושע שימלא חיבורו חן בעיני קוראיו, ויבואו לדקדק ביותר
בעניניס אלו, ותרבה החסידות בישראל.

בכבוד,

צבי שכטר

אלול תשע"ז

RABBI SIMCHA SCHEINBERG
Rosh HaYeshiva Yeshivas Torah Ore

הרב שמחה שייינברג

ראש הישיבה, ישיבת תורה, אור ירושלים

בן מרן רבי חיים פינחס שיינברג זצוק"ל

ט"ו תמוז תשע"ח

בס"ד

מכתב ברכה

בא לפני ידי"נ היקר הרב הגאון ר' יהושע פריילִיך שליט"א מתלמידינו החשובים לשעבר, שהיה קרוב מאוד לאאמו"ר זצוק"ל ותלמודו בידו תכריך כתבים על עניני ברכות הראיה השבח והודאה, ועתה רחש לבו לדבר טוב להוציאם לאור העולם בשפת אנגלית לתועלת הציבור הרחב שיהיה יותר קל להם ללמוד ולהבין בשפה זו.

וניכר מתוך הכתבים כמה הוא השקיע בעניינים אלו את הדקדוק בכל פרט ופרט כדי לזכות את אחינו בני ישראל לקיים הלכות אלו כדת וכדין.

וברכתי ותפילתי ליד"נ שיזכה לברך על המוגמר ושהספר יתקבל ברצון בכרם בית ישראל להרבות כבוד שמים להגדיל תורה ולהאדירה, ושיזכה לכתוב עוד חיבורים חשובים מתוך מנוחת הנפש והרחבת הדעת

הכו"ח לכבוד התורה ולומדיה

6 Panim Merot Street• Jerusalem, PO Box 6967 • 02.537.2928
רחוב פנים מאירות 6 ירושלים ת.ד. 6979 טל.02.537.2928. ישראל

Rabbi Chaim Walkin

7 Kassuto St.
Jerusalem

הרב חיים וואלקין

רחוב קאסוטו 7
ירושלים

כבוד ידיד נפשי יקר יקרים מלא בתורה ויראת שמים טהורה מרביץ
תורה לעדרים, הרב ר' יהושע פריילִיך היו'
אחדשה"ט באה"ר

קבלתי הקונטרס בעניני ברכת הודאה וברכת השבח ונתפעלתי מאד
מדבריך, מבהירות וסידור הדברים, ושם שאלות העולות על הפרק שנדונו
בטוטו"ד וזה יהיה לתועלת גדולה בכל בית.

יתן השי"ת שתזכה בעמלך בתורה לחבר חיבורים מועילים
לזכות את הרבים.

והננו עומדים לקראת השנה החדשה, תזכו אתה וביתך לכוח"ט בספפשצ"ג,
שיתמלאו כל משאלות לבכם לטובה ולברכה, אתם וביתכם וכל אשר לכם.

אשר זעליג וייס
כגן 8
פעיה"ק ירושלם ת"ו

בס"ד

הן ראיתי את הספר הנפלא על ברכות השבח והראיה שחיבר ידידי יקירי
איש מהיר במלאכתו מלאכת לימוד הרה"ג ר' יהושע פריילינך שליט"א. ספר
זה ערוך בשפת האנגלית לתועלת הרבים דוברי שפה זו.
מן המעט שראיתי בספר אכן נוכחתי (לראות) שהספר מקיף מאוד, מצטיין
בבהירות ובישרות, ויש בו גם חכמה וגם מלאכה, והכל ערוך בטוב טעם
ודעת. בטוחני שרבים יהנו מספר יקר וחשוב זה שיש בו הוראה למעשה
בהלכות עמוקות אלה.
ברכתי להרב המחבר שליט"א שיזכה תמיד להגדיל תורה ולהאדירה
בשמחה, שלוה ונחת.

YOUNG ISRAEL OF RIVERDALE
4502 Henry Hudson Parkway ∽ Riverdale, New York 10471

Rabbi Mordechai Willig
718.796.8208

בס"ד

[handwritten Hebrew text]

הנה ידיד ש"ב הר"ר יהושע פרייליך שליט"א חבר ספר על ברכות ראייה וברכות שבח והודאה, והוא ליקוט מדברי שו"ע או"ח ונושאי כליו, וכן מספרי ודברי פוסקי זמננו. ויש בו ידיעות חשובות להלכה ולמעשה, ונכתב בסגנון בהיר לדוברי אנגלית. ויהי רצון שכולנו נזכה להודות להלל לשבח לה' אלקינו ע"פ הלכה ובכונה ראוי', ושהמחבר שליט"א יזכה להמשיך ללמד תורה ולקדש שם שמים מתוך בריאות נחת והרחבה עמו"ש.

[handwritten signature]

About the Author

Rabbi Yehoshua Freilich has been a leading force in women's education for over forty years. As dean and founder of Bnot Chayil Seminary and subsequently Baer Miriam Seminary in Yerushalayim, he has been a constant inspiration to thousands of students, many of whom are prominent leaders in Klal Yisrael today. He has given halachah *shiurim* to students in many of the yeshivos and seminaries in Yerushalayim, as well as to the local women in the Bayit Vegan neighborhood.

In the United States, he studied with Rav Yisroel Eliezer Kanarek, *zt"l*, in the Ohr Hameir Yeshiva of New Rochelle. From there, he continued his studies in Yeshivas Rabbeinu Yitzchak Elchanan, studying with Rav Y.B. Soloveitchik, *zt"l*, and Rav Dovid Lifshitz, *zt"l*. After making aliyah, he became a devoted student of Rav Chaim Pinchas Scheinberg, *zt"l*, studying in Yeshivas Torah Ore. He had a very close relationship with various *rabbanim* in Yerushalayim and a very special relationship with Rav Yehoshua Neubert, *zt"l*, from whom he received much guidance in halachah.

Recently, Rabbi Freilich became the Rosh Kollel of the Dr. Bank Kollel, a *kollel* for English-speaking *baalei batim* in Bayit Vegan. He has been the *rav* of the Acheinu Bnai Yisrael congregation in Bayit Vegan for many years, where he continues to inspire many every Shabbos.

Rabbi Freilich can be reached by phone at (0)54-984-9181 or by email at yfreilich1@gmail.com.

Table of Contents

Acknowledgments

I would like to express my immense thanks for everything connected to this work. First, I thank Hashem for giving me the strength, endurance, and wisdom to prepare these *halachos*. Then, I must thank all who have had a meaningful influence upon me from my early years, beginning with my parents, and later on in life, my in-laws. My father has been a pillar of spiritual light to me. He is an outstanding example of appreciating Torah to the fullest, with *hasmadah* (diligent continuity of study) in learning and true *harbatzas Torah*, sharing the words of Torah with all. *Hakaras ha'tov* (feeling and expressing gratitude) is one of his major themes. He should be well and healthy for many good years. My mother, may she rest in peace, in addition to nurturing me throughout my early years, continued to inspire me spiritually—first, as a *baalas middos* (person of character) par excellence; second, as a model of *tefillah* and *shirah* (joyful praise to Hashem); and finally, as an outstanding example of *kevius* (faithful timely good practice). Mom had a *seder kavua* (set study session) every morning from 5:30am–6:30am studying one *pasuk* of *Tehillim* with all the commentaries; in the course of ten years, she concluded the entire *Tehillim*—a massive learning project that she wrote up in notebooks and which has already been printed.

While unfortunately I did not have the privilege to meet my father-in-law, Yehuda Mandel, *z"l*, a Holocaust survivor, stories about him have taught me worlds of what it means to be an *ish ha'emes*, a person of truth, and a *true* baal *bitachon*. My mother-in law, Yehudit Kohn Mandel Novack, of blessed memory, was a living miracle. A survivor of the concentration camps, followed by other major challenges, she remained a model to all, myself included, as an unmatched pillar of strength. Her fortitude and pride as a Jewess were exceeded only by her incredible positive, optimistic attitude to life. Her legendary autobiography, *The Lilac Bush*, was recommended as a Mussar *sefer* by many great Rabbis. Honorable mention, too, goes to Rabbi Yehuda (Julius) Novack, who was part of our family for so many years. His good spirit, inspiration, and words of Torah will continue to inspire us always.

I must thank Hashem for all the *rebbeim* from my early schooling who made such a strong, positive impression upon me. Later, I was blessed with encounters with great *Gedolim*, who helped me become a true *ben Torah* and who influenced me on the path of a Torah life. These include Rav Reuven Aberman, *zt"l*, Rav Naftali Friedler, *zt"l*, Rav Leib Heiman, *zt"l*, Rav Yisrael Kanarek, *zt"l*, Rav David Lifshitz, *zt"l* , Rav Yehoshua Neuwirth, *zt"l*, Rav Yaakov Perlow (the Novominsker Rebbe), *zt"l*, Rav Chaim Pinchas Scheinberg, *zt"l*, Rav Shimon Schwab, *zt"l*, and Rav Yoseph Dov Soloveitchik, *zt"l*.

More recently, I am grateful for the constant partnership in Torah with Rav Meir Chazan, Rav David Cohen, Rav Aharon Feldman, Rav Yisrael Gans, Rav Yisroel Ber Kaplan, Rav Zev Leff, Rav Yeshayahu Rottenberg, Rav Hershel Shechter, Rav Simcha Scheinberg, Rav Asher Weiss, Rav Chaim Walkin, and Rav Mordechai Willig. A special thanks to Rabbi Ari Enkin, Rabbi Zeev Kraines, Mrs. Esther Trevor (who was also very helpful in the preparation of the seven volumes of *Tehillas Esther*, as well as the *About Bubbie* book), Ms. Dena Rand, and Mrs. Michal Steinberg for their serious editing of the manuscript. Much thanks as well to Rabbi Emanuel Feldman, Rabbi Yaakov Feldheim, Rabbi Michael Kaufman, Rabbi David Refson, Rabbi Sinai, Rabbi Abba Wagensburg, Rabbi Yoel Yehoshua, Rabbi Yehuda Fierstein, Rabbi David Kahn, Rabbi Tzvi Goodman, Mr. Barnea Selavan, and Reb Simcha Steinhauer for their helpful advice. A very special thanks to Rav Zvi Rosen and Rav Efrayim Polikoff for the many hours they spent reviewing the halachic aspects of the manuscript.

I also thank Hashem, of course, for my many good friends who are always a constant support, including Dr. Moshe and Mindy Engelberg, Mr. Melvin Friedman, Rabbi Yaakov Itskowitz, Dr. David and Vivian

Luchins, Rabbi Menachem Kasdan, Dr. David Koenigsberg, Rabbi Avraham Portnoy, Rabbi Yaakov Roseness, and Rabbi Levi Ohrbach and his rebbetzin at Be'er Miriam Seminary.

Additionally, it would be totally ungrateful not to recognize those who gave me great inspiration during my formative youthful years as a National Advisor and later on as Regional Director for NCSY. These were personalities whose great leadership changed the face of American Jewry today. These include Rabbi Pinchas Stolper, Rabbi David Cohen, Rabbi Baruch Taub, and Rabbi Louis Ginsberg, *zt"l.*

As one who grew up in the small Jewish community of Mount Vernon, New York, it is always amazing to recount the quality of various products who were raised there (my childhood friends) and went on to become leaders of Jewish communities and projects all around the United States. Special thanks to them for their part in advising me on different parts of this project. These include Rabbi Herbert Cohen (who was also very involved in helping produce the *About Bubbie* book and *Tehillim*), Rabbi David Friedman, and Rabbi Yoseph Wikler.

I would also like to thank my dear friend for so many years, Rabbi Yaacov Haber, as well as Rabbi Doron Kornbluth, Mrs. Sherie Gross, and the entire Mosaica staff for helping me turn my work into a most beautiful *sefer*.

Finally, the greatest support to me is my own family. This includes my two model *mechanchim*-(educators)-par-excellence brothers-in-law, Rabbi Hillel Mandel (and his wife Adina), and Rabbi Noach Orlowek (and my sister Rena). Reb Hillel, a most outstanding "*mechanech* of *mechanchim*," was always there to give me much-needed "support" and encouragement whenever the goings were getting difficult. I also want to thank my brother Rabbi Akiva and his wife, Yosepha Rochel, who are heavily involved as pillars of *harbatzas Torah* in Milwaukee. May they have continued success in their *avodas ha'kodesh* (holy endeavors), and may they see much *Yiddishe nachas* together with their beautiful families.

I thank Hashem, too, for my wonderful children and their spouses: Yehuda and Gitti Freilich, Pesach and Shira Borak, Eli and Yael Freilich, Asher and Hadassa Kidorf, Elazar and Chava Freilich, and Moshe and Tovi Freilich. I would not be where I am without their constant support and help. May we all merit to see much *Yiddishe nachas* from their delightful children.

Acharon acharon chaviv (saving the best for last) is my dear wife, Miriam, who stands with me through rain and snow. *Sheli shela v'shela sheli*. Without her constant encouragement and advice, this project would never have been completed. She is an ideal of the dedicated wife and devoted mother and grandmother to our very beautiful family. She is an outstanding example of a *yarei Shamayim* (God-fearing person) with a most sensitive heart to the needs of all of Klal Yisrael (the Jewish people). May we merit to live many good and healthy years together.

Introduction

BLESSING HASHEM FOR THE PLEASURES WE OBSERVE

All too often we turn a blind eye to Hashem's natural wonders all around us. Yet, knowing Hashem through His extraordinary world is one of the great responsibilities of a Jew. It is part of the mitzvos of *emunah baShem* (faith), *ahavas Hashem* (loving Hashem), and *deveikus baShem* (cleaving to Hashem). Especially in today's skeptical age, when Hashem's magnificent creations are commonly brushed off as works of "nature," it is all the more important to recognize, internalize, and proclaim the handiwork of Hashem regarding natural occurrences.

There is a wealth of tools for reaching this appreciation. These start with *sefarim* (Torah books), both classics such as *Chovos Halevavos* and recent ones like those of Rav Avigdor Miller, *zt"l*. These *sefarim* detail methodologies for using the universe to attain heights of closeness to Hashem.[1] More immediate is *iyun tefillah*, learning the meaning of the prayers, particularly the *Tehillim* in *Pesukei D'zimra*, which bring an awareness of Hashem's wondrous world. Most directly, Chazal (the Talmudic Sages) instituted the *Birchos Re'iyah*, blessings for wonders that we see, to help us focus on their innate blessedness. Considering how often people turn a blind eye to Hashem's natural wonders, these simple *berachos* (blessings) prove not to be simplistic at all.[2]

Birchos Re'iyah come in a palette of types. There are blessings for impressive panoramas: oceans, mountains, and deserts. There are blessings for dramatic weather formations, such as rainstorms, lightning, thunder, and the rainbow. Some *berachos* focus on beauty, others

---

1   Many other *sefarim* also address the issue, including the *Rambam* in *Mishneh Torah*, the *Chazon Ish* in *Sefer Emunah U'bitachon*, and *Kehilos Yaakov*, *Chayei Olam*.

2   The great *tzaddikim* tell us it is one of Hashem's greatest miracles that He hides all His unbelievable wonders in a way that people aren't struck by them.

on natural phenomena, like elephants, monkeys, dwarfs, and giants. Impressive people also warrant a *berachah*: these include *Gedolei Torah* (Torah sages), monarchs, and leading scholars. Finally, the Land of Israel holds a special place: there are *berachos* for the holy cities, new communities, and *l'havdil*, destroyed ones.

Recently, I had the good fortune to be inspired by the *sefer Sha'ar Ha'ayin* (*A Gate for the Eye*) by Rabbi Eliyahu Ariel from Modi'in Ilit, which delves into the *halachos* (laws) and *hashkafos* (theological concepts) of the *Birchos Re'iyah*. From the first perusal, it was clear how much there is to know and how important it is to study these laws and concepts. As he writes, there is a great deal of ignorance when it comes to these *berachos*. Many people have never learned them, neither from the Gemara nor the *Shulchan Aruch*.

The *Shaar Ha'ayin*'s thesis is that, contrary to the common attitude, one should not be lenient about reciting these blessings. Considering how much they add to the crucial mitzvos of *emunah* and *ahavas Hashem*, people should be reciting them more often than not. This approach, in fact, has been encouraged by leading *poskim* (halachic arbiters).[3]

He explains and refutes many common misconceptions that have led to the present laxness. For example, even when the *poskim* dispute certain details or qualifications for a particular *berachah*, they still recommend that it at least be said in an abridged form (*bli Shem u'Malchus*, without saying Hashem's Name). This reservation has led some people to mistakenly conclude that, in such cases, saying even the truncated *berachos* is questionable. However, the *poskim* clearly state the opposite; namely, that reciting these *berachos* in reduced form is the "proper and laudatory behavior of a Jew."[4]

This confusion likely has arisen from the difference in this regard between *Birchos Ha'nehenin*—blessings over physical pleasure—and *Birchos Re'iyah*—blessings over Hashem's wondrous creations. When

---

3   See recommendations in *Shaar Ha'ayin*, including those by Rav Chaim Kanievsky, Rav Moshe Sternbuch, Rav Avraham Genichovsky, Rav Moshe Karp (Kiryat Sefer).

4   See various examples: *OC* 218:9, *OC* 219:3:9 *Nisim*, *OC* 225:2 *Bar Mitzvah*, *OC* 224:10 *Mishnah Berurah* 14; *Matziv Gevul Almana*, *OC* 225:10:32 *Shekachah Lo B'olamo* (beautiful things), *OC* 225 *Mishna Berurah* 31, *Meshaneh Habriyos* (animals).

there is a doubt whether one needs to recite one of the *Birchos Ha'nehenin*, such as *Hamotzi*, the *halachah* is not to recite it.[5] However, for *Birchos Re'iyah*, the duty to praise Hashem is the greater, and, therefore, one looks for ways to recite them even when in doubt.[6]

Indeed, many people hesitate reciting them when in doubt. There is a widespread notion that these *berachos* are always optional (*reshus*). One possible source for this mistake is in *Eruvin* (40b), where the *berachah* of *She'hecheyanu* is ruled optional (*reshus*); however, *Magen Avraham* (*Orach Chaim* 225:6) and *Mishnah Berurah* (*Orach Chaim* 225:9) clarify that this is true **only** for the *berachah* of *She'hecheyanu* (and the related *berachah Hatov V'ha'meitiv*). Moreover, they say, the word *reshus* (optional) means only that one is not punished for failing to recite the *She'hecheyanu*. It still remains "most praiseworthy" to take advantage of any opportunity to do so.

Finally, some people assume that the obligation to say *berachos* upon seeing wondrous sights is predicated on feeling some excitement (*hispaalus*). Since almost everything today is familiar and people rarely feel excited, they assume the obligation does not apply.

However, many *poskim* explain that one's feelings are only relevant to the *berachos* of *She'hecheyanu* and *Hatov V'ha'meitiv*, whose obligations are based on the happiness that comes from newness.[7] In contrast, Chazal made *Birchos Re'iyah* incumbent based on objective standards.[8] Regardless of any amazement one may or may not feel, they are considered obligatory by most authorities.[9]

---

5   Because of the principle *"safek berachos l'hakel."*

6   See *P'nei Yehoshua, Berachos* 54a, *Tzlach* and *Rambam, Hilchos Berachos* 10:26.

7   See *OC* 223:3:4.

8   *Mishneh Torah, Berachos* 10; *OC* 218:3, *Mishnah Berurah* 12, 13. Various *berachos* show the power of Hashem in different ways (e.g., *Oseh maaseh vereishis, She'kocho u'gevuraso malei olam, Meshaneh ha'berios, She'asah nissim*).

9   The role of inspiration may be a factor in questionable situations; however, whenever the necessary criteria are met, one is obligated to recite the *berachah* regardless. Nevertheless, inspiration may be connected to the halachah that in many cases one only recites a *berachah* if one has not seen the phenomenon within thirty days. For a full discussion of this point, see *Shaar Ha'ayin*, pp. 30, 48.

Seeing the *Birchos Re'iyah* in this light inspired me to undertake the present *sefer*, to provide guidance for the English-reading public for when to recite these crucial *berachos*. Besides *Shaar Ha'ayin* and its *mekoros* (sources), I referenced other halachic works, spoke to *poskim*, and appended select comments on *hashkafah*. Additionally, I expanded the scope of the work to include *berachos* and *tefillos* (prayers) similar in concept to the *Birchos Re'iyah*, such as *Kiddush Levanah*, the laws of visiting the *Kosel* (the Western Wall), cemeteries, procedures pertaining to sleep, and a whole section on *Birchos Shevach V'hodaah* (Blessings of Praise and Thanksgiving), including the all-purpose "joy" *berachah*, *She'hecheyanu*.

The *berachos* of *Shevach V'hodaah* mark specific occasions, ranging from surviving potentially fatal circumstances to celebrating lifecycle events[10] to receiving good news. In truth, the *Birchos Re'iyah* address particular scenarios. But our thanksgiving and praise should never be confined only to prescribed occasions. We are enjoined constantly to strive higher, to further sensitize ourselves to appreciate the "great" good and extraordinary wonders that Hashem provides us ("*Modim anachnu lach*"). As Chazal teach, the wise will naturally take wisdom further ("*Ten l'chacham veyechkam od*," Mishlei 9:9).[11]

Wherever a person travels, two phrases should be part of his vocabulary: "*Ma rabu ma'asecha Hashem*—How **numerous** are your wondrous creations, Hashem" (Tehillim 104:24), and "*Ma gadlu ma'asecha Hashem*—How **great** are your wondrous creations, Hashem" (Tehillim 92:6). And whenever a person receives special benefits, he must remember and balance the other two classic verses: "*Bishvili nivra ha'olam*—The world was created for me," and "*Anochi afar ve'efer*—I am

---

10   *Bris, pidyon ha'ben*, certain birthdays, and so on.

11   The *sefarim* suggest a three-pronged approach. First, we need to simply **look**; we tend to not even see the special things around us and about us. Second, we must **think** about how special they are and stop taking them for granted. We must consider how almost every system, both in the human body and outside us, is so complex; just realizing their brilliance will bring us to a completely different view of the world. This will make it easier to remind ourselves that objects are not just physical, but are works of Hashem. Third, after raising our awareness, our emotions can chime in, so that we feel **excited and amazed** about the creations of Hakadosh Baruch Hu.

dust and ashes." Hopefully, these *pesukim* (verses) together with the blessings taught in this *sefer* will bring us closer to a world in which we are truly cognizant of and grateful for the beautiful kingdom of *Hashem Yisbarach*.

A NOTE ABOUT THE HALACHAH IN THIS SEFER

As the author of this halachic *sefer*, *hineni he'ani mi'maas,* I feel a degree of trepidation as we go to press. There is a special *tefillah* which is recited by many before Torah learning every day, praying to Hashem *"shelo ekashel b'dvar halachah*—that I should not stumble in matters related to halachah." Two major concerns emerge in writing a *sefer* on halachah. First, that we may not be relating the correct halachah; and second, that the halachah may not be transmitted clearly. I pray to Hashem that I should not be guilty of any of these deficiencies.

In our halachic system, many times we find a multitude of opinions. I have tried to list the more accepted opinions followed by additional opinions either in the text or notes. The *sefer* provides many sources that enable the reader to further research the material. I have tried to enhance the halachah with some *sevara*, especially in the notes, so that one should be able to appreciate the logic of the halachic process. In this regard, I have included numerous halachic Sephardic opinions as well, since the Sephardic world of halachah is as variegated and as colorful as the Ashkenazic.

In conclusion, I have tried to present some halachic guidelines so that one can become familiar with the basic halachic parameters of these *berachos*. With all the above in mind, I recommend that one consult a *rav posek* to clarify the proper way of action.

Chazak chazak v'nischazek.

Birchos Re'iyah

Chapter One

Birchos Re'iyah

A. GENERAL HALACHOS OF *BIRCHOS RE'IYAH*

1. The Obligation

Birchos re'iyah are considered obligatory by many authorities.[1]

One who is clearly obligated to recite the *berachah* must say it with *Shem u'malchus* (Hashem's name and kingship). If he says the abridged version without *Shem u'malchus* (e.g., *Baruch oseh maaseh vereishis*), he has not fulfilled his obligation and must still recite the full *berachah*.[2]

Among the Sephardic communities, there are two customs in this regard. Some follow the ruling of Rav Ovadiah Yosef, who writes that **many** of these *berachos* should be recited in full, in accordance with the opinion of *Shulchan Aruch*.[3] Others follow the opinion of *Ben Ish Chai* and recite many of the *berachos* in the abridged version.[4]

One who is unsure whether the *berachah* is necessary should still recite the abridged version in order to praise Him. In general, when one is forced to recite *birchos re'iyah* and *shevach* in their abridged version because of halachic doubt, they must still be treated with the same devotion and seriousness as regular *berachos*.[5]

---

1 *Shaar Ha'ayin, Iyunim,* sect. 6; *Shulchan Aruch OC* 218:3; *Piskei Teshuvos* 218:1, especially note 4; *Rambam, Mishneh Torah, Berachos* 1:4; cf. *Hasagos Raavad* ad loc.; *Rif, Berachos* 44.

2 *Shaar Ha'ayin,* p. 38.

3 For discussion on this subject, see *Yalkut Yoseph* 3, p. 622, and *Shaar Ha'ayin,* p. 38.

4 *Ben Ish Chai (Eikev* 1:16) *See Ohr L'Tzion* 2:14:47; *Shaar Ha'ayin,* p. 38, note 12.

5 *Shulchan Aruch OC* 218:9, 219:3, 9; *Rama OC* 225:2, 224:14; *Mishnah Berurah* 225:32. *P'nei Yehoshua, Berachos* 54a, points out that since we derive the concept of *Birchos Hodaah* from Yisro, who expressed an abridged version of a *berachah* in *Shemos* 18:1 by reciting a special praise to Hashem for saving the Jewish People, one fulfills the basic idea of blessing in this form. For a full discussion on this matter, see *Shaar Ha'ayin,* p. 39, note 15, and *Iyunim,* p. 191.

9

2. Who Is Obligated?

Men and women are equally obligated to recite *birchos re'iyah*. Some authorities question whether women are exempt from *Birkas Ha'chamah* and *Kiddush Levanah* because they must be recited at a particular time (time-bound *berachos*).[6]

A blind person is generally exempt from most *birchos re'iyah* and does not recite any *berachah*. However, there are two *berachos* where there is basis for him to recite them. In the case of the *berachah* over seeing kings, if the blind person feels the atmosphere of the visit, he should recite the full *berachah*.[7] Similarly, he should also recite the *berachah* of *Kiddush Levanah*.

An *aveil*, even in the *shivah* period, is not exempt from *birchos re'iyah*. However, an *onein* is exempt until burial.[8]

A minor should be trained to recite *birchos re'iyah*.[9]

3. Degree of Inspiration

- Most authorities opine that one should recite a full *berachah* on phenomena that are considered objectively inspirational and worthy of praise according to the criteria of the Sages, even if one is not personally inspired. For example, even if one does not get excited upon seeing great oceans or very tall mountains, he should still recite the *berachah*.[10]

- However, there are "gray" areas where certain phenomena may be inspirational to some individuals but not others. In such cases, authorities rule that those who are inspired may recite a full *berachah*.[11] For example, some authorities assert that one

---

6   See *Shaar Ha'ayin*, pp. 45, 107 for more details.

7   *Mishnah Berurah* 224:11; *Shaar Ha'ayin*, p. 45, 143, and *Iyunim* 13. This is based on the fact that this *berachah* is recited on the "honor" that is displayed to the king and not necessarily upon seeing the "actual" person. The *Pri Megadim* points out that if he is blind from birth, he should recite the abridged *berachah*.

8   *Piskei Teshuvos* 229:6; *Kaf Hachaim* 229:8; *Halachah Berurah* 229/11.

9   *Shulchan Aruch OC* 215:3.

10 *Shaar Ha'ayin*, p. 48. See also Rabbi Yisroel Pinchos Bodner, *Halachos of Brochos for All Seasons*, p. 570.

11 *V'Zos Haberachah* (p. 155) explains that all authorities agree that a *berachah* is required on exceptional mountains even if the individual is not personally moved by seeing them. But

may recite the full *berachah* on any **tall** mountain that personally inspires one to feel the greatness of Hashem. (See section B2a on mountains for examples.)

There are various authorities who point out that one who lives right near a particular phenomenon, such as an ocean or a desert, may not be required to recite the *berachah*, even if he hasn't actually seen the sight within the last thirty days, because of his (over)familiarity with the site. Even according to this opinion, this does not apply to one who lives in another area of a city that is far from the site.[12] However, many opinions hold that as long as one has not seen the phenomena for at least thirty days, he is required to recite the *berachah*.[13]

4. Standing or Sitting

Although it is praiseworthy to stand while reciting *Birchos Re'iyah*, one is not halachically required to do so.[14] However, one should stand for *Kiddush Levanah*, as it is likened to *hakbalas p'nei haShechinah* (greeting the Divine Presence).[15] *Birkas Ha'gomel* should also be recited while standing because it is compared to the bringing of the *korban todah* (thanksgiving offering) in the Beis Hamikdash and because of

---

there is also a "subjective standard" requiring a *berachah* (without *Shem u'malchus*) upon seeing mountains and natural phenomena only if one is personally moved by their appearance. Outstanding peaks usually have individual names. It is reported that the Brisker Rav and the Steipler Rav recited the *berachah* the first time they saw the Judean Hills on their first trip to Yerushalayim, but not when seeing them thereafter (*Peninei Halachah, Harchavos*, p. 216; *Shaar Ha'ayin*, p. 92:4; *Vayehi Binsoa*, p. 85).

12   *Halichos Shlomo, Tefillah* 23:28; *Shaar Ha'ayin*, p. 44; *Iyunim*, pp. 259. For a full discussion, see the opinion of Rav Elyashiv in *Shaar Ha'ayin* that this principle only applies to the *berachah* over *avodah zarah* (*Shulchan Aruch OC* 224) but not to other *berachos*. I heard from Rav Mordechai Willig that the principle of "familiarity" with various phenomena can be applied today even when only seen in books, encyclopedias, and other media. This is among the reasons why several authorities are lenient regarding reciting these *berachos* nowadays. For an extensive treatment of this topic, see *Shaar Ha'ayin*, Introduction, pp. 27–31, and *Nesivos Haberachah*, p. 421, note 16, and p. 435, note 68.

13   *Nesivos Haberachah* 29:10, note 16.

14   *Shaar Ha'ayin*, p. 48, note 44; also see *Shut Chut Shani* (*Birchas Hodaah*), p. 183, where he writes that the *minhag ha'olam* is to stand unless one is in the middle of learning Torah.

15   *Sanhedrin* 42a; *Rambam, Mishneh Torah, Berachos* 10:17.

kavod ha'tzibbur (honor of the congregation).[16] (See Chapter 15, "Birkas Ha'gomel.")

5. View

Ideally one should attempt to get the best view of the phenomena. Many opinions permit one to recite the *berachah* even if it is observed from a great distance, such as from the window of an airplane, as long as one can see it clearly.[17] In addition, many authorities rule that one may recite the *berachah* even if one cannot see the entire phenomena, as long as one sees clearly a substantial part of it (i.e., the ocean or desert, etc.).[18] However, if it is foggy and one cannot see it clearly, one should not recite the *berachah*. Even if one only sees the phenomena through binoculars or a telescope, they may still recite the *berachah*.[19]

Presence

One should recite the *berachah* as long as he is still in the presence of the site. Once he has left, most authorities rule that the *berachah* may no longer be recited. Nevertheless, one does not necessarily need to be looking at the site when reciting the *berachah*; it suffices for him to be adjacent to it. As such, he may recite the *berachah* from a siddur. Similarly, one may still recite the *berachah* even if the site is temporarily covered by a cloud.[20] However, if it is foggy and one cannot see the phenomena clearly, a *berachah* is not recited.

---

16 *Sanhedrin* 42a; *Rambam, Mishneh Torah, Berachos* 10:8, with *Kesef Mishnah* commentary; *Chasam Sofer OC* 511. See *Pri Megadim*, introduction to *Hilchos Berachos*; *Shaar Ha'ayin*, p. 48 note 44 and *Nesivos Haberachah* 29:3.

17 *B'Tzeil Hachochmah* 2:16; *Shaar Ha'ayin* 2:2, note 3, and *Iyunim* for more discussion, but see note 8, where he quotes the *Shevet Halevi* who disagrees.

18 *B'Tzeil Hachochmah* 2:16; *Shaar Ha'ayin* 2:5; *Shaar Ha'ayin*, p. 48, *Iyunim* 9 (p. 244–45) and 18. This is the view of many authorities, including Rav Elyashiv. See *Shaar Ha'ayin* 2:5, which quotes Rav Elyashiv and Rav Chaim Kanievsky.

19 *Shaar Ha'ayin*, p. 52 (2:11). However, if the telescope uses mirrors to reflect images to the eye, one may not recite the *berachah*.

20 As long as one did not take one's mind off the site (*Shaar Ha'ayin*, p. 58). If one falls asleep during a drive or while on a beach, he may still recite the *berachah*.

Night

Many authorities rule that one may recite the *berachah* at night if one can still clearly see the site, i.e., water or desert.[21]

6. How Often?

In general, *birchos re'iyah* may not be recited if one has seen the particular phenomenon within the last thirty days.[22] Most authorities rule that even if one did not recite the *berachah* upon seeing it the first time, he may only make the *berachah* on a second sighting if thirty days have passed.[23]

7. Interruptions

One may recite *birchos re'iyah* even in the middle of saying the blessings before and after the reading of the *Shema* (*birchos k'rias Shema*), though preferably one should make the *berachah* at the break between the sections.[24]

One should interrupt one's Torah learning in order to recite these *berachos* when seeing these phenomena.[25]

8. On Behalf of Others (*Motzi*)

One person may make these *berachos* with the intention of fulfilling the obligation of others who listen to his words. Those present must also intend that their personal obligation will be met by their listening.

---

21   *Shaar Ha'ayin* 2:5 quotes Rav Elyashiv and Rav Chaim Kanievsky. See *Halichos Shlomo, Tefillah* 23:26, which adds that one may only recite the *berachah* if he can see well enough to be truly inspired by the site. See also *Shaar Ha'ayin*, p. 100, who quotes the *Maharsham* that one may recite a *berachah* on a rainbow at night. However, see the opinion of *Shevet Halevi*, quoted in *Shaar Ha'ayin*, p. 245, that seeing in a non-conventional way does not require a *berachah*.

22   One does not make *berachos re'iyah* upon seeing the same type of sight within less than thirty days because there is not enough *hispaalus* (excitement) in seeing the phenomena. There are some exceptions to this rule (e.g., lightning, thunder, rainbow, cemeteries, etc.) which will be explained in further chapters.

23   *Shulchan Aruch OC* 224:12; *Biur Halachah* 218, s.v. *Ba'makom ha'zeh*; *Shaar Ha'ayin*, p. 42. Cf. *Minchas Shlomo* (1:73) who permits one who has already left the place to recite a *berachah* under certain conditions.

24   *Mishnah Berurah* 66:19; *Shevet Halevi* 11:58. See also the laws of lightning and thunder, below.

25   See *Shaar Ha'ayin*, p. 68, note 41, for further discussion.

However, it is questionable whether one who has already made his *berachah* may recite it again to be *motzi* (fulfill for others) people who have not yet recited it.[26]

9. Similar Phenomena—Including Future Items

As mentioned above, one does not recite *birchos re'iyah* on a particular item unless he has not seen the item within thirty days. There is discussion among the *poskim* whether one needs to recite a new *berachah* when he will be seeing either **similar** (but not the same exact one) or different phenomena that require the same *berachah* in the course of the day (or within thirty days).[27] For example:

- When seeing mountains and deserts while traveling
- When seeing different cemeteries
- When seeing various animals at a zoo or game park
- When seeing different kings

a. Natural Phenomena

Natural phenomena can be divided into four categories: (a) bodies of water; (b) mountains; (c) steep cliffs;[28] and (d) deserts.

Two Different Categories with Same Berachah

If one knows that on the same day he will be seeing two **different** categories (i.e., mountains and later an ocean, or cliffs and later a desert), one should definitely recite a new *berachah* on the second sighting, even though the text of that *berachah* is the same as the *berachah* made on the first sighting.

---

26   *Mishnah Berurah* 46:13. See discussion in *Shaar Ha'ayin* (pp. 46–47). Rav Elyashiv and Rav Chaim Pinchas Scheinberg are of the opinion that *areivus* (mutual responsibility) does not apply under these circumstances, and one may not make a *berachah* for another person.

27   *Mishnah Berurah* 224:17. There are two questions to be asked: (1) Does seeing a similar item, i.e., two different bodies of water or two different cemeteries, require a new *berachah*? Or do we consider the general category as one? (2) Can one recite a *berachah* on an item (that has the same *berachah*) when it is not immediately in front of them?

28   Note: Many authorities consider cliffs and mountains as two distinct phenomena.

Same Category

If the additional phenomena will be in the **same** category (i.e., additional but different bodies of water, sets of mountains or cliffs, etc.), there are different opinions among the *poskim* whether one is required to recite a new *berachah*. Many authorities opine that one should still recite individual *berachos* on each item as they experience it,[29] while other authorities opine that in these situations, one should avoid reciting the full *berachah* upon the second item.

b. Animals, Cemeteries, and Kings

There is a similar discussion among the authorities whether one who sees **different** animals (especially monkeys and later elephants) or two cemeteries must recite a new *berachah* on the second sighting.[30]

See individual *berachos* for more details and examples.

See the individual categories for more examples.

B. *OSEH MAASEH VEREISHIS*—WHO MAKES THE WORK OF CREATION

1. Introduction

עַל יַמִּים וּנְהָרוֹת, הָרִים וּגְבָעוֹת וּמִדְבָּרִיּוֹת, אוֹמֵר: בָּרוּךְ...עוֹשֶׂה
מַעֲשֵׂה בְרֵאשִׁית.

---

29   *Orchos Rabbeinu* 1:182, quoting *Chazon Ish*; *Ashrei Ha'ish* 38:23, quoting Rav Elyashiv; *Chazon Ovadiah*, p. 467; I heard this from Rav Goelman in the name of Rav Chaim Pinchas Scheinberg. This was also the opinion of Rav Shlomo Zalman Auerbach. Rav Vosner recited *berachos* on a different set of mountain ranges in the Alps each day (heard from Rav Ganz). See also *Aruch Hashulchan OC* 224:8, and *Ahaleich B'Amitecha* 16:20, 17:10 and 18:7, 9 (see notes there). Rav Betzalel Stern says that to avoid halachic doubt, when one makes a *berachah* on one item, he should intend to exclude all other items. See *V'Zos Haberachah*, pp. 155–56. See *Shaar Ha'ayin*, p. 43, and *Iyunim* 11, p. 256), and *Peninei Halachah, Harechavos*, p. 220, about including Hashem's name. For a full discussion on this matter, see *Sh'ar Ha'ayin*, p. 243, 251–58; and *Nesivos Haberachah*, p. 751.

30   Based on *Mishnah Berurah* 224:17. See discussion in *Piskei Teshuvos* 224:11, notes 57, 58, and 225:23; *Shaar Ha'ayin* pp. 42–43. Some authorities want to make a distinction between more stationary items (i.e., oceans and mountains) which would not require a new *berachah*, and mobile items (i.e., animals, kings, cemeteries, etc.), which would require a new *berachah*. Some authorities disagree and suggest reciting the *berachah* without including Hashem's name.

> Upon oceans, rivers, mountains, hills, and deserts, one says, "Baruch...Oseh maaseh vereishis—Blessed...Who makes the work of Creation."[31]

The Sages teach that one who witnesseses natural phenomena that evoke a feeling of the greatness and power of HaKadosh Baruch Hu should recite the *berachah* of *Oseh maaseh vereishis*. These phenomena include oceans, rivers, lakes, mountains, hills, deserts, and other exceptional sights.[32]

One should seek opportunities to behold these wonders in order to be able to recite the *berachah*. *Rambam* writes:

> What is the path [to attain] love and fear of Him? When a person contemplates His wondrous and great deeds and creations and appreciates His infinite wisdom that surpasses all comparison, he will immediately love, praise, and glorify [Him], yearning with tremendous desire to know [Hashem's] great name, as David stated: "My soul thirsts for Hashem, for the living God." (Tehillim 42:3)[33]

Thus one should seek opportunities to behold these wonders in order to be able to recite the *berachah* and have a greater appreciation of Hashem. Contemporary authorities have written that our sense of awe and amazement when encountering Hashem's creations, unfortunately, is not as strong nowadays as it was in earlier generations. Hopefully, a proper deeper study of these subjects and halachos of these *berachos* will arouse within us a heightened awareness of Hashem's magnificent universe.

---

31 *Shulchan Aruch* 228:1.

32 *Berachos* 54a.

33 *Rambam, Mishneh Torah, Yesodei HaTorah* 2:2. *Tzelach* (*Berachos* 54a) explains that the *berachah* is worded "*oseh*" (in the present tense) rather than "*asah*" (in the past tense) because it is also recited upon seeing lightning and hearing thunder, which are happening in the present. See, however, *Magen Giborim* (as quoted in *B'Seiser Raam*, p. 2, note 6) who suggests that the language "*oseh*" refers to the concept of "ongoing creation" i.e., "*ha'mechadesh b'tuvo b'chol yom tamid maaseh vereishis*—Every moment the world is considered newly created." See *Rambam* ibid., 1:1–5, and *Ohr Hachaim, Bereishis* 2:3.

2. Mountains, Craters, and Other Natural Wonders

a. Mountains

One who sees exceptionally high mountains (or mountain ranges) that are awe-inspiring should recite the *berachah* of *Oseh maaseh vereishis*:

- Some authorities write that this *berachah* may only be recited upon seeing the world's most outstanding mountains, such as Mount Everest, the Alps, the Pyrenees, the Andes, the Rockies, the Himalayas, and Mount Hermon.[34]

- Other authorities assert that one may recite the full *berachah* on any tall mountain or mountain range that personally inspires one to feel the greatness of Hashem. In Israel, this may include the mountains of Edom (seen in Eilat on the Jordanian side), Mount Meron, Mount Tavor, and Mount Carmel.[35] In the United States, this may refer to the Catskills,[36] Bear, and Pocono Mountains, among others. (For a more extensive list, see end of section).

In this case, if one is in doubt of his level of inspiration, one should recite the *berachah* without *Shem u'malchus*: *Baruch atah oseh maaseh vereishis*.[37]

b. Unique Rock and Mountain Formations

One who sees unique rock or mountain formations (*geva'os*),[38] craters, or very steep (hanging) cliffs should at least recite the abridged version of the *berachah*. If one is very moved by them, one may recite the *berachah*

---

34   *Shulchan Aruch OC* 228:3; *Aruch Hashulchan OC* 228:1.

35   The midrash (*Yalkut Shimoni, Shoftim* 47, based on *Yirmiyahu* 46:18), teaches that Mount Tavor and Mount Carmel vied for the opportunity to be the mountain upon which the Torah would be given, based on their great size. (They were both rejected because of their arrogant character.) See *Tehillim* 68:17 and 89:13. See also *Shaar Ha'ayin*, p. 93.

36   I heard in the name of Rav David Feinstein that one may recite a *berachah* upon seeing the Catskills. See also *V'Dibarta Bam*, p. 112,where it seems that this was the opinion of Rav Moshe Feinstein.

37   See earlier for a fuller discussion on this topic

38   *Shulchan Aruch OC* 228:3; *Peninei Halachah*, p. 304; *Shaar Ha'ayin*, p. 375. For a discussion on the differences between *harim* and *geva'os*, see *Ahaleich B'Amitecha* 16:3, *Shaar Ha'ayin*, p. 94, and *Halachos of Brochos for All Seasons*, p. 569. See also *Mor U'Ketzia* 228, which connects the word *givah* to *migba'as*, referring to the pointy hat of the Kohen that resembles a sharp cliff. See *Halachah Berurah*, p. 480, for other differences.

in full. This includes steep and wide canyons in the Grand Canyon, very high cliffs in Yosemite National Park, and the special rock formations in Zion National Park (Utah).[39] In Eretz Yisrael, this might include places like Mount Gamla (which has the form of a camel), Masada (which has very high cliffs), and Mount Arbel. Upon seeing the cliffs of Rosh Hanikra and craters in southern Israel, such as the *Machtesh Ha'gadol*, *Machtesh Ha'katan*, and *Machtesh Ramon*, the abridged version of the *berachah* should be recited.

c. Similar Phenomena

There is a halachic basis for one to recite a full *berachah* upon seeing a new mountain range even though he has recited the *berachah* on a different one within the last thirty days. However, some authorities question this practice.[40]

In the case of seeing two different types of phenomena, such as one who first sees mountains and then steep cliffs, a full *berachah* may be recited for each. Examples of this would be one in Eretz Yisrael who sees the steep cliffs at Mount Arbel and later on sees Mount Hermon or seeing Massada and later on the mountains of Edom (Eilat). Similarly, one who is touring National Parks in the United States (e.g., Grand Canyon, Zion National Park, Yosemite, etc.) and sees a variety of phenomena may make separate *berachos* on each experience.[41]

---

39   A number of authorities (Rav Dovid Cohen and others) rule that one may recite the full *berachah* on these places. See *Nesivos Haberachah*, p. 438.

40   See before for more discussion. See *V'Zos Haberachah*, pp. 155–56. According to Rav Shlomo Zalman Auerbach, one may recite the full *berachah* on a different set of mountains. This was also the opinion of Rav Chaim Pinchas Scheinberg (heard from Rav Goelman). Rav Vosner recited *berachos* on a different set of mountain ranges in the Alps each day (heard from Rav Ganz). See also *Aruch Hashulchan OC* 224:8 and *Ahaleich B'Amitecha* 16:20. Some authorities disagree and suggest reciting the *berachah* without including Hashem's name. See *Shaar Ha'ayin*, pp. 43–15, and *Iyunim* 11, p. 256, and *Peninei Halachah, HaRechavos*, p. 220, for a full discussion.

41   Especially in the Grand Canyon, Zion National Park, or Yosemite Park, etc.

3. Bodies of Water

a. The Ocean

The Mishnah in *Berachos* tells us that one must recite *Oseh maaseh vereishis* on seas and rivers. It then quotes the opinion of Rabbi Yehudah, who says that one should recite a special *berachah* of *She'asah es ha'yam ha'gadol* on the *"yam ha'gadol"* (the "great sea"). The question among the commentaries is whether the *yam ha'gadol* is the major water body that surrounds the world, i.e., the Atlantic and Pacific Oceans, etc., or whether it refers to the Mediterranean Sea, which is next to Eretz Yisrael, which is the "Great Land."

Many authorities rule that one recites the *berachah* of "'ברוך אתה ה אלוקינו מלך העולם שעשה את הים הגדול...—*she'asah es ha'yam ha'gadol*" when seeing any section of the ocean. This includes the following interconnected bodies of water: the Atlantic, Pacific, Indian, Arctic, and Antarctic Oceans, the Caribbean and North Seas, the Gulf of Mexico, and the Long Island Sound. These authorities opine that the words *yam ha'gadol* refer to any part of the great ocean surrounding the globe.[42] Other authorities rule that one should only recite the *berachah* of *Oseh maaseh vereishis*.[43]

b. The Mediterranean Sea

Many authorities rule that one recites the *berachah* of *Oseh maaseh vereishis* on this sea.[44]

---

42 *V'Zos Haberachah*, p. 154, in the name of Rav Yosef Shalom Elyashiv; *Minchas Yitzchak* 1:110; *Mishnah Berurah* 228:2, *Shaar Hatziyun* §3; *V'Aleihu Lo Yibol* (Rav Shlomo Zalman Auerbach), p. 123. This is also the view of Rav David Feinstein as well as many Sephardic authorities, cited in *Halachah Berurah* 228:2. However, see *Yalkut Yosef* 228:4, who recommends saying the abridged *berachah* (without the name of Hashem).

43 Based on *Mishnah Berurah* 228:2, also heard in the name of Rav Chaim Pinchas Scheinberg; *Shaar Ha'ayin*, p. 80, also quotes this as the opinion of Rav Chaim Kanievsky.

44 Based on *Mishnah Berurah* 228:2, also heard in the name of Rav Chaim Pinchas Scheinberg; *Chayei Adam* 63; *Aruch Hashulchan OC* 228:4. *Shaar Ha'ayin*, p. 80, quotes that this is also the view of Rav Yosef Shalom Elyashiv and Rav Chaim Kanievsky.

However, other authorities, including various Sephardic opinions, rule that one should recite the special *berachah* of *She'asah es ha'yam ha'gadol* upon sighting the Mediterranean Sea.[45]

Various authorities **recommend** that, when seeing the Mediterranean, it is proper to combine the two *berachos* in the following way:

בָּרוּךְ...עוֹשֶׂה מַעֲשֵׂה בְרֵאשִׁית שֶׁעָשָׂה אֶת הַיָּם הַגָּדוֹל.

Baruch...oseh maaseh vereishis she'asah es ha'yam ha'gadol."[46]

c. Seas

One recites the *berachah* of *Oseh maaseh vereishis* upon seeing large seas, such as the Black Sea, the Baltic Sea, the Persian Gulf, and in Eretz Yisrael, the Red Sea,[47] the Sea of Galilee,[48] and the Dead Sea.[49] Some authorities rule that one omits Hashem's name when making a *berachah* upon seeing the Dead Sea.[50]

---

45   The opinion of the *Shulchan Aruch OC* 228:1 is that the title "*Yam Ha'gadol*" is appropriate for the Mediterranean Sea due to its proximity to Eretz Yisrael, which is also called *gadol* (great). See *Bamidbar* 34:7 and *Rashi, Devarim* 1:7. See also *Shevuos* 47b. Rav Yaakov Kamenetsky (based on the *Shiltei Giborim*) argues that the Mediterranean is an extension of the Atlantic, and therefore the appropriate *berachah* would also be *She'asah es ha'yam ha'gadol*. The Sephardic opinion recommended in *Halachah Berurah* 228:2 is to recite a combination of the two *berachos*, as brought in the body text, but see *Birkas Hashem* 3:2, *Kaf Hachaim* 228:5, *Ohr L'Tzion* 2:14:40, note 40, which opine reciting only the *berachah* of *Oseh maaseh vereishis*.

46   *Minchas Yitzchak* 1:110. This is also the view of Rav Shlomo Zalman Auerbach (*V'Aleihu Lo Yibol*, p. 126.) Regarding whether such "add-ons" constitute a *hefsek* (interruption), see *Shulchan Aruch YD* 328, with *Shach, Taz,* and *Perishah* 328:2, concerning the *berachah* over *hafrashas challah*, and whether one should say *l'hafrish terumah challah* (*Shach* rules that it is permitted, while *Taz* says that it is forbidden). See *Shaar Ha'ayin*, p. 81, note 11, and *Piskei Teshuvos* 228:2.

47   *Shaar Ha'ayin* 8:21. Cf. *Halachically Speaking*, vol. 2, who cites Rav Yisrael Belsky as saying that no *berachah* is recited.

48   *Shaar Ha'ayin* 8:21; *Mor U'Ketzia* (*Yaavetz*) 228; *Chazon Ovadiah*, p. 469; *Halichos Shlomo, Tefillah* 23–27.

49   *Ohr L'Tzion* 2:14:40. I personally heard this in the name of Rav Neuwirth. See *Birkas Shmuel*, p. 501; Rav Elyashiv, *Ashrei Ha'ish* 38-14; Rav Nissim Karelitz, *Chut Shani*, p. 185. They hold that a sea does not need to be from the Days of Creation—as long as it is not man-made. (see Addendum 1)

50   Rav Chaim Pinchas Scheinberg suggests reciting the *berachah* without including Hashem's name. See *Halichos Shlomo* 23, note 43, and *Shevet Halevi* 9:47, who holds that no *berachah* is necessary. *Chazon Ovadiah*, p. 469, recommends thinking the words of the *berachah* (*hirhur*).

The Dead Sea

There is an interesting discussion among the authorities whether seeing the Yam HaMelach (Salt Sea, or Dead Sea) warrants reciting the *berachah* of *Oseh maaseh vereishis*. Some rule that the criterion for the *berachah* is that the phenomenon must date back to the Six Days of Creation. This seems to be indicated by the *berachah*'s translation: "Who makes the work of Creation."

It is unclear whether the Yam HaMelach was around at the time of Creation. The Torah writes: "The Valley of *Sidim*, which is the Salt Sea" (*Bereishis* 14:3). *Rashi* there explains, "Eventually, when Sodom and Amorah are overturned, water [from the Jordan River] will enter into it and it will become the Salt Sea."[51] Similarly, *Malbim* (*Bereishis* 13:10) comments that the Salt Sea was formed from the waters of the Jordan River in the same way that the overflow of the Nile in Egypt inundates the surrounding land. These sources would imply that the Yam HaMelach is a later development and was not in existence from the Six Days of Creation.

However, a number of other sources indicate that the Yam HaMelach existed from the Six Days of Creation. The Talmud (*Bava Basra* 74b) mentions seven bodies of water, among them the *Yama D'Sedom*—the Sea of Sodom, which surrounded Eretz Yisrael from the time of Creation. This is based on the verse in *Tehillim* (24:2) that states: "He established it [Eretz Yisrael] upon seas." Rav Yaakov Emden, in his work *Mor U'Ketzia*, suggests that the Yam HaMelach was originally a small body of water that later became the larger one we see now, and therefore one can definitely recite a *berachah* on it.

In truth, one may ask whether *any* body of water can be traced back to the Six Days of Creation. We know that there were various floods in history that may have altered the world's bodies of water.[52] The most famous is the flood in the days of Noach. There was also the less-famous flood in the days of Enosh, when the waters of the Great Ocean

---

Some authorities suggest that to avoid doubt, one should recite the *berachah* when he can also see the Judean Desert and/or the Jordanian mountains at the same time. See addenda at the end of this section.

51   *Rashi, Bereishis* 14:3, based on *Bereishis Rabbah* 42:5.
52   See *Malbim, Bereishis* 8:22.

inundated one third of the world's surface. According to the Talmud (*Yerushalmi, Shekalim* 6:2), the water from these floods filled up various seas and oceans, including parts of the Mediterranean, right up to the shores of Akko and Yaffo, as well as various points along the Italian coastline (see *Rashi, Bereishis* 6:4).

Thus, there are various authorities who rule that the *berachah* of *Oseh maaseh vereishis* may be recited even on sights and wonders that were not actually around at the time of Creation, as long as they came about as a result of **Hashem's direct intervention** and not as a result of human activity.[53] This would include any phenomena (bodies of water [rivers, lakes], rock formations, and craters, etc.) that seem to have been formed as a result of "natural" consequences. They support their opinion with the following observations:

- We recite *Oseh maaseh vereishis* on lightening, even though the bolt one sees was not around at the time of Creation.
- The wording of the *berachah* may be understood as praising Hashem as the Creator at the time of Creation.

In addition, some authorities rule that we may assume that all major natural phenomena were around at the time of Creation unless we know otherwise.[54] In conclusion, there is a basis for one to recite the full *berachah* of *Oseh maaseh vereishis* on the Yam HaMelach.[55]

I heard that Rav Yehoshua Neuwirth offers an interesting suggestion. He says that in order to avoid halachic doubt, one should try to recite the blessing from a vantage point where one can see the Yam HaMelach and the Judean Desert (or the Jordanian Mountains) at the same time.[56]

d. Rivers

Many authorities rule that one may recite the *berachah* in full when seeing the massive rivers of the world, such as the Nile (4,258 miles—the

---

53   See *Shaar Ha'ayin*, p. 314, for further discussion.

54   *Shaar Hatziyun* 228:8.

55   *Mor U'Ketzia* 228, *Ashrei Ha'ish* (*Birkas Re'iyah*), *Chut Shani* (*hodaah*), p. 185, and I heard that Rav Neuwirth held this opinion. Other authorities suggest reciting the *berachah* without *Shem u'malchus*; (see *Shaar Ha'ayin*, p. 85).

56   *Shaar Ha'ayin* 8:8, note 22.

longest river in the world), the Mississippi-Missouri (3,900 miles), the Amazon (4,000 miles), the Volga (2,266 miles), the Danube (1,800 miles), and even the Hudson River (315 miles).[57]

Other authorities question this practice and suggest that one recite the *berachah* without including Hashem's name.[58] Many Sephardic authorities rule that one does not recite the *berachah* on most rivers today.[59]

e. Lakes

Many authorities opine that one who sees huge lakes that are not man-made should recite the *berachah* of *Oseh maaseh vereishis*. These include, for example, the Great Lakes and the Great Salt Lake in the United States, and Lake Victoria in Africa.

f. Similar Phenomena—Different Bodies of Water

As mentioned above, one does not recite the *berachah* if one has seen the same body of water within the last thirty days, even if he did not recite the *berachah* the first time.[60]

Many authorities opine that one who makes a *berachah* upon seeing a specific body of water, and then sees a different one within thirty days, may recite a full *berachah*. For example, one who sees the Mediterranean and later sees the Sea of Galilee, or one who sees the Atlantic Ocean and then sees Lake Michigan, may recite a new *berachah*.[61] Others question

---

57 See *Shaar Ha'ayin*, p. 90, note 7; *Mishnah Berurah* 228:4, *Shaar Hatziyun* §8; *Aruch Hashulchan OC* 228:2. This is the ruling of Rav Chaim Kanievsky and many other authorities.

58 *Shaar Ha'ayin*, p. 90. See *Eishel Avraham* 228, which points out that many rivers may not be from the time of Creation, or are man-made (even partially—Rav David Feinstein), and therefore a *berachah* is not recited on them. Moreover, perhaps they are merely the runoff from the melted snow of nearby mountains. Some stipulate that the river must be very wide. This might be why *Kitzur Shulchan Aruch* and *Chayei Adam* do not mention rivers. See *Berachos* 59b.

59 See *Shulchan Aruch OC* 228:2. They only allow the *berachah* to be recited upon seeing the four rivers emanating from Eden (*Bereishis* 2:11–14), which might include the Nile, Euphrates, and Tigris rivers. For full discussion, see *Shaar Ha'ayin*, p. 91, note 8.

60 *Mishnah Berurah* 228:2. If one already saw it and did not recite a *berachah*, many opinions say that one can no longer recite the *berachah*; see *Biur Halachah* 218, s.v. *Ba'makom ha'zeh*, but see the opinion of Rav Shlomo Zalman Auerbach in *Minchas Shlomo* 1:73, that one may still recite the *berachah* (*Shaar Ha'ayin*, p. 42).

61 *Halichos Shlomo*, *Tefillah* 23:26; *Peninei Halachah*, *Harchavos*, p. 21, rules that one may recite the *berachah* on separate bodies of water. See also *Shaar Ha'ayin*, p. 86, who rules that one traveling from the Mediterranean to the Atlantic can recite the *berachah* of *She'asah es ha'yam ha'gadol*.

this practice and would recommend that one should recite the *berachah* without including Hashem's name.[62] However, all authorities agree that if one sees the Atlantic Ocean and later sees the Pacific Ocean, a new *berachah* should not be recited (as it is all considered the same ocean).

Travel from Eretz Yisrael to America

As people travel from Eretz Yisrael overseas to North or South America, they pass over two major bodies of water (first the Mediterranean Sea and then the Atlantic Ocean), which may have different *berachos*, as discussed above. Various authorities rule that **one** *berachah* of *Oseh maaseh vereishis* for both should be said.[63] Other authorities rule that one says *Oseh maaseh vereishis* on the Mediterranean and *She'asah es ha'yam ha'gadol* on the Atlantic Ocean.[64]

Travel from America to Eretz Yisrael

Many authorities suggest that one recites one *berachah* of *She'asah es ha'yam ha'gadol*[65] (or *Oseh maaseh vereishis*) for both bodies of water at the beginning of the trip.[66] Other authorities are of the opinion that one should recite the *berachah* of *She'asah es ha'yam ha'gadol* on the Atlantic Ocean and *Oseh maaseh vereishis* on the Mediterranean.[67]

---

62 *Shaar Ha'ayin* 8:9. The question is whether two bodies of water are too alike to warrant a separate *berachah*. See *Piskei Teshuvos* 228:2, note 17.

63 *V'Zos Haberachah*, p. 154, in the name of Rav Moshe Shternbuch, says that when one says *Oseh maaseh vereishis*, he should add the words *she'asah es ha'yam ha'gadol*.

64 *Shaar Ha'ayin*, p. 86, quotes this in the name of Rav Chaim Kanievsky, Rav Elyashiv. But see *B'Tzeil Hachochmah*, which says that one recites one *berachah* of *She'asah es ha'yam ha'gadol* for both. See *Peninei Halachah, Harchavos*, p. 211, for a discussion of whether one *berachah* can be recited for phenomena not in front of them.

65 *Shaar Ha'ayin*, p. 86, note 28, brings the opinion of Rav Elyashiv and others; also *V'Zos Haberachah*, p. 154, in the name of Rav Shternbuch. The *berachah* of *She'asah es ha'yam ha'gadol* includes the future bodies of water. Others explain this *p'sak* that it seems to take into account the opinion of the *Levush* that the Mediterranean is considered a continuation of the Atlantic Ocean, and therefore one *berachah* is recommended, based on the principle of *safek berachos l'hakel* (Rav Zvi Rosen). This was also the opinion of Rav David Feinstein. The opinion of Rav Chaim Pinchas Scheinberg was to recite one *berachah* of *Oseh maaseh vereishis* and add the words *She'asah es ha'yam ha'gadol*.

66 *Shaar Ha'ayin*, p. 86:11; *Chedvasa D'Hilchasah*, p. 186. This was also the opinion of Rav David Feinstein and Rav Moshe Shternbuch (to say *She'asah es ha'yam ha'gadol*), while Rav Chaim Pinchas Scheinberg recommended saying *Oseh maaseh vereishis*.

67 *Peninei Halachah, Harchavos*, p. 211, considers it two separate oceans.

4. Deserts

One who sees a desert should recite the *berachah* of *Oseh maaseh vereishis*.[68] Halachically, a desert is defined according to the following criteria:

- It has existed since the Days of Creation.[69]
- It is not naturally suitable for habitation because of its dangerous and oppressive heat (or cold).[70]
- Its soil is not suitable for the growth of any "normal" vegetation.[71]

This would include major deserts such as the Sahara in North Africa, the Colorado Plateau, the Mojave (in California, Nevada, Utah, and Arizona), Death Valley (California and Nevada), the Atacama, the Judean Desert,[72] the Sinai, the Negev, as well as the Antarctic,[73] and the Arctic Circle.

There are grounds to recite the full *berachah* upon seeing even a small section of a desert or when seeing it from a great distance (e.g., from an airplane).[74]

5. Other Exceptional and Unusual Sights

a. Volcanoes, Geysers, Waterfalls, and Caves

There are different opinions among the authorities as to whether the full *berachah* may be recited when seeing other natural phenomena that offer a magnificent sight of natural power and beauty. This would

---

68 Some rule that one must be in the middle of the desert, while others rule that it is sufficient to simply get a good look at the desert, such as by standing in Neve Yaakov or other sections of Yerushalayim and looking out at the Judean Desert (*Peninei Halachah*, p. 213).

69 See *Rashi* (*Yeshayahu* 40:12) who writes that the world was "one-third desert at the time of Creation."

70 *Iyov* 38:26: "A desert in which there is no man." See *Metzudas David* ibid.

71 *Bamidbar* 20:5: "No water to drink." There is hardly any rainfall (no more than 10 in/25 cm per year).

72 *Midbar Zif*, also called *Midbar Yehudah*. See *Radak*, *Tehillim* 63:1.

73 See notes in *Shaar Ha'ayin*, pp. 97, 484, regarding whether it is considered a desert or an ocean.

74 *Shaar Ha'ayin*, p. 45.

include phenomena such as volcanoes,[75] geysers,[76] outstanding "beautiful" waterfalls,[77] and stalagmite caves.[78] There seems to be an interesting *machlokes* among the authorities whether the list mentioned in the Talmud includes only examples of the more common phenomena, or whether this is the full list upon which the Sages established the *berachah*. There are grounds to recite a full *berachah*.[79] Most authorities agree that one may definitely recite the full *berachah* upon seeing Niagara Falls.[80]

b. Eclipses

Some authorities rule that when seeing a solar or lunar eclipse, the *berachah* is recited without including Hashem's name.[81]

---

75 Ibid., p. 76, note 41, quoting Rav Nissim Karelitz. I heard this also in the name of Rav Yisrael Ber Kaplan. *Tehillim* 104 begins and concludes with the words, "*Barchi nafshi es Hashem*—My soul, bless Hashem!" and includes the praise, "*Hamabit la'aretz va'tirad, b'harim v'ye'eshanu*—He Who looks at the earth and it quakes; He touches the mountains and they emit smoke."

76 I heard this from various authorities, including Rav Yisrael Ber Kaplan.

77 *Shaar Ha'ayin*, p. 76, reports that Rav Vozner recited the *berachah* upon beautiful waterfalls.

78 *Shaar Ha'ayin*, p. 76:10. See also *Ohr L'Tzion* 2:88:62, who rules that the *berachah* is recited in full. Rav Ovadiah Yosef (*Halachah Berurah* 228:7) questions whether they were in existence from the Days of Creation.

79 Rav David Cohen and Rav Aharon Feldman told me that the phenomena listed in *Shulchan Aruch* are only meant as the more common examples. This is also the view of Rav Shmuel Vosner (quoted in *Shaar Ha'ayin*, p. 77). See also *Peninei Halachah*, p. 311.

80 The *berachah* on Niagara Falls is based on either its amazingly beautiful and majestic appearance (see previous note) or, as others point out, the *berachah* may be said because of its position as the continuation of a river (Niagara) between two major lakes, Erie and Ontario. See *Shaar Ha'ayin*, p. 76; see *Halachos of Brochos for All Seasons*, p. 568, especially notes 103–4.

81 See the discussion in *Shaar Ha'ayin*, p. 76, whether a *berachah* may be recited upon something (like an eclipse—*Sukkah* 29a) that is a *siman kelalah* (a bad omen). See *Aruch L'Ner* (*Sukkah* 29a) and *Gilyonei HaShas* (Rav Yosef Engel, *Berachos* 54a) for interesting discussion on this topic. *Chazon Ish* and Rav Chaim Kanievsky hold that a *berachah* is not recited on a *siman kelalah*; see *Berachos* 6:3. Others disagree (including Rav Elyashiv, *Yissa Yosef*, vol. 3, *OC* 2:56). In any case, it is important that one should be inspired from all the acts of Hashem and not only from the things that we are accustomed to see; see *Chovos Halevavos*, *Shaar Cheshbon Hanefesh* 3:23.

Chapter Two

The Berachos over Lightning and Thunder

A. INTRODUCTION

עַל הַזִּיקִין, וְעַל הַזְּוָעוֹת, וְעַל הַבְּרָקִים, וְעַל הָרְעָמִים, וְעַל הָרוּחוֹת
אוֹמֵר: בָּרוּךְ...שֶׁכֹּחוֹ וּגְבוּרָתוֹ מָלֵא עוֹלָם

On comets, on earthquakes, on lightning, on thunder, and on storms one recites: "Baruch...she'kocho u'g'vuraso malei olam—Blessed...Whose strength and might fill the world."

The Talmud tells us that Hashem produces certain powerful and frightening natural experiences so as to "wake us up" and arouse us to revere him and come closer to him:

אמר ר' אלכסנדרי אמר ר' יהושע בן לוי לא נבראו רעמים אלא
לפשוט עקמומית שבלב שנאמר (קהלת ג, יד) והאלהים עשה
שייראו מלפניו.

Rav Alexandri said in the name of Rav Yehoshua ben Levi, "Thunder was only created to [arouse fear and thus] straighten the crookedness of the heart."[1]

---

1   *Berachos* 59a.

B. BASIC HALACHOS

1. Which *Berachah*?

The common custom is to recite the full *berachah*[2] of *Oseh maaseh vereishis* upon seeing lightning,[3] and *She'kocho u'gevuraso malei olam* upon hearing thunder.[4]

Nevertheless, if one reversed the *berachos* and recited *Oseh maaseh vereishis* upon hearing thunder, or *She'kocho u'gevuraso malei olam* upon seeing lightning, one has fulfilled one's obligation.[5]

If one sees lightning and hears thunder at the same time,[6] he should only recite *Oseh maaseh vereishis*. In this case, if one mistakenly recited *She'kocho u'gevuraso malei olam*, he has fulfilled his obligation.[7]

If there is a time gap between observing lightning and hearing thunder, a separate *berachah* should be recited on each, even if one hears the thunder while he is reciting the *berachah* on lightning.[8]

---

2 Note: Certain Sephardic communities will only recite the short *berachah* (**without** *Shem u'malchus*), based on the *Ben Ish Chai* (*Ekev* 1:16) but see *Yalkut Yoseph* Volume 3-227:2 note 2 for full discussion on this issue.

3 Lightning is the natural consequence of friction between cold air and hot air fronts. Some suggest that this conflict is symbolic of the clash between good and evil forces. *B'Seiser Raam*, p. 68, quotes the Vilna Gaon, who describes lightning as a reflection of a heavenly fire connected to the original fire of Creation. This interpretation is reflected in the language of the *berachah*—*Oseh maaseh vereishis*. *Malbim* (*Tehillim* 135:7, s.v. *Berakim l'matar asah*), writes that the source of lightning came into being with the creation of rain. See *B'Seiser Raam* (ibid.) for a full discussion.

4 *Shulchan Aruch OC* 227:1; *Mishnah Berurah* 227:5. The *berachah* of *She'kocho u'gevuraso malei olam* is very appropriate for thunder, as the roaring sound of the thunder permeates the atmosphere and is a true expression of the power and strength of Hashem.

5 *Shulchan Aruch OC* 227:1; *Mishnah Berurah* 227:5.

6 I.e., within 2–3 seconds of seeing the lightning. This concept is known as "*toch k'dei dibbur.*"

7 *Shulchan Aruch OC* 227:1; *Mishnah Berurah* 227:5. See also *Be'er Heitev* 227:1, s.v. *Ein marbim b'verachos*; *B'Seiser Raam* 5:5. There is discussion among the *poskim* in the case where one hears the thunder immediately after he started the *berachah* over the lightning (i.e., after he said the word "Hashem"). Rav Chaim Sanzer (*Hagahos, Shulchan Aruch* 227) explains that based on the general *minhag* to recite *Oseh maaseh vereishis* only on lightning, one can make a separate *berachah* on thunder as it was not included in the first one. Cf. *Chayei Adam* 63:7, who writes that only one *berachah* is recited (see also *Dirshu* 227, note 3).

8 *Mishnah Berurah* 227:5; *B'Seiser Raam* 5:5. But see *Aruch Hashulchan* 227:2, which would seem to suggest reciting only one *berachah*.

2. A Reflection

Many authorities rule that one may recite the *berachah* over lightning as long as he sees the reflection of the lightning on a wall or through a translucent frosted glass window or sees the sky light up.[9] Other authorities disagree and require that one see the actual flash.

3. Heat Storms

Most authorities rule that one does not recite the *berachah* if he sees lightning that is the result of a heat storm.[10]

4. Lightning without Thunder

Since thunder is a reliable sign that the lightning did not come from a heat storm, some have the custom to delay their *berachah* on lightning until they actually hear the thunder. However, many authorities rule that if it is clear that the source of the lightning is a rainstorm, one may recite the *berachah* on lightning without thunder. Additionally, one may assume that lightning flashes in the far distance are from a rainstorm, and the *berachah* may be recited on them.[11]

5. Making the *Berachah* Immediately

One must recite the *berachah* immediately after seeing the lightning or hearing the thunder. If more than two or three seconds have elapsed, one must wait until the next occurrence to make the *berachah*.[12]

---

9   *Minchas Shlomo* 2:4:34; *Emes L'Yaakov OC* 227. *B'Seiser Raam*, p. 67, suggests that the main point of the *berachah* is to feel the hand of Hashem in creation, and therefore he may bless even if he did not see the actual lightning bolt. Indeed, *Tzitz Eliezer* 12:21 notes that the Mishnah (*Berachos* 9:2) speaks about a blessing "on lightning" and not "upon *seeing* lightning." Cf. *Avnei Yashfe* 4:36:3, who cites opinions that one only recites the *berachah* when seeing the *actual* lightning bolt.

10   *Shulchan Aruch OC* 227; *Mishnah Berurah* 227:3; *Halichos Shlomo, Tefillah* 23, note 39; *Minchas Shlomo* 2:4:34. Cf. *Aruch Hashulchan OC* 227:1 and *Avnei Yashfe* 4:36:3, who are stringent. *Shaar Ha'ayin* (4:8, cited also in *Mishnah Berurah* [*Dirshu*] 227:1) quotes Rav Chaim Kanievsky, in the name of *Chazon Ish*, who said that one does recite a *berachah* on lightning from a heat storm. *B'Seiser Raam*, p. 30, points out that, curiously, the Mishnah (*Berachos* 9:2) mentions thunder before lightning, even though lightning is usually seen before thunder. He suggests that this could imply that one recites the *berachah* even upon seeing lightning that does not produce to thunder, i.e., from a heat storm. Some suggest that one should recite the abridged *berachah* (without *Shem u'malchus*) on this type of lightning.

11   *Shaar Ha'ayin* 4:5. I also heard this from Rav Yehoshua Neuwirth.

12   *Shulchan Aruch OC* 227:3; *Mishnah Berurah* 227:12.

6. How Loud/Bright?

It is not necessary to delay the *berachah* until one hears a very loud thunderclap or sees a very bright bolt of lightning.[13]

7. How Long is the *Berachah* Valid?

The initial *berachos* remain valid as long as the sky has not cleared from the storm clouds. Even if a few clouds still remain, one may recite the *berachos* again if the thunder and lightning return.[14] For example, if one is traveling through a storm on a highway, and the sky clears, he may recite a new set of *berachos* as he drives into a new storm.

The *berachos* remain valid for the entire day until one goes to sleep.[15] One who woke up in the middle of the night and recited these *berachos*, even if he went back to sleep, does not recite them again during the day on the same storm.[16]

8. Standing or Sitting

Although it is preferable to stand while reciting these *berachos*, they may be said when sitting if necessary.[17]

9. Interruptions

One who is in the middle of learning or teaching Torah when he hears the thunder or sees the lightning should interrupt momentarily in order to recite these *berachos*.[18]

The following rules apply to one who sees lightning or hears thunder while engaged in *tefillah*:

---

13   *Shaar Ha'ayin* 4:12, s.v. *Sevara.*
14   *Shulchan Aruch OC* 227: 2; *Shaar Ha'ayin* 4:15. See *Avnei Yashfe* 4:36:4.
15   *Shaar Ha'ayin* 4:18. Some recite the abridged *berachah* after a daytime nap. The *Ketzos Hashulchan* 66, note 23, rules that daytime sleep is not considered to be an interruption. The common custom is not to recite a new *berachah.*
16   *Shaar Ha'ayin* 4:18; *Halichos Shlomo, Tefillah* 23:25; *Ishei Yisrael* 6:28. Oral ruling from Rabbi Y. B. Kaplan.
17   *Shaar Ha'ayin* 4:20; *Rivevos Ephraim* 6:409. See also *Aleinu L'Shabei'ach*, vol. 2, pp. 597–8.
18   *Shaar Ha'ayin* 4:21, note 41. This is unlike the prohibition to interrupt one's learning to say "Bless you" when someone sneezes (*Shulchan Aruch YD* 246:17).

- During *Pesukei D'zimra*—One may recite these *berachos*.[19]
- During *Birchos K'rias Shema* or *K'rias Shema* itself—They may only be recited in the paragraph breaks and in between the *berachos*.[20]
- During *Shemoneh Esreh*—One may not recite these *berachos*. However, one may recite them during *chazaras ha'shatz*, *Kedushah*, and *Kaddish*.[21]
- During the *berachah* of *Asher yatzar*—One may not recite these *berachos*.[22]
- During *Birkas Hamazon*—Many authorities rule that one should only recite these *berachos* in between the *berachos* of the *Birkas Hamazon*.[23]
- After *Ha'mapil*—Most authorities allow one to recite these *berachos*,[24] though others forbid it.[25]

One who is awakened by thunder should clean his hands by wiping them on any surface before reciting the *berachah*.[26]

There are grounds to allow one to recite these *berachos* even if he feels a slight urge to relieve himself.[27]

---

19   *Mishnah Berurah* 66:19; *Shaar Ha'ayin* 4:24.
20   *Shaar Ha'ayin*, ibid. Cf. *Kitzur Shulchan Aruch* 6:3, who cites opinions allowing this interruption even in the middle of a *berachah*.
21   *B'Seiser Raam* 8:6.
22   *Chayei Adam* 5:13.
23   See *Shaar Ha'ayin* 4:45; *B'Seiser Raam* 8:5; *Shaarei Berachah* 21:56. See also *Piskei Teshuvos* 183, note 58.
24   The *Biur Halachah* 239, s.v. *Samuch l'mitaso*, quotes the *Chayei Adam*, who holds that *Ha'mapil* is a *Birkas Ha'shevach* and not a *Birkas Ha'nehenin*. According to this approach, one is permitted to speak about an important matter after saying *ha'mapil*.
25   *Biur Halachah* (ibid.) himself is of the opinion that the *berachah* of *Ha'mapil* is a *Birkas Ha'nehenin*, and therefore no interruptions are allowed. See *Mishnah Berurah* (*Dirshu*) 239:30, who writes in the name of *Chazon Ish* that one who has recited *Ha'mapil* is not even allowed to recite *Asher yatzar* after relieving himself. *Shaar Ha'ayin* 4, note 45.
26   *Yalkut Yosef* 227:3.
27   *Mishnah Berurah* 92:4, 227:10; *B'Seiser Raam* 7:5.

C. RAINBOWS

1. Introduction

The rainbow is a sign of the covenant that Hashem made with Noach that He will never again destroy all of mankind by means of a flood (or in any other way), even if our behavior warrants annihilation.[28]

Some commentaries explain that the form of a rainbow represents an imaginary bow directed away from earth as a sign of peace.[29] This is said to be an expression of Hashem's great patience and His hope that we will use His world in a more constructive way. The rainbow's beautiful spectrum of colors could symbolize the hope that all people, despite their differences, will ultimately unite with one another to create a brilliant array of all hues.

The *Shelah Hakadosh* points out that the rainbow symbolizes the fact that even when clouds of evil block the sun from appearing, the radiant light of righteousness still shines through, and man can become the projector to reveal that splendor.[30]

Note: It is especially important to study this *berachah* by heart, for many times a siddur may not be available.

---

28   *Seforno, Bereishis* 9:16; *Ohr Hachaim, Bereishis* 9:11; *Ibn Ezra, Bereishis* 9:11.

29   Commentary of Rav S. R. Hirsch, *Bereishis* 9:12.

30   *Piskei Teshuvos* 229:2, note 8, 9. The *Shelah* says that he heard from the *Rama* that if we were more meritorious, rain would only fall at night and a rainbow would never appear, just as was the case in the days of Chizkiyahu and Rabbi Shimon Bar Yochai. The *Zohar* points out that the three colors of the rainbow represent the meritorious acts of the three segments of the Jewish People—Kohanim, Levi'im, and Yisraelim, and should stir us to repentance. The source of the rainbow is a white light (the original *Ohr Eloki*), which is refracted by the clouds. Rav Kook explains that the message for us is that we are not yet on the level to absorb this very strong light directly, but rather it must be weakened by means of the clouds (*Ein Ayah*, pp. 154–56). Nevertheless, Hashem waits patiently for us to work on ourselves because of His covenant with us. Rav Moshe Shapiro, *Maamakim, Vayikra*, p. 27, explains that the symbolism of the beautiful colors is that they distract mankind from the holy white light behind it all—Hashem. He adds that the rainbow is surrounded by the sky, which is the color of *techeiles* (sky blue) to remind us of our "*tachlis*" to be "sky-bound." The color *techeiles* is not found in the rainbow as it is reserved for holy things like tzitzis, etc.

2. How to Make the *Berachah*

One who sees a rainbow in the sky (which comes as the result of rain),[31] should recite:

בָּרוּךְ...זוֹכֵר הַבְּרִית נֶאֱמָן בִּבְרִיתוֹ וְקַיָּם בְּמַאֲמָרוֹ.

Baruch...zocheir ha'bris ne'eman b'vriso v'kayam b'maa-maro—Blessed...Who remembers His covenant, is trust-worthy in His covenant, and fulfills His word.[32]

This means that Hashem restrains Himself from destroying the world—even when it is filled with many wicked (Jewish)[33] people.

Before making the *berachah*, one should only take a quick look at a rainbow, as it is forbidden to gaze at it.[34] The Talmud says that gazing at the rainbow is compared to looking at the Glory of Hashem, which the rainbow also symbolizes.[35] *Tosafos Rid* adds that just as it is hard to distinguish in a rainbow the point where one color ends and the next color begins, so too, one cannot precisely discern the various qualities of the Divine Presence.[36]

One should endeavor to see the entire half-circle span of the rainbow before reciting the *berachah*. However, as long as the basic form of the rainbow is identifiable, the *berachah* may be recited.[37] It is questionable whether one should recite the *berachah* over a partial rainbow. Therefore, in that case one should recite the abridged *berachah* (without *Shem u'malchus*).[38]

---

31 *Siach Nachum* 13.

32 *Shulchan Aruch OC* 229:1.

33 *Piskei Teshuvos* 229, note 9. See discussion there.

34 *Chagigah* 16a. The Talmud compares gazing at a rainbow to gazing at the face of Hashem, implying that this is a disrespectful act. See *Yeshayahu* 1:28; *Mishnah Berurah* 229:5. See also ArtScroll, *Kiddushin* 40a, note 26.

35 *Chagigah* 16a.

36 *Tosafos Rid, Chagigah* 16a.

37 See *Biur Halachah* 229, s.v. *Ha'roeh*; *Shaar Ha'ayin* 12:7; *V'Zos Haberachah*, p. 156; *Chazon Ovadiah*, p. 473.

38 *Biur Halachah* 229, s.v. *Ha'roeh*. See *Birkas Shmuel*, p. 505, who notes that even seeing part of the rainbow reminds us of the covenant.

There is no limit to the number of times that one can recite the *berachah*, as long as the skies have cleared up before a new rainbow appears.[39]

3. Telling Others

The appearance of a rainbow is considered a "bad omen" in that it reminds us that Hashem may have wanted to destroy the world due to our bad behavior and only relented due to His covenant.[40] Consequently, there is a custom not to tell others about the appearance of a rainbow. Some authorities permit one to hint to others that there is a rainbow in the sky, for example, by saying, "It is now possible to recite the blessing over the rainbow," or by showing someone the *berachah* in a siddur.[41] Most Sephardic authorities permit directly telling others that there is a rainbow in the sky.[42] One who is asked to point out where a rainbow is located in the sky is permitted to answer.[43]

D. OTHER NATURAL PHENOMENA

1. Storms, Hurricanes, Tornados, Typhoons

If one feels or hears unusually strong winds,[44] especially if they have the power to knock down trees or move very heavy items (e.g., a car),

---

39   *Mishnah Berurah* 229:2. Cf. *Ketzos Hashulchan* 66:26; *Shaar Ha'ayin* 12:5; *Birkas Habayis* 29:19; *Shaarei Berachah* 21, note 70.

40   *Mishnah Berurah* 229:1. Some explain that this may be so as not to cause people pain or discomfort, as the verse, *"U'motzi dibah hu kesil"* (*Mishlei* 10:18) indicates. *Shulchan Aruch YD* 402:1 rules that one should not inform others of a death unless it is for a productive purpose. The *Chasam Sofer* (*Pesachim* 4a) discusses how even just saying negative things can have a negative effect upon a person and even cause the *Shechinah* to depart from him. So too, spreading bad news shows a lack of sensitivity, and may even be a form of *lashon hara* against Hashem. People must be more careful when sharing negative information about the world and it should be for a positive purpose. Rav Aharon Feldman suggests that perhaps one would be permitted to tell somebody about the appearance of the rainbow and add a piece of *mussar*, i.e., how we really have to work on ourselves.

41   *Shaarei Berachah* 21:28.

42   *Chazon Ovadiah*, p. 472. *Halachah Berurah*, p. 485, points ot that it is an opportunity to thank Hashem that he made a covenant not to destroy the world and to emphasize the importance of doing *teshuvah*.

43   *Pesachim* 3b; *Shaar Ha'ayin* 12:7.

44   This generally refers to winds over 60 km/74 miles per hour, which have the power to break branches and sway cars. Hurricanes usually have winds of over 120 km/hr. See *Shaar Ha'ayin*, p. 71, and *Iyunim* 30.

one recites *Oseh maaseh vereishis*. On hurricanes or tornadoes, one may alternatively recite the *berachah* of *She'kocho u'gevuraso malei olam*.[45]

2. Earthquakes

One who feels the shockwaves of an earthquake (or sees objects shake and move because of one) should recite either *Oseh maaseh vereishis* or *She'kocho u'gevuraso malei olam*.[46]

The *berachah* must be recited within two or three seconds after experiencing the earthquake.[47] If there are additional quakes (aftershocks) that follow soon after, a new *berachah* should not be recited. However, a new *berachah* is required on aftershocks felt later in the day.[48] If one missed the opportunity to recite the *berachah* the first time, he may recite the *berachah* on aftershocks that may follow.

---

45   *Shulchan Aruch OC* 227:1; *Shaar Ha'ayin*, p. 71.

46   *Shulchan Aruch OC* 227:1; *Shaar Ha'ayin*, p. 72; *Piskei Teshuvos* 227:4.

47   *Shaarei Teshuvah* 227:1. A *segulah* for protection during an earthquake is to say the verse, "*Kadosh, kadosh, kadosh Hashem...*" (*Piskei Teshuvos* 227:2).

48   *Shaarei Teshuvah* 227:1. This would seem to depend on whether there was *hesach ha'daas* (a distraction of the mind) in the interim.

Chapter Three
The Heavenly Bodies

A. *BIRKAS HA'CHAMAH—BERACHAH* OF THE SUN

1. Introduction

The Sages teach that the sun's very first appearance in history occurred in Nissan, and that spring was the beginning of the cycle of the four seasons. According to the Jewish calendar, every twenty-eight years the sun returns to the original position it occupied at the moment it was placed in the cosmos on the fourth day of Creation.

In celebration of this anniversary of the sun's creation, the Sages instituted that we recite the *berachah* of *Oseh maaseh vereishis* after sunrise on the first Wednesday morning after the vernal equinox (*tekufas Nissan*). *Birkas Ha'chamah* was last recited in 2009 and is due to be recited in 2037, 2065, and 2093.[1]

In addition to the *berachah*, various chapters of *Tehillim*, including *Hallelu es Hashem min ha'shamayim* (*Tehillim* 150), and other *tefillos* are also recited.[2]

2. How Clear

Ideally, one should be able to see the sun itself before making the *berachah*. However, as long as one can still see the impression of the sun through clouds, he can recite the *berachah*. If the sun is totally covered all morning with clouds, an abridged *berachah* (without *Shem u'malchus*) should be recited shortly before midday. If the sun becomes visible later on during the day, the abridged *berachah* should again be recited.[3]

---

1   *Berachos* 59b; *Shulchan Aruch OC* 229:2.
2   *Mishnah Berurah* 229:8.
3   Ibid.; *Shaar Ha'ayin* 13:8. *Shaarei Teshuvah* 229 cites *Panim Meiros* who opines that one can recite the *berachah* even if the sun is totally covered. *Teshuvos Chasam Sofer* (56) rules that

3. How Early

Ideally, one should recite the *berachah* as early in the morning as possible. However, it is also preferable to delay the *berachah* in order to say it in the presence of a multitude of people, or at least in a minyan (ten people).[4] The custom is to recite this *berachah* after *Tefillas Shacharis*.[5]

4. How Late

One should recite the *berachah* by the end of the fourth hour of the day. If case of necessity, it can be recited until *chatzos* (halachic midday).[6]

5. Women

The authorities debate whether the obligation to recite *Birkas Ha'chamah* is time-bound. Although there are various opinions in this regard, nowadays many women have the custom to recite this *berachah*.[7]

---

if the impression of the sun is recognizable, one can recite the *berachah*. It is reported that *Chazon Ish* waited until the sun came out a little bit from behind the clouds before making the *berachah*.

4   *Mishnah Berurah* 229:8; see *Shaar Ha'ayin* 13:2, note 5, who discusses the prioritization of *b'rov am*—doing a mitzvah together with a multitude of people, versus *zerizus*—doing a mitzvah at the first opportunity. See *Shulchan Aruch OC* 426:2, who discusses how this applies to *Kiddush Levanah*. See also *Rama OC* 426:2 and *Biur Halachah* ibid., s.v. *Ela ten*, for a discussion of whether *b'rov am* applies even in the presence of only two people.

5   *Mishnah Berurah* 229:8. Actually, the sun appeared in the world on the evening of the fourth day (i.e., Tuesday evening) at approximately 6:00 PM.

6   Ibid.

7   *Shaar Ha'ayin* 13:12. The question is whether this *berachah* falls into the category of *mitzvos asei she'ha'zeman grama*, from which women are exempt. A secondary question raised is whether women are allowed to voluntarily recite the *berachah* when the only mitzvah is the *berachah* itself. Because of these factors, several Sephardic *poskim* rule that the *berachah* not be recited and suggest that she should listen to the *berachah* of a man who has her in mind. Among the *poskim* who hold that women are obligated are *Maharil Diskin, Chazon Ish*, and Rav Chaim Kanievsky. The *minhag Yerushalayim* is that women do recite the *berachah*. For further discussion, see *Magen Avraham OC* 296:11, and *Biur Halachah* 296, s.v. *Lo*, concerning the *berachah* of *Borei me'orei ha'eish*. See also *Halichos Beisah*, p. 125; *Halichos Bas Yisrael*, p. 178; *Mishnah Berurah (Dirshu)* 229:2.

B. *KIDDUSH LEVANAH*—SANCTIFICATION OF THE NEW MOON

1. Introduction

Kiddush Levanah is an opportunity to bless Hashem once a month for the reappearance and renewing of the moon.[8] Of all the celestial bodies, the moon is the closest and most visible to us. Therefore, it is a link between the upper world and the lower world. The Sages teach that the moon symbolizes the presence of Hashem in our world, either because of its amazing cycle of constant renewal or because of the light that it reflects. They thus assert that reciting *Kiddush Levanah* is comparable to greeting the Divine Presence.[9] As such, its reappearance brings us to a greater awareness and recognition of the greatness of the Creator.[10]

In addition, *Darchei Moshe* writes that this monthly reunion with Hashem can be compared to the joy of a wife who has been distanced from her husband for an extended period of time. Indeed, the custom of jumping when reciting the words, *"K'sheim she'ani rokeid k'negdeich"* is intended to symbolize dancing at a wedding!

The moon is also an important symbol: Every month it appears, reaches its climax, and then slowly wanes until it completely disappears. It is then reborn and eventually regains its former status.

This is comparable to the Jewish People, who regularly appear on the scene of history, reach the climax of their "light" and influence, and

---

8   See the discussion in *Ishei Yisrael*, p. 442, and *The Commentators' Rosh Chodesh*, pp. 185–88, whether *Kiddush Levanah* is considered: (a) a *Birkas Shevach V'hodaah*, thanking Hashem for His wondrous creations (*Rabbeinu Yonah*); (b) a *Birkas Ha'mitzvah*—an extension of the mitzvah of *Kiddush Ha'chodesh* (*Tanna D'bei Rabbi Yishmael*); or (c) a *Birkas Ha'nehenin*, acknowledging the enjoyment and benefit we receive from the light of the moon (*Sanhedrin* 42a). See also *Hegyonei Haparashah* (*Shemos*, p. 132), who discusses whether it should be called *Kiddush Levanah* or *Chiddush Levanah*.

9   *Sanhedrin* 42a. See *Hegyonei Haparashah* (*Shemos*, p. 133) for various explanations of this concept. See *Maharal* (*Chiddushei Aggados* 3:158 and *Nesiv Ha'avodah* 13), who explains in what sense the Gemara equates greeting a person (and *hachnasas orchim*) to greeting the Divine Presence. In a similar vein, the Gemara (*Kiddushin* 31b) relates that when Rav Yosef heard the footsteps of his mother, he would say, "I must arise in front of the *Shechinah*" (i.e., a mother is the representative of the *Shechinah*).

10   As we say in *Maariv*, "*U'mesader es ha'kochavim b'mishmeroseihem.*" See also *Rabbeinu Yonah*, *Berachos*, end of *Tefillas Ha'shachar*. This also explains the custom of saying *Aleinu* (*Biur Halachah* 426, s.v. *U'mevarech me'umad*).

then slowly "wane" until it seems as if they've disappeared. Still, despite all our hardships and challenges, Hashem constantly gives us new opportunities to do *teshuvah*, revitalize, and pick ourselves up. *Kiddush Levanah* inspires us to look forward to a brighter day when the glory of the Jewish People will be restored, and we will regain our sovereignty among the nations.[11]

This idea is also reflected through the life of David HaMelech. Although he was despised and belittled, he always picked himself up again. This is one reason why we say *"David melech Yisrael chai v'kayam"* as part of the *Kiddush Levanah* ceremony.

On an even deeper level, *Kiddush Levanah* symbolizes that the Jewish People are destined to be reunited ("remarried") with Hashem and shine like the light of the original sun, emanating a Divine light—*"Ohr Eloki."*[12]

2. *Kiddush Ha'chodesh*

The Jewish calendar is based primarily on the cycle of the moon.[13] Our *Kiddush Levanah* ceremony is a commemoration of the mitzvah of *Kiddush Ha'chodesh* that was performed by the Great Sanhedrin in Jerusalem each month. The mitzvah of *Kiddush Ha'chodesh* has three parts:

---

11   The *berachah* states, "To the moon He said that it should renew itself as a crown of splendor for those [Israel] born from the womb." The Sages teach that the moon's renewal is a sign to the Jewish People that they have a chance to be redeemed from the *galus* experience.

12   The Sages (*Bereishis Rabbah* 1:16 and *Chullin* 60a) famously teach that the diminishing of the moon is a result of its sin: When the world was created, the moon could not accept the fact that the sun was the same size as it, so Hashem punished it by causing it to wane monthly. Nevertheless, this will be rectified in the future, as one of prayers of *Kiddush Levanah* states: "May the light of the moon be like the light of the sun and like the light of the seven days of Creation." *Teshuvos V'Hanhagos* (1:203) writes that Kabbalistic sources compare the moon's returning to its full white color to a bride returning to her husband in her purified state each month. This symbolizes the great reconnection between Hashem and the Jewish People each month, which is a *simchah* worthy of dancing.

13   The Jewish calendar is based on several factors. While the main consideration is the astronomical cycle of the moon, it is also dependent on two witnesses who must actually see the moon. The calendar also must be kept in sync with the solar seasons, which is why leap months are proclaimed every few years. This is in contrast with other calendrical systems that are exclusively either solar or lunar. The Sages compare the Sanhedrin's role in *Kiddush Ha'chodesh* to a groom (Hashem) deciding the general time for the wedding, but letting the bride (the Jewish People) decide the exact date. See *Peninei Halachah*, Rosh Chodesh, p. 24.

- Examining the witnesses to see if there was an actual "birth" of the moon
- Declaring the new month
- Communicating the date of the new month to the Jewish People

3. *Birkas Ha'chodesh* (Shabbos before Rosh Chodesh)

There are two main variations of the text of *Birkas Ha'chodesh*:

- The Sephardic version is a straightforward announcement of the new month's arrival and an instruction to the congregation as to which days are to be observed as Rosh Chodesh.
- Ashkenazic siddurim include additional prayers asking Hashem that the new month be blessed with manifold blessings and that we should merit witnessing the final redemption.[14]

4. From When Can It Be Recited?

Technically, one may recite *Kiddush Levanah* on the first night that one can actually see the new moon. Consequently, one who recited *Kiddush Levanah* before three days have passed has fulfilled his obligation.[15]

Nevertheless, there are two customs as to the earliest time that one should recite *Kiddush Levanah* each month:[16]

- In many Ashkenazic communities, the custom is to recite it from three days (a full seventy-two hours) after the astronomical "birth" (*molad*) of the new moon.[17]

---

14 Interestingly, although the custom of reciting the monthly *Birkas Ha'chodesh* prayer is mentioned in the *Shulchan Aruch* (*OC* 284), it is not found in the section that deals with Rosh Chodesh. It seems to have its source in the siddur of Rav Amram Gaon.

15 *Halichos Shlomo*, Rosh Chodesh 1, note 108.

16 There are three opinions regarding from when the *berachah* may be recited: (a) The *Rambam* (*Berachos* 10–16) is of the opinion that the *berachah* may be recited from the first night when one sees the new moon; (b) *Talmidei Rabbeinu Yonah* are of the opinion that it may only be recited after three days have elapsed from when the new moon made its appearance (*molad*); (c) Rav Menachem Azaryah, quoted in the *Beis Yosef* (*OC* 426), rules that at least seven days must pass before *Kiddush Levanah* may be recited.

17 *Mishnah Berurah* 426:20. This was the custom of *Chazon Ish*, Rav Chaim Kanievsky, and Rav Shlomo Zalman Auerbach. See also *Aruch Hashulchan OC* 426:13.

- Other communities (primarily Chassidim and Sephardim) recite it only after seven days have passed.[18]

Kiddush Levanah should only be recited after dark, so that one can fully benefit from the moonlight.[19]

It is a widespread custom to recite *Kiddush Levanah* on Motzaei Shabbos. This custom is based on two ideas:

- *Kiddush Levanah* is compared to greeting the Divine Presence. Because of this, it is appropriate to recite it when we are dressed in our finest Shabbos clothes.
- It is easier to gather people together right after *Maariv* on Motzaei Shabbos.

Others have the custom to recite *Kiddush Levanah* immediately after three days have passed from the *molad*, especially in the winter, when there is a danger that it will not be visible on Motzaei Shabbos due to cloud cover.[20]

5. How Many People

When necessary, *Kiddush Levanah* may be said alone. However, since it is preferable to recite *Kiddush Levanah* with at least three people,[21] and optimally with a minyan,

6. Until When

One may recite *Kiddush Levanah* all night until dawn, when necessary. Some authorities rule that it may be recited even after dawn, as long as one can still see the moon clearly.[22]

---

18 *Shulchan Aruch OC* 426:4; *Chasam Sofer OC* 102; *Sdei Chemed, Eretz Yisrael*. Some permit already on the seventh night (*Mishnah Berurah [Dirshu]* 426, note 26).

19 *Shulchan Aruch OC* 426:1. Cf. *Mishnah Berurah (Dirshu)*, note 5, and *Ishei Yisrael* 40:2. This is based on Kabbalistic reasons. For more details, see *Kaf Hachaim* 426:61.

20 *Kitzur Shulchan Aruch* 97:10; *Mishnah Berurah* 426:20; *Shaar Hatziyun* 426:21. *Sefer Hachassidim* says that one should not delay it even in order to recite it in a group at a later time. Cf. *Biur Halachah* (426, s.v. *Ela*), who suggests waiting up to ten days in order to recite it with at least three people.

21 *Mishnah Berurah (Dirshu)*, note 20; *Biur Halachah* (167, s.v. *Echad*) writes that even two people may have the status of *b'rov am*. *Igros Moshe* (*OC* 1:144) writes that even two have some value in making *Kiddush Levanah* more significant.

22 *Mishnah Berurah (Dirshu)* 426, note 5.

One may recite *Kiddush Levanah* until mid-month, which is approximately the fifteenth of the month.[23] The entire fifteenth day is included, even after the exact midpoint of the month has passed.[24]

It is questionable whether one is permitted to recite *Kiddush Levanah* on the sixteenth day of the month, when the moon is already waning. Common custom is to recite the abridged *berachah* in such a case.[25]

7. Determining the Exact Moment of the *Molad*

The *molad* is the first moment that the moon begins to wax. This is an astronomical calculation not observable to the naked eye from earth.

Although this moment will obviously occur at different times around the world, most authorities rule that the global *molad* is defined as the time it occurs over Yerushalayim. As such, in order to know the start time, as well the deadline for reciting *Kiddush Levanah* in one's own time zone, one must consider the time differential between his position and Yerushalayim. For example, if the *molad* is at 8:00 PM in Eretz Yisrael, in New York it will be at 1:00 PM.[26]

Other authorities rule that if it occurs at 8:00 PM in Eretz Yisrael, it is fixed as 8:00 PM local time anywhere in the world.[27] This would also affect the latest time that one may recite *Kiddush Levanah* in the various localities.

8. How Clearly Must the Moon Be Seen?

It is preferable to recite *Kiddush Levanah* when the sky is clear. However, one may still recite it on a cloudy night as long as there is

---

23   *Shulchan Aruch OC* 426:3; *Mishnah Berurah* 426:19. Note: A month is considered to be 29 days, 12 hours, and 793 *chalakim*. Thus, mid-month is approximately 14 days, 18 hours and 22 minutes.

24   *Biur Halachah* 426. Note: The *Shulchan Aruch* holds 15 full days, while the *Rama* holds 14½ days. When necessary, we rely upon the opinion of the *Shulchan Aruch*.

25   See *Mishnah Berurah* (*Dirshu*) 426:18, note 40; *Biur Halachah*, s.v. *V'lo tes'zayin b'chlal.* Some suggest reading the relevant Talmudic passages (*Sanhedrin* 42a) or *Tur/Shulchan Aruch* passages in this case and have in mind either the *berachah* or learning the subject. In this way, one can recite a *berachah* without saying the name of Hashem in vain.

26   *Mishnah Berurah* (*Dirshu*) 426, note 35.

27   Ibid., where it quotes in the name of Rav Yonah Mertzbach (*Aleh Yonah*, p. 31).

enough light from the moon to benefit from.[28] It is sufficient to see only part of the moon clearly.[29]

If one began to recite the *berachah*, and the moon suddenly became covered by clouds, he should complete the *berachah*.[30]

One must see the actual moon; it does not suffice to merely see its reflection.[31] One may use binoculars or a telescope to look at the moon.[32]

9. Looking at the Moon

One should briefly look at the moon before reciting the *berachah*. Some authorities consider it improper to stare at the moon.[33] If one did not look at the moon before reciting the *berachah*, but there are others in one's group who did, one still fulfills the mitzvah.[34]

10. Where to Make the *Berachah*

One should preferably recite the *berachah* outside under the open sky, and not under a roof.[35] However, in extenuating circumstances, one may recite *Kiddush Levanah* inside a house, as long as he can clearly see the moon through a window.[36]

11. When in Doubt

There are differing opinions on what to do if one is unsure whether he recited *Kiddush Levanah* already that month.[37] Various authorities point

---

28   *Mishnah Berurah* 426:3. *She'arim Hametzuyanim B'Halachah* (97:7) discusses whether one may recite the *berachah* if he can merely recognize the impression of the moon behind the clouds. See also *Hegyonei Haparashah, Shemos*, p. 121.

29   *Halichos Shlomo, Rosh Chodesh* 1:44.

30   *Mishnah Berurah* 426:3.

31   *Mishnah Berurah* (*Dirshu*) 426, note 13.

32   *Hegyonei Haparashah, Shemos*, p. 127.

33   *Mishnah Berurah* 426:13. It is considered as staring at the face of the *Shechinah* (see Introduction to this section). Some authorities rule that one may look at the moon the entire time. *Shelah* writes that one should only look at the moon before beginning the *berachah*.

34   *Halichos Shlomo, Rosh Chodesh* 1:30. *Maharshal* teaches that the *berachah* is recited over the renewal of the lunar cycle and not necessarily upon **seeing** the moon.

35   *Kitzur Shulchan Aruch* 97:8; *Levush* 426:4. It is more respectful to greet the King in this way. *Chazon Ish* rules that it is permitted to recite it outdoors under a covering. See *Ishei Yisrael* 40:9.

36   *Shaar Hatziyun* 426:4; *Shaarei Teshuvah* 426:1.

37   See *Sdei Chemed, Asifas Dinim, Berachos* 1:18:3; *Rivevos Ephraim*, vol. 6, p. 251. *Mishnah*

out that in this case the best thing would be to be *yotzei* from another person or to mentally concentrate (*hirhur*) on the *berachah*.[38]

12. Women's Obligation

The custom is that women do not recite *Kiddush Levanah*. While some authorities permit women to recite it voluntarily, others rule that (for Kabbalistic reasons) it is not appropriate for them to say it.[39]

13. Children

Parents should train their sons gradually to recite *Kiddush Levanah* from ages six to seven, but certainly from age twelve.[40]

A child who will become bar mitzvah in a particular month does not need to wait until his bar mitzvah to recite *Kiddush Levanah*.[41]

A blind person is obligated in *Kiddush Levanah*. However, it is preferable for someone to recite it with him in mind, and for him to respond with Amen.[42]

14. Mourners

A mourner during the *shivah* week should not recite *Kiddush Levanah* unless he will not be able to do so after *shivah*.

Part of the standard text of *Kiddush Levanah* includes saying *shalom aleichem* to three Jews. There are different opinions regarding whether one is allowed to say *shalom aleichem* to a mourner during the twelve months of mourning for a parent (or the thirty days of mourning for

---

Berurah (Dirshu) 426, note 39. Part of the question is whether the principle of *safek berachos l'hakel* ("when in doubt, do without") applies when the *berachah* is the entire mitzvah.

38   *Shut Shevet Hakehasi* 2:166; see *Sefer Ha'chodesh V'Halevanah*, p. 484.

39   *Sanhedrin* 42a; *Mishnah Berurah* 426:1; *Aruch Hashulchan, OC* 426:14; *Igros Moshe CM* 2:47:2; *Halichos Beisah*, p. 240. Some say that it is immodest for women to go outside to recite *Kiddush Levanah*.

40   For a full discussion on this matter, see *Mishnah Berurah (Dirshu)* 426:1, notes 3–4. Also see *Mishnah Berurah (Dirshu)* 70:8, note 21, where this discussion applies to the mitzvah of *k'rias Shema*—whether *chinuch* in this case (where a father may not be home at these times) begins from ages six to seven or age twelve. See there *machlokes* between *Rashi* and *Rabbeinu Tam*.

41   *Halichos Shlomo* 15:11; *Ishei Yisrael* 40:1. Cf. *Yabia Omer* 3:27 seems to suggest that one should wait until bar mitzvah. For full discussion, see *Halachos V'Halichos Bar Mitzvah*.

42   *Mishnah Berurah* 426:1; *Biur Halachah* 426, s.v. *V'nehenin*.

other close relatives).[43] However, it is permitted for a mourner to say *shalom aleichem* to others.

15. Recited Standing

The Talmud teaches that reciting *Kiddush Levanah* is like greeting the Divine Presence.[44] Therefore, the custom is to recite it while standing.[45] Some make a point of keeping their feet together.[46]

16. Which Direction to Face

There are various customs regarding which direction one should face while reciting *Kiddush Levanah*. While one custom is that one should face the moon when reciting *Kiddush Levanah*, others have the custom to face east or to focus on the direction of the synagogue.[47]

17. Additional Passages and Prayers

There are various passages that are added to *Kiddush Levanah*. Common custom is to say "*Shalom aleichem*" three times, even when reciting it alone.[48] Three represents resolve and emphasis. The Ashkenazic custom is to say it to three different individuals, while the Sephardic custom is to say it to the group. One then responds with "*Aleichem shalom*" (unless he is in the middle of the *berachah* of *Kiddush Levanah*).

There are different explanations why *shalom aleichem* is said at this time. Some explain that it serves as a response to the preceding words, "*Tipol aleihem eimasah v'fachad...*," which ask Hashem to bring fear and

43 *Mishnah Berurah* 426:11. See *Shemiras Shabbos K'Hilchasah* 65, note 163; *Halichos Shlomo* 1:31; *Gesher Hachaim* 21:13; *Kol Bo, Aveilus.* Those who are lenient assert that in this instance, *shalom aleichem* is a prayer rather than a greeting, i.e., "May Hashem bring 'peace' upon you."

44 *Sanhedrin* 42a.

45 See *Shulchan Aruch OC* 426:2; *Nesivos Shalom, Parashas Bo*, pp. 86–88.

46 *Yesod Shoresh V'Avodah* 9:4.

47 *Avnei Yashfe* 3:50.

48 Ibid.

horror on our enemies.[49] As such, saying *shalom aleichem* expresses our hope that the Jewish People should be blessed with peace.[50]

It is also customary to say the words "*David melech Yisrael chai v'kayam.*" This is because the kingdom of David is compared to the moon, and we are praying that one day it will renew itself like the moon with the coming of the Mashiach.[51]

Many have the custom of **dancing** by jumping slightly when saying the words "*K'shem she'ani rokeid k'negdeich...*" as an expression of joy.[52] It is also customary to dance at the conclusion of *Kiddush Levanah* while singing the words "*Tovim me'oros...*" from the *Keil Adon* prayer sung in *Shacharis* of Shabbos.

Many have the custom to recite *Aleinu* at the end of *Kiddush Levanah*.[53] This is to emphasize that we are praying to Hashem and not to the moon or any heavenly body.

---

49   The *pasuk* of "*Tipol...*" is also said three times but in reverse order. One of the reasons for saying it backward is to alert us to the fact that although Hashem generally runs the world in a rational order and process using "natural" means, sometimes He reverses "nature" and performs miracles to protect us from the evil schemes of those who try to harm us (*World of Prayer*, vol. 2, p. 99).

50   *Mishnah Berurah* 426:16. See *Shalom Rav*, p. 195, who explores the various reasons offered for this custom. *Kaf Hachaim* 426, based on the *Ari*, explains that at such a joyous time, when we are greeting the Divine Presence, it is appropriate to join in friendship. It also corresponds to the strained relationship between the sun and the moon mentioned earlier. As such, we pray that we should not be affected by this negative attitude. (Just as the sun continues to share its light with the moon, so too, we should be able to share our love with fellow Jews.) The Sephardic custom is to say it at the end of *Kiddush Levanah*. See also *Minhagei Yeshurun* 100.

51   See *Rosh Hashanah* 25a; *Tehillim* 87:38–39. See also *Maharsha, Sanhedrin* 38a.

52   *Rama* (OC 426) says that jumping is also a type of dancing. See *Meiri, Sanhedrin* 42a. Some explain that there are two types of dancing: *rikud* and *machol*. *Rikud* is an upward movement like jumping, trying to connect and reach closer to the heavens and to Hashem, while *machol* is a circle dance. For an original interpretation of the deeper meaning of the word *rikud*, see *Shem MiShmuel, Korach (chasunah)*, p. 265. It may be related to *meraked* (sifting) because of the jumping motion of the sifter. On a deeper level, it is also may be seen as an expression of separating purities from impurities. Similarly, when one dances at *Kiddush Levanah*, he is showing his yearning to separate himself from the material world (*gashmiyus*) and uplift himself to the spirituality (*ruchniyus*) of Heaven. *Machol* is the word to describe dancing in a circular motion, which symbolizes the unity of the group (in term representing the Jewish People). This may explain the custom to include both types of dance during *Kiddush Levanah*.

53   *Ishei Yisrael* 40, note 83, especially when in a group.

18. Tishrei, Av, and After Fast Days

Many have the custom to wait until after Yom Kippur in order to recite *Kiddush Levanah* in a joyous mood. Some recite *Kiddush Levanah* immediately after Yom Kippur, even before putting on proper shoes or eating. On the other hand, others have the custom to recite it before Yom Kippur in order to add an extra mitzvah to our slate before Heavenly judgment.[54]

Most people wait until after Tishah B'Av in order to recite *Kiddush Levanah* in a happier state. Some recite *Kiddush Levanah* immediately after Tishah B'Av, even before putting on proper shoes or eating. Others are careful to eat and put on shoes first.[55]

While most people recite *Kiddush Levanah* after a fast day, others have the custom to wait another day.[56]

19. Friday Night and Yom Tov Night

If one is concerned that by waiting until after Shabbos or Yom Tov he might miss the deadline to recite *Kiddush Levanah*, he may recite it on Friday night or Yom Tov night. In such a situation, one does not say the supplementary prayers.[57]

C. COMETS, FALLING STARS, AND SHOOTING STARS

1. Introduction

In the first *berachah* of the daily *Maariv* service, we praise Hashem as "He who arranges the stars in their constellations according to His will." Also, every month, as we sanctify the new moon, we declare: "A decree

---

54 *Shulchan Aruch OC* 426:2. Rav Shlomo Zalman Auerbach and Rav Chaim Kanievsky recited it during the *Aseres Yemei Teshuvah*; *Shalmei Mo'ed*, p. 13.

55 *Mishnah Berurah (Dirshu)* 426:11, note 24. The *Arizal* explains that since Mashiach is born on Motzaei Tishah B'Av, by reciting *Kiddush Levanah* at that time, we are informing the moon and the Jewish People that there will be a renewal. Some wait until the eleventh of Av, while others recite it before Tishah B'Av. The latter approach was the custom of the Vilna Gaon, *Chazon Ish*, Rav Chaim Kanievsky, and Rav Shlomo Zalman Auerbach. *Halichos Shlomo, Mo'adim—Nine Days* 14, note 38.

56 *Mishnah Berurah* 426:11.

57 *Mishnah Berurah* 426:12; *Shaar Hatziyun* 426:12; *Aruch Hashulchan, OC* 426:10; *Minchas Yitzchak* 2:120:2. The issue is that we are afraid that one might transgress Shabbos by carrying a siddur in the public domain.

and a schedule he gave them [the light bodies] that they should not alter their appointed task." Thus, the faithful regularity of the hosts of stars attests to Hashem's supreme mastery over all Creation.

Yet, the Sages also understood that certain irregularities in that order, such as comets and shooting stars, are also signs from Hashem's constant attention to His universe and are worthy of *berachah*. What is the difference?

- A comet is a fast-moving rock formation with a "fiery" tail of gas, which can be seen in the night sky as it comes close to the earth.
- A "shooting star" or "falling star" is a streak of light caused by a meteor colliding with the atmosphere or by tiny bits of dust and rocks that light up. These shooting stars burn up as they get closer to the earth. (If it falls to the ground, it is called a "falling star.")

2. Halachos

One who sees a comet or a shooting star should recite the *berachah* of *Oseh maaseh vereishis*. Alternately, one may recite *She'kocho u'gevuraso malei olam*.[58]

One recites the *berachah* even if one sees these things with the aid of binoculars or a telescope, as long as the image is not reflected to the eye from a mirror.[59]

One should not recite these *berachos* more than once per night.[60]

---

58 *Shulchan Aruch OC* 227:1; *Shaar Ha'ayin* 7:1 (p. 74).

59 *Shaar Ha'ayin*, p. 75.

60 *Shulchan Aruch* ad loc.; *Shaar Ha'ayin* ad loc.; *Mishnah Berurah* 227:2 and *Shaar Hatziyun* ibid.

Chapter Four

Birkas Ha'ilanos—
the Berachah on Trees

A. INTRODUCTION

אמר רב יהודה האי מאן דנפיק ביומי ניסן וחזי אילני דקא
מלבלבי אומר ברוך שלא חיסר בעולמו כלום ובָרא בו בריות
טובות ואילנות טובות להתנאות בהן בני אדם. (ברכות מג:)

*Rav Yehudah said: "One who goes out during Nissan and sees
trees that are blossoming recites: 'Blessed...who has withheld
nothing from His world and has created in it beautiful creatures and trees for human beings to enjoy.'" (Berachos 43b)[1]*

The essence of the *berachah* on trees is to recognize the annual
renewal of the agricultural world that has been dormant during the
winter months. The Sages wanted us to recite this *berachah* specifically
on fruit-bearing trees because fruit represent the most pleasurable
food provided naturally by Hashem. This can be seen in the wording of
the *berachah*:

בָּרוּךְ...שֶׁלֹּא חִסַּר בְּעוֹלָמוֹ כְּלוּם וּבָרָא בּוֹ בְּרִיּוֹת טוֹבוֹת וְאִילָנוֹת
טוֹבוֹת לְהַנּוֹת בָּהֶם בְּנֵי אָדָם.

*Baruch...she'lo chisar ba'olamo k'lum u'vara vo b'riyos tovos
v'ilanos tovos l'hanos ba'hem b'nei adam—Blessed...Who*

---

[1] The *Ben Ish Chai* explains why the words *b'riyos tovos* (beautiful creations/people) are added
to this *berachah*: This is to indicate that in the same way a tree (which seems to die in the
winter) refreshes itself in the spring, similarly a human being should take a lesson from the
tree, who in the course of his life should strengthen himself to rejuvenate by doing *teshuvah*
when he finds himself weakening in his observance (*K'Chol Asher She'alta, Pesach*, p. 11).

> *has made nothing lacking in His world, and created in it goodly creatures and **goodly trees for human beings to enjoy.***

B. GENERAL HALACHOS

1. When Is the *Berachah* Made?

One should recite the *berachah* during the month of Nissan when fruit-bearing trees are beginning to blossom.[2] One first gazes at the flowers (or the buds of the fruit) and then recites the *berachah*. Although it is customary for one to recite the *berachah* during the month of Nissan, it may also be recited earlier during the months of Adar and Shevat or later during the month of Iyar if one sees trees beginning to blossom at that time.[3] Some Sephardic authorities, however, rule that for Kabbalistic reasons, the *berachah* may only be recited during Nissan.[4]

Some authorities hold that the *berachah* may even be recited on a tree that does not produce flowers, such as a grapevine.[5]

---

2 *Ahaleich B'Amitecha* 17:2 discusses the application of this halachah to fragrant trees that do not produce fruit. See *Maasei Chemed*, p. 184, which incudes lemons and *esrogim* in the list of fruit trees. However, see discussion there concerning papaya, passion fruit, raspberry, and date trees.

3 *Mishnah Berurah* 226:1 and *Har Tzvi* (*OC* 118) write that the best time to say the *berachah* is when **most** trees are beginning to blossom, which is generally in Nissan or a bit earlier. However there is basis for reciting the *berachah* even earlier when one sees the almond (*shekeidiyah*) trees are beginning to blossom (during Shevat), *Maasei Chemed*, p 94-95; *Rivevos Ephraim* (4:173) reports that Rav Moshe Feinstein recited the *berachah* during the month of Iyar.

4 *Kaf Hachaim OC* 226:1; *Yechaveh Daas* (1:1) cites others who rule that it may still be recited afterward.

5 *Shulchan Aruch OC* 226:1. *Mishnah Berurah* 226:2 points out that the *berachah* cannot be said upon just seeing new leaves. However, see *Halichos Shlomo, Nissan*, note 10, which records that Rav Shlomo Zalman Auerbach would recite the *berachah* even if the flowers have already fallen off and even on trees that do not have flowers. *V'Aleihu Lo Yibol*, vol. 1, p. 124; *Eishel Avraham* (*OC* 226) writes that one may even recite the *berachah* on the new leaves. See also *Maasei Chemed*, p. 113:34, notes 85–86.

How Late

Although the *berachah* should be recited the first time one sees a blossoming tree, it may be recited at a later time.[6] Indeed, the *berachah* may be recited as long as the fruit buds have not yet fully ripened.[7]

Additional Halachos

One may recite the *berachah* on a tree that is growing in a hothouse or in a pot.[8]

Women should also recite this *berachah*.[9]

There are different opinions concerning one who is becoming a bar mitzvah during the month of Nissan. While some authorities recommend that he should recite the *berachah* as early as possible,[10] others say that he should wait until after his bar mitzvah.[11]

One may recite the *berachah* at night as long as he can see the blossoms.[12]

The *berachah* may be recited on Shabbos. There is even a custom in many Sephardic communities to specifically recite it on Shabbos Chol Hamoed Pesach when more people are gathered together.[13] This is based on the principle of *B'rov am hadras melech*, which teaches that doing mitzvos together with others brings greater honor to Hashem.

---

6   *Mishnah Berurah* (226:5) writes that the *berachah* is on the renewal of the spring season. See *Chazon Ovadiah, Pesach*, p. 25; *V'Zos Haberachah*, p. 157.

7   *Mishnah Berurah* 226:4:5.

8   See *Piskei Teshuvos* 226:5.

9   The *poskim* point out that this *berachah* is not considered under the category of obligations that are time-bound (from which women are generally exempt). They point out that this *berachah* is dependent upon the the seasons of growth, but not a specific date or time (see *Har Tzvi OC* 1:118).

10   Rav Chaim Kanievsky (quoted in *K'Chol Asher She'alta*, Pesach/Yom Tov, p. 8) points out that the principle of *zerizin makdimim l'mitzvos* takes priority.

11   *Yabia Omer* 3:27; *Halachos V'Halichos Bar Mitzvah* (Rav Adler) 8–13 for full discussion on this matter.

12   *Piskei Teshuvos* 226:3, notes 28, 34. One who is blind should hear the *berachah* recited by someone else and respond with Amen. *Shaar Ha'ayin* 14:13; *Tzitz Eliezer* 12:20.

13   See *Shaar Ha'ayin* 14:14.

2. Southern Hemisphere

In parts of the world where trees blossom during other months of the year, such as in the Southern Hemisphere, one may recite the *berachah* at the appropriate time in that location.[14]

One only recites the *berachah* once a year. One who travels to a place where the seasons are different is not required to recite the *berachah* again.[15]

3. How Many Trees?

While many authorities rule that the *berachah* may be recited upon seeing even one tree,[16] there are those who say that one should endeavor to recite the *berachah* upon seeing at least two trees in a field or an orchard.[17] Indeed, it is noted that the blessing is worded in the plural: "*ilanos tovos.*"

4. Grafted Trees

There is a difference of opinion among the authorities whether one may recite the *berachah* on a grafted tree.[18] All agree, however, that one may recite the *berachah* on a tree that was planted from the seeds of a fruit from a grafted tree.[19]

5. *Orlah*

There is a difference of opinion among the authorities whether one may recite the *berachah* on a tree in its first three years, as its fruits are forbidden because of the mizvah of *orlah*.[20]

---

14   *Piskei Teshuvos* 226:2; *Har Tzvi* 1:118; *Minchas Yitzchak* 10:16.

15   *Mishnah Berurah* 226:3; *Shaar Hatziyun* 226:1 regarding the question as to whether the year is considered from one Tu B'Shevat to the other. *Ahaleich B'Amitecha* 17:4; *Maasei Chemed*, p. 96; *Shaar Ha'ayin* 14:7 quotes the opinion of Rav Moshe Shternbuch that if one moves to another region, he would be required to recite it again.

16   *B'Tzeil Hachochmah* 6:36, 14:26; *Shaarei Berachah* 23, note 59.

17   See *Halachos Ketanos* 2:28.

18   *Shaar Ha'ayin* 14:15; *Halachos Ketanos* (1:60) says that one may not recite *She'hecheyanu* on a grafted fruit since it is forbidden to graft diverse species. The same logic should apply here. *Biur Halachah* (225) brings both opinions.

19   *Maasei Chemed* 3:12; *Shaar Ha'ayin* 14:27; *Piskei Teshuvos* 226:6. For a full list and discussion on this matter, see *V'Zos Haberachah*, chaps. 17–18.

20   *Maasei Chemed* 3:13 quotes Rav Chaim Kanievsky as permitting one to recite the *berachah*;

6. Kabbalistic Customs

Some of the various Kabbalistic customs that are associated with reciting this *berachah*[21] include:

- To recite it specifically during the month of Nissan
- To recite it in a field or orchard where there are many blossoming trees
- To recite it together with a minyan
- To add a series of additional prayers and readings before and after reciting the *berachah*
- To give *tzedakah* before reciting the *berachah*

---

however, *Minchas Yitzchak* 3:25 does not allow it. They discuss the appropriateness of the *berachah*'s wording: *"lei'hanos ba'hem b'nei adam"* in this context.

21   *Piskei Teshuvos* 226:1; *Kaf Hachaim OC* 226:8; *Teshuvos V'Hanhagos* 1:191. On a Kabbalistic level, reciting this *berachah* is considered to be a *tikkun* to elevate the holy sparks of souls hovering between various "worlds." These sparks are said to be found in trees.

Chapter Five

The Berachos on Exceptional Creations

A. EXCEPTIONALLY BEAUTIFUL CREATIONS

1. Introduction

הרואה בריות טובות אומר ברוך שככה לו בעולמו. (ע"ז כ:)

One who sees beautiful creations recites: "Baruch…She'kachah lo b'olamo—Blessed…Who has (created) such 'things' in His world."
(Avodah Zarah 20a)[1]

One recites the *berachah* of *"She'kachah lo b'olamo"* ("…Who has such" things" in His world") when seeing exceptionally beautiful creations.[2] This *berachah* is said upon seeing especially beautiful people, animals, birds, fish,[3] or exceptionally tall trees. Hashem created beautiful things in this world in order to open our eyes to another dimension of His revelation through the natural world. Seeing beautiful things should uplift a person to feel closer to Hashem, who is the ultimate Source of all beauty.[4] Nowadays, there is a wealth of opportunity to recite this

---

1   See also *Berachos* 58b.
2   *Shulchan Aruch OC* 225:10; *Avodah Zarah* 20a. See *Abudraham*, who says this is based on the verse *"Ashrei ha'am she'kachah lo"* (*Tehillim* 144:15) and on the verse in *Mishlei* (16:4): *"Kol po'al Hashem le'maaneihu*—Hashem created every 'thing' that they should praise Him (or show His greatness)." These beautiful qualities should be associated to Hashem.
3   *Rosh Hashanah* 31a. The *Shir Shel Yom* recited every Thursday starts with the word *"Harninu*—Sing joyously!"* as it refers to the birds and fish created on that day. See also *Avos D'Rabi Nassan* 1:8; *Rosh, Tamid* 7:4; *Ahaleich B'Amitecha*, p. 172, note 14.
4   See *Avos* 3:7, with *Rambam* commentary; *Yalkut Yosef* 225:29; *Peninei Halachah*, p. 319, and *Harchavos*, p. 223.

berachah (even if only the abridged version) by visiting parks, zoos, botanical gardens, and the like.

2. General Halachos

The *Mishnah Berurah* points out that since the exact level of beauty required in order to recite this *berachah* is hard to define, one should say the *berachah* in an abridged form without including Hashem's name.[5] Some authorities point out that if the sight is so unique that it is visited by tourist groups—and one is truly inspired by it—a full *berachah* may be recited.[6]

Based on the above, one should recite the *berachah* (in full or abridged version, as per the discussion above) over the following sights if one finds them especiaaly beautiful:

- Unusually tall trees, such as the trees in Sequoia Park (some are over 100 meters high) and eucalyptus trees in Australia (some are over 150 meters high).[7]
- Beautiful birds, such as peacocks (especially with their wings open), very colorful parrots, pheasants, cranes, flamingos, penguins, hummingbirds, and butterflies.
- Beautiful fish, turtles, and frogs. These can be seen in underground observatories, dolphiniums, and aquariums.[8]
- Beautiful animals, such as leopards, tigers, stallions, polar bears, and gazelles.

---

5   *Mishnah Berurah* 225:32; *Shaar Hatziyun* 225:33 remarks that it is hard to determine what level of beauty warrants the *berachah*. *Chayei Adam* 63:1 rules that one only recites the *berachah* the first time that he sees the sights unless he sees a much more beautiful sight (which is not common today as we see all these things all the time). See also *Kitzur Shulchan Aruch* 61:15 and *Birkas Habayis* 29:13.

6   Some authorities rule that there are times when the *berachah* may be recited in full. For example, *Yalkut Yosef* 225:29 rules that one may recite the *berachah* in full upon seeing a peacock. See discussion in *Peninei Halachah*, *Harchavos*, pp. 231–33.

7   See *Shaar Ha'ayin*, chap. 15, note 28, regarding whether exceptional height is considered beautiful. See *Mor U'Ketzia* 225 regarding seeing a giant.

8   I personally heard that both Rav Aharon Feldman and Rav Avigdor Nebenzhal rule that one may recite the *berachah* in full. There are thousands of different types of fish, including clown fish, lionfish, bubble fish, butterfly fish, angel fish and rainbow parrot fish—just to mention a few.

Some authorities include beautiful sights, such as spreads of very colorful blossoming flowers,[9] beautiful formations of migrating birds, and the like.[10]

B. SEEING UNUSUAL ANIMALS OR INDIVIDUALS

הרואה פיל קוף וקפוף אומר ברוך משנה את הבריות.

One who sees an elephant, monkey, or kipof recites, "Baruch meshaneh ha'berios — One who makes strange creatures."

(Berachos 58b)

Many times, we take for granted the fabulous creation of animals and humans by Hashem. At times, Hashem implants into the creation unusual-looking animals and people in order to make us more aware of Him. People may look at these "exceptions" and "deformities" as though they are "mistakes" in Creation. The truth is quite different: *Berachos* are recited in order to give us another opportunity to recognize Hashem and to know that there is a purpose to everything (even if we cannot comprehend all the reasons).[11]

1. Monkeys, Elephants, and More

One who sees an elephant or a monkey (or a *kipof*, see note) should recite the *berachah* of *Borei meshaneh ha'berios*.[12] Some commentators explain that this *berachah* was established by the Sages so that we should recognize "unusual creations" in the animal world that Hashem

---

9   *Peninei Halachah, Berachos*, p. 231.

10   There is some discussion whether the *berachah* must be recited on a tangible "object" of beauty (heard in the name of Rav Aharon Feldman and Rav Tzvi Rosen), or whether it is sufficient to merely see a "sight" of beauty (*Peninei Halachah, Berachos*, p. 231).

11   See especially the laws of "deformities," where the *berachah* of *Dayan ha'emes* is recited.

12   *Shulchan Aruch OC* 225:8. Some identify the *kipod* (or *kipof*) mentioned by the Talmud as a porcupine, a vulture, or a bat. Interestingly, the vulture has a jaw that resembles the jaw of a human being. I heard in the name of Rav David Feinstein that the *kipod* is an owl (*ozniyah*). See *Mishnah Berurah* (*Oz V'Hadar*) 225, note 106, for further discussion. Various authorities opine that a separate *berachah* should be made on each animal. This is the view of *Chazon Ish* (*Orchos Rabbeinu* 116) and Rav Yosef Shalom Elyashiv (*Ashrei Ha'ish* 38:23). This is also the opinion of Rav Ovadiah Yosef, as stated in *Yabia Omer* 4:200 and *Yalkut Yosef* 3:225:21.

has created.[13] Others explain that the *berachah* is an acknowledgment that Hashem created various animals with characteristics that are most similar to human beings, yet are still very distinct creations.[14]

Some authorities rule that the *berachah* may be recited on any animals that have very outstanding features and characteristics, for example, giraffes, kangaroos, and crocodiles.[15]

Many authorities rule that one may recite this *berachah* on the same species[16] of animal once thirty days have passed since the last sighting.[17]

---

13 The question is whether the *berachah* is meant to express our recognition of how these animals are distinct from other animals, or whether it is pointing out the difference between these animals and Man.

14 There is a fascinating discussion about this question: As we saw, the Gemara (*Berachos* 58b) tells us that upon seeing a monkey, an elephant, or a *kipof*, one recites the *berachah* of *Meshaneh ha'berios*. The commentators question whether this short list is exclusive, and thus one may only recite the *berachah* on these specific animals, or whether it is merely a sampling, and one may recite the *berachah* on all exotic animals, such as giraffes and kangaroos. *Rashi* (*Berachos* 57b) points out that the distinctiveness of these specific animals is their appearance. For example, elephants are distinct because of their extraordinary size (they are 10–12 ft tall and weigh 4–7 tons) and form (their trunk is out of proportion to the rest of their body). A monkey's unique characteristic is that it is very similar to a human being. Using *Rashi*'s criteria, some authorities include the giraffe, due to its extended neck, and the kangaroo, due to its very short legs and its pouch. On the other hand, the *Meiri* (*Berachos* 58b) understands that the monkey and the elephant were singled out because they possess characteristics very similar to those of human beings. For example, the elephant has a large brain, is very intelligent, and has hairless skin. The monkey is similar to human beings in its appearance, behavior, emotions, and capabilities. The *Meiri* also quotes the *Yerushalmi* that says that a monkey can be taught seventy languages. See *Eruvin* 31b and *Me'ilah* 21a. Other authorities suggest that the *berachah* may be alluding to a time when Hashem actually turned people into various animals. For example, the *Meleches Shlomo* (*Kilayim* 8:6) says that there were people who were turned into elephants or monkeys during the generation of the Flood. See also *Bereishis Rabbah* 23:6 and *Sanhedrin* (109a) for more on the transformation of people into monkeys. *Piskei Teshuvos* 225, note 140. See also *Ahaleich B'Amitecha*, p. 173; *Peninei Halachah*, p. 324 and *Peninei Halachah, Harchavos*, p. 236.

15 *Halichos Shlomo, Tefillah* 23:35; *Shaar Ha'ayin*, chap. 15:6, note 17. This is also the view of Rav Nissim Karelitz and Rav Moshe Shternbuch. However, see *Yalkut Yosef* 225:21, *Chayei Adam* 63:14, and *Shaar Ha'ayin*, chap. 15:6, note 3817, who quotes Rav Yosef Shalom Elyashiv and Rav Chaim Kanievsky, who follow the opinion of the *Rambam* and *Meiri* and rule that the *berachah* may only be recited on a monkey or elephant.

16 But not the exact same animal. *Shaar Hatziyun* 225:32.

17 *Shulchan Aruch OC* 225:9; *Yalkut Yosef* 225:21; *Aruch Hashulchan OC* 225:13; see *Shaar Ha'ayin* 15:7, who quotes this as being the opinion of the *Chazon Ish* and Rav Chaim Kanievsky, who hold that even the *Mishnah Berurah* would agree to this. *Tzitz Eliezer* 12:22; *Piskei Teshuvos*

Other authorities rule that the *berachah* may only be recited the first time that one sees it in his life.[18]

2. Visiting a Zoo: *Halachah Lemaaseh*

In addition to being a fun experience, a trip to the zoo can be a religious experience as well.[19] It is an opportunity to contemplate and appreciate the creations of Hashem and to fulfill the mitzvos of *ahavas Hashem* and *yiras Hashem*.[20] It is always appropriate to proclaim: "*Ma rabu maasecha Hashem*—How numerous are Your works, *Hashem!*"[21] and "*Ma gadlu maasecha Hashem*—How great are Your works, Hashem!"[22] Don't miss out!

Upon entering a zoo or safari, some authorities opine that one should recite a separate *berachah* upon the first monkey and elephant that he sees.[23] However, **many authorities** suggest that one should recite a **full berachah** on the first elephant or monkey that one sees, and should have in mind to include all the other unusual animals that one will see there.[24] Rav Shlomo Zalman Auerbach opines that one recites the *berachah* on

---

225, note 149; *Chut Hashani*, p. 189. I also heard this opinion from Rav Moshe Shternbuch, and in the name of Rav David Feinstein, as well as many other *poskim*.

18   *Shulchan Aruch OC* 225:9; *Piskei Teshuvos* 225:23.

19   See *Kum His'haleich B'Aretz*, p. 164, for an interesting discussion about visiting zoos or other parks. According to some authorities, it may be a mitzvah to be familiar with what animals look like. See *Rashi* and *Mizrachi*, *Vayikra* 1:46–47, and *Rambam*, *Mishneh Torah*, *Maachalos Assuros* 1:1. See also *Yechaveh Daas* 3:66 for more on this subject. *Midbar Kedeimos* 2:22 cites a report that *Terumas Hadeshen* went to visit lions, and the *Chida* visited the zoo in London. The Steipler took children to a park in Ramat Gan and recited the *berachah* on monkeys. See also *Shalhei D'Kaita*, p. 106, and *L'Horos Nassan* 4:68 for more. See *Piskei Teshuvos* 225:21, note 46, regarding reciting the *berachah* on two different animals.

20   See *Rambam*, *Yesodei HaTorah* 2:2:5. See *Vayehi Binsoa*, p. 81, for a discussion on snakes.

21   *Tehillim* 104:24.

22   Ibid., 92:6. The verse: "*Ma rabu maasecha Hashem!*" is recited daily as part of our morning tefillah in the *berachah* of *Yotzeir ohr*, while "*Ma gadlu maasecha Hashem!*" is recited on Shabbos in *Mizmor shir l'yom haShabbos*. Whereas on a weekday we marvel at the diversity of Creation ("*Mah rabu*—How numerous!"), on Shabbos we look at the "big picture"—how everything fits in to one "great" system ("*Ma gadlu*—How great!").

23   This is the view of *Chazon Ish* (*Orchos Rabbeinu* 116) and Rav Yosef Shalom Elyashiv (*Ashrei Ha'ish* 38:23). See also *Yabia Omer* 4:200 and *Yalkut Yosef* 3:225:21. *Orchos Rabbeinu* 3:25 reports that *Chazon Ish* told Rav Chaim Kanievsky that if one does not see them together, one should recite two separate *berachos*.

24   I heard this from Rav Moshe Shternbuch, Rav Yisrael Ganz, and other authorities.

the first unusual animal that one sees, and has in mind to include all subsequent animals. Upon seeing any other unusual animals, one may recite the *berachah* again, this time without including Hashem's name.[25]

One must make sure that the place where one recites the *berachah* is clean and should not have a bad odor.

There are some who have the custom that pregnant women do not visit a zoo.[26]

3. Deformities from Birth

One who sees a person who has a serious deformity from birth recites the *berachah* of *Meshaneh ha'berios*.[27] Deformities in this category include the following people: Someone whose hands or arms are not

---

25 *Halichos Shlomo, Tefillah* 23:35, note 135, writes that one can include in one *berachah* all other animals in the zoo. (It is interesting to note that the opinion of Rav Shlomo Zalman Auerbach is that one can recite a *berachah* on any strange-looking animals, i.e., giraffe, hippopotamus, etc. In a discussion with Rav Ganz, he suggested that perhaps the reason for this *p'sak* is due to the fact that the many animals in the zoo may be included in this genre; the zoo is *mitztaref* [combines] all the animals together, so one *berachah* is sufficient.) This not the same case as different cemeteries, where he opines that separate *berachos* are recited, since there is no connection between them. See *Ahaleich B'Amitecha* 17:10 and 18:7, who says that to avoid halachic doubt, when one makes a *berachah* on an item, he should intend to exclude all other items. For more on this, see *Yalkut Yosef, Berachos* 225:21, and *Vayehi Binsoa*, p. 83. Cf. *Shulchan Aruch OC* 178:3 and 174:5. *Ahaleich B'Amitecha*, p. 173, and *Piskei Teshuvos* 225:2, note 146, suggest that one should have in mind to exclude the other animal when reciting the *berachah* so one can definitely recite a new *berachah* upon seeing the latter ones. See also *Peninei Halachah*, p. 235. After reciting the first full *berachah*, some *baalei mussar* recommend that upon seeing any other unusual animals, one should recite the *berachah* without including Hashem's name.

26 See *Vayehi Binsoa*, p. 81. The sight of impure animals can have an effect upon the embryo. See *Shemiras Haguf V'Hanefesh*, p. 419 (142:4). There is a similar custom about not visiting a cemetery.

27 *Shulchan Aruch OC* 225:8, 9. According to Rav Shlomo Zalman Auerbach and *Chazon Ish*, one recites the *berachah* in full. According to the *Mishnah Berurah*, one recites the *berachah* without including Hashem's name. *Peninei Halachah*, p. 322, writes that the *berachah* is a sort of *tzidduk ha'din*, justifying the decrees of Hashem. We are stating our belief that these things are part of Hashem's great plan and thus avoiding a false interpretation that they are just a freak accidental occurrence. It would seem that deformities from birth are meant as a positive lesson to people.

proportional to his body, one who has fewer or more fingers than normal or who has no feet, one who is blind in both eyes,[28] and Siamese twins.[29]

The *Shulchan Aruch* also points out that this *berachah* was also established when seeing people with an uncommon skin color. Examples of this include an Albino as well as "blue" people coming from Kentucky.[30] The custom today is to recite the shortened *berachah*.[31]

4. People of Unusual Size or Height—Midgets

At times, one may see midgets or exceptionally tall people. The *berachah* of *Meshaneh ha'berios* is to be recited. When visiting a circus, this *berachah* may be very relevant.

- Many authorities are of the opinion that the *berachah* may be recited again as long as one has not seen the unusual individual in the last thirty days.[32]

- Other authorities rule that one may only recite the *berachah* in full the first time one sees such an individual, and never again.[33] Thus some suggest that one should recite the (shortened) *berachah* without including Hashem's name when seeing one of these individuals a second time.[34]

---

28   *Mishnah Berurah* 225:22–23. Perhaps the blessings are to make people appreciate how fortunate we are to have full mobility and full faculty of our various organs.

29   *Shevus Yaakov* 1:4.

30   *Shaar Ha'ayin* 15:7. It seems that in earlier times, it was a true rarity to encounter an individual whose external features were noticeably different from those of the "locals." Therefore, there was greater significance in making the *berachah* than today, when there is such diversity that it's less likely for us to be amazed by someone's external appearance.

31   See *Kaf Hachaim OC* 225:65; *Shaar Ha'ayin* 15:1; *Ahaleich B'Amitecha* 17:16; *Chayei Adam* 63:1.

32   *Rama OC* 225:8; *Chayei Adam* 63:14; *Shaar Ha'ayin* 15:2,7; *Halichos Shlomo* 23:26; *Minchas Shlomo* 1:73. This is also the view of *Chazon Ish* (*Orchos Rabbeinu* 3:224). See *Peninei Halachah*, pp. 206–35. I heard this from Rav Moshe Shternbuch. Rav David Feinstein opined that the *berachah* is only recited on midgets, not giants.

33   *Shulchan Aruch OC* 225:9; *Shaarei Berachah* 21:17.

34   *Mishnah Berurah* 225:31; *Kaf Hachaim, OC* 225:65; *Peninei Halachah, Harchavos*, p. 235, says that one can recite the *berachah* in full at least once in one's lifetime.

5. Deformities from Accidents or Operations

One who sees a Jew with deformities that are not from birth but are the result of some accident or operation, and is **pained** by the sight,[35] should recite the *berachah* of *Dayan ha'emes*. This would include the deformities mentioned above, as well as the loss of sight in one eye.[36] The custom would be to recite the shortened *berachah* (if one has not seen the person within thirty days).

6. General Halachos

It is not necessary to recite the *berachah* in front of the person. If one is in doubt concerning the source of the deformity, one should recite both *Baruch Dayan ha'emes* and *Baruch meshaneh ha'berios* without including Hashem's name.[37]

---

35   *Shulchan Aruch OC* 225:9; *Mishnah Berurah* 225:26–27. The *berachah* of *Dayan ha'emes* is recited whenever one is exposed to *"ra"* (evil) things in this world. The purpose of the *berachah* is to dispel the idea that these events happen for naught. There is an aspect of *middas ha'din* that Hashem demonstrates in this world for a variety of reasons (heard from Rav Aharon Feldman). For a deeper understanding of these matters, see *Ramchal, Daas Tevunos*. *Dayan ha'emes* seems to be said only in a situation where one **sees** these acts of *ra* brought upon people by Hashem. This is in contrast to the *berachah* of *Meshaneh ha'berios*, where one sees a naturally **completed** act of Hashem, i.e., blind from birth etc. See *Yad Hamelech* (in *Mishneh Berurah Oz V'Hadar* 225:118).

36   *Shaar Hatziyun* 225:26.

37   *Shaar Ha'ayin*, p. 121, note 14. See *Levush* 225:9. It would seem that in this case, the *berachah* is a way of "sharing their pain." Perhaps *Meshaneh ha'berios* is also a "weaker" form of *Dayan ha'emes*.

Chapter Six

The Berachos on Seeing Kings, Rulers, and Distinguished People

A set of special *berachos* were established by the Rabbis upon seeing important personalities such as kings, great leaders, *talmidei chachamim*, and great scholars.

A. *BIRKAS HAMELECH*—ON KINGS AND RULERS

1. Introduction

ת"ר...הרואה מלכי ישראל אומר ברוך שחלק מכבודו ליראיו מלכי עובדי כוכבים אומר ברוך שנתן מכבודו לבריותיו.

א"ר יוחנן לעולם ישתדל אדם לצאת לקראת מלכים ולא לקראת מלכי ישראל בלבד אלא אפילו לקראת מלכי עובדי כוכבים שאם יזכה יבחין בין מלכי ישראל למלכי עובדי כוכבים. (ברכות נח)

The Rabbis taught...one who sees kings of Israel recites: "Blessed...Who has shared of His glory with those who revere Him." One who sees kings of the other nations of the world recites: "Blessed...Who has given of His glory to flesh and blood."

Rabbi Yochanan said: One should always strive to run toward kings of Israel to greet them. And not only should he run toward kings of Israel, but also toward kings of the nations of the world, so that if so he will be privileged to distinguish between the (honor bestowed upon) kings of Israel [Mashiach] and the kings of the nations of the world.

(Berachos 58a)

Hashem's majesty is reflected through His many messengers in this world. A king is considered to be an agent of Hashem's Providence, representing His dominion over this world. The Sages thus instituted *berachos* to be recited upon seeing kings as an opportunity to express our recognition of Hashem's glory, which is reflected through the human majesty.

Some explain that by creating these blessings, our Sages were teaching that by witnessing the honor bestowed on a mortal king, we will be able to appreciate the greater honor that will be bestowed on the Mashiach in the future. and certainly to the King of kings![1]

One who sees a non-Jewish king or great ruler recites the *berachah* of *She'nasan mi'kevodo l'vasar v'dam*—Who has given of His glory to flesh and blood.

2. Criteria Required for *Berachah*

- Many opinions point out that the king should have the authority to decide on life-and-death issues, including the power to pardon people from the death penalty, and thus to confirm death penalties.[2] He must also have the executive power to send soldiers to war without the interference of any other governing body.[3]
- Various opinions say that it is sufficient that the title of authority be hereditary (even if they do not have full power of authority).[4] Others apply it to any ruler who exhibits degrees of power (see previous point), even if self-appointed (e.g., a dictator) or elected.

---

1   See *Rashi, Berachos* 58, where he discusses how this will bring a person to realize how rewarding the experience will be.

2   *Mishnah Berurah* 224:12. This seems to be the truest test of a king demonstrating full power. The Queen of England's signature is required for pardons and executions, even though it is a purely ceremonial gesture. The President of the United States has the power to pardon criminals and can issue orders for soldiers to go to war (*She'arim Hametzuyanim B'halachah* 160:10:6).

3   See *Shulchan Aruch OC* 224; *Mishnah Berurah* 12; *Magen Avraham* 224:5.

4   See *Shaar Ha'ayin*, p. 359, for discussion.

- Various opinions say that he must be a "good" king or leader. See the note concerning an evil king or leader like Pharaoh, Hitler, Stalin, and the like.[5]
- *Kavod malchus*—The authorities discuss the degree of royal honor that must be displayed.[6] This may include a royal entourage, being attended to by a large army escort, masses of people, royal dress, in the royal palace,[7] or in a special limousine.

3. Other Halachos

Based on the above principles, the following rules apply:

a. An Absolute Monarch

One may recite a full *berachah* upon seeing an absolute monarch—of hereditary lineage who has absolute power—wearing full regalia or surrounded by another display of royal honor. This would apply nowadays to the kings of Saudi Arabia, Oman, United Arab Emirates, Swaziland, Qatar, and the kings of some other African and Middle Eastern countries. If the king is considered to be evil, some authorities write that one should recite the *berachah* without Hashem's name.[8]

b. A Limited Monarch

Some authorities rule that a full *berachah* may be recited if one sees a limited monarch—of hereditary lineage but with limited power as long as he is wearing full regalia or is surrounded by another display of royal honor.[9] Other authorities would suggest reciting the *berachah* without including Hashem's name.[10] This category would include the kings of

---

5   See *Shaar Ha'ayin*, p. 358, for a discussion. *Lev Chaim* 3:55 writes that the *berachah* is recited in consideration of the honor due to his position, regardless of his ethical standards. *Minchas Elazar* 5:7 rules that it does not apply to an evil king or leader. See also *Halachah Berurah*, p. 302; *Maharsha, Zevachim* 102, s.v. *Va'yeshanes*; *Rashi, Shemos* 6:13 and 11:8.

6   This is because the *berachah* uses the word "*kavod*" (honor). See *Birkei Yosef* 224:3 and *Yalkut Yosef* 225:12.

7   See *Yechaveh Daas*, vol. 2, p. 107; *Teshuvos V'Hanhagos* 2:139; *Kitzur Shulchan Aruch* 60:10.

8   *Shaar Ha'ayin*, p. 358. Concerning a dictator, see *Orchos Rabbeinu* 1:180.

9   *Shevet Halevi* 1:35. If the monarchy is hereditary, he is considered a king of the country, even if he does not have the authority to kill.

10 *Be'er Moshe* 2:9; *Avnei Yashfe* 1:47.

Holland, Denmark, Norway, Sweden, Jordan, Morocco, Thailand, the emperor of Japan, and the princes of Monaco and Lichtenstein.

c. A Queen

According to some authorities, the *berachah* may be recited in full, even if she is a limited monarch.[11] Other authorities do not require any *berachah*,[12] but they recommend reciting the *berachah* without Hashem's name.[13] This would include the Queen of England.

d. A President

According to many authorities, a *berachah* may be recited upon the elected leader of a country who has executive powers to kill or pardon a condemned criminal.[14] Other authorities rule that the *berachah* should be recited without Hashem's name.[15] This category would include the President of the United States.

e. A Leader of a Country

The authorities opine that no *berachah* is required for an elected or appointed leader of a country with limited power. However, there are various authorities who point out that it is **proper** to recite the *berachah* without Hashem's name.[16] This would include seeing a prime minister, an ambassador, or major administrative leaders such as governors of a state.[17]

---

11   *Shevet Halevi* 1:35; *Avnei Yashfe* 1:47; *Teshuvos V'Hanhagos* 2:139; *B'Tzeil Hachochmah* 2:19; *Be'er Moshe* 2:9. Rav Gurwitz of Gateshead notes that in the case of the Queen of Engand, a death penalty requires her confirmation, even if only symbolic.

12   *Shaar Ha'ayin* 19:5.

13   Based on *Mishnah Berurah* 224:12.

14   *She'arim Hametzuyanim B'Halachah* 60:6:1; *Be'er Moshe* 2:9; *Yechaveh Daas* 2:28; *Chazon Ovadiah, Berachos*, p. 313; *Orchos Rabbeinu* 1:180. I heard that this is also the view of Rav Yosef Dov Soloveitchik (especially if the meeting takes place in the White House).

15   *Rivevos Ephraim* (3:540:4) reports that the Chafetz Chaim did not recite the *berachah* on seeing the president of Poland.

16   Based on *Mishnah Berurah* 224:12. Rav Efraim Polikoff explained to me that the Prime Minister of Israel and a governor of a state in the USA have certain military powers, and the ambassador of a country represents the *kavod* of the ruling authority. It seems that the *Mishnah Berurah* is suggesting an abbreviated form of *berachah* is an appropriate praise of Hashem in cases where one sees personalities who have various degrees of military power or clearly represent the "ruling" authority.

17   *Noam*, vol. 16; *Shaarei Halachah*, p. 133; *Be'er Heiteiv* 224:6.

3. Jewish Kings

If the king or ruling authority is an observant Jew, then one recites the following *berachah*: *She'chalak mi'kevodo li'rei'av*—Who has shared of His glory with those who revere Him. However, if the ruler is a nonobservant Jew, many authorities would say that one recites the *berachah* of *She'nasan mi'kevodo l'vasar v'dam*.[18]

4. Seeing the Mashiach

When seeing the Mashiach, one recites the following *berachos*:

- *Chacham Ha'razim*—Who knows all secrets.
- *She'chalak mei'chochmaso li'rei'av*—Who has shared of His wisdom with those who revere Him.
- *She'chalak mi'kevodo li'rei'av*—Who has shared of His glory with those who revere Him.
- *She'hecheyanu...*[19]—Who has kept us alive...

5. Additional Halachos

- One may only recite the *berachah* on the same ruler once in thirty days. However, one may recite the *berachah* again within that period when seeing a different king or ruler.
- Many authorities point out that it is not necessary to see the ruler's actual face before making the *berachah*, but that it is sufficient to see the honor displayed to the king, such as the royal car or the masses of assembled people.[20]
- One must see these things with one's eyes, or with the aid of binoculars or a telescope. However, one does not recite the *berachah* if he only sees them via television or other similar technology.[21]

---

18   *Halachah Berurah*, p. 303; *Kaf Hachaim OC* 224:29. See *Mishnah Berurah* 224:9, who defines the words as *"she'chalak"*—*she'am Hashem hem chelek elokah* **u'd'veikim bo** (is an extension of Hashem and cleaves to Him). This does not seem to apply to a nonobservant Jew. However, see *Rashash, Berachos* 58a, s.v. *Malchei Yisrael*.

19   See *Minchas Shlomo* 1:91:27.

20   See *Shaarei Teshuvah OC* 224:5 and his proofs; *Kitzur Shulchan Aruch* 60–10; see *Shaar Ha'ayin*, p. 144, for other opinions.

21   *B'Tzeil Hachochmah* 2:19; *Piskei Teshuvos* 218:2, 224:6.

- One who was born blind may only recite the *berachah* without Hashem's name. However, one who became blind later in life may recite the *berachah* if he feels the honor of the occasion.[22]
- It is a mitzvah to see the honor and glory bestowed on earthly rulers, even if this will mean interrupting one's Torah studies. Some explain that this is in order to appreciate the difference between the honor shown to an earthly king and the greater honor that will be shown to the Mashiach upon his arrival. Others explain that it is to allow one a preview of the type of honor that will be given to the Mashiach.[23]

B. GREAT LEADERS

1. Great Torah Scholars

When seeing the greatest Torah leaders of the Jewish People, one recites the *berachah She'chalak mei'chochmaso li'rei'av*.[24]

There are many authorities who opine that this *berachah* is fully applicable nowadays, though it is sometimes difficult to determine who is considered to be among the greatest Torah leaders.[25] Others argue

---

22 *Shulchan Aruch OC* 224; *Mishnah Berurah* §11.

23 *Shulchan Aruch OC* 224:9; *Halachah Berurah*, p. 312.

24 *Shulchan Aruch OC* 224:6. It is important to note the difference in the wording of the *berachah* for a Torah scholar ("He *shared* of His wisdom to *those that revere Him*") and a secular scholar ("He *gave* of His wisdom to *flesh and blood*"). The *Maharsha, Berachos* 58, explains that when one engages with Torah learning, Hashem is, so to speak, sharing of His Divine wisdom in an intimate relationship. Because of this, *yiras Hashem* (reverence) is a prerequisite to acquiring Torah knowledge. On the other hand, the acquisition of secular knowledge, though it also comes from Hashem, is something more external and less spiritually connected. It is thus not sharing, but a gift. See *Levush* 224:7 for an additional interpretation.

25 *Shevet Halevi* 10:13 defines a leading Torah scholar as someone who is accepted as wise in Torah learning, who learns *lishmah*, and, perhaps, someone who is learned in Kabbalah. *Shaar Ha'ayin* 17:2 adds someone who is familiar and able to discuss all sections of Torah and is accepted as one of the greatest leaders of the generation. See *Shulchan Aruch YD* 243:2 and *Birkei Yosef CM* 153 for the definition of a *talmid chacham*. Rav Azriel Auerbach told me that one should recite the *berachah* upon seeing Rav Yosef Shalom Elyashiv and Rav Chaim Kanievsky. Rav Baruch Ezrachi recited the *berachah* on Rav Aharon Leib Shteinman. Rav Chaim Kanievsky also told people to recite it on Rav Aharon Leib Shteinman. Rav Sinai (from Seminar Be'er Miriam) told me that Rav Yosef Shalom Elyashiv told Rav Yitzchak Zilberstein to recite the *berachah* when going to visit Rav Ovadiah Yosef. Rav Yehoshua

that we no longer have scholars on the level of greatness and erudition necessary in order to warrant reciting this *berachah*, and therefore it should only be recited without Hashem's name.[26] There are various opinions who suggest reciting the *berachah* of She'hecheyanu (without *Shem u'malchus*) upon seeing a great Torah *gadol* for the first time.

No *berachah* is recited when seeing famous religious leaders of other faiths.[27]

2. Secular Scholars

One who sees one of the greatest non-Jewish scholars of secular knowledge recites the *berachah* of She'nasan mei'chochmaso l'vasar v'dam. The *berachah* is recited on scholars whose contributions have greatly helped humanity. Some authorities rule that the definition of a scholar is one with expertise in one of the seven classical branches of knowledge,[28] while others rule that the *berachah* may be recited on any scholar as long as he is an expert in any one area of knowledge.[29]

In our rapidly changing world, it is very hard to define who is a true scholar. For this reason, most authorities agree that this *berachah* is no longer recited with Hashem's name. Some authorities suggest, nonetheless, that one should recite an abridged *berachah* on any major secular scholar.[30]

In addition, some authorities rule that the scholar must believe in God and observe the Seven Noachide Commandments.[31] There is a

---

Neuwirth told me that he recited the *berachah* when he saw the *Chazon Ish*. See also *Chayei Adam* 63:5; *Shaar Ha'ayin* 17:3; *Beis Hillel* 38, p. 31, note 1; *Chazon Ovadiah*, p. 405, and *Yechaveh Daas* 4:16. It has been reported that Rav Chaim Kanievsky applied this title to Rav Avigdor Nebenzhal.

26   *Aruch Hashulchan, OC* 224:6; *Shaar Ha'ayin*, p. 136. I heard this from Rav Chaim Pinchas Scheinberg. *Kaf Hachaim* 224:19; *Ohr L'Tzion* 2:46:61.

27   *Shaar Ha'ayin*, chap. 18:2.

28   *Shulchan Aruch OC* 224:7; *Shaar Ha'ayin*, chap. 18, note 4; *Midbar Kedeimos* 8:18. The seven major branches of knowledge are: Logic (Language), Mathematics, Geography, Medicine (Science), Music, Philosophy (History), and Astrology. See *Mishnah Berurah (Oz V'Hadar)* 224:56 for a discussion concerning the exact list and how it applies to medicine.

29   *Mor U'Ketzia* 224; see *Mishnah Berurah (Oz V'Hadar)* 224:56.

30   *Ahaleich B'Amitecha* 14:4; *Minchas Elazar* 5:7:4; *Teshuvah Mei'ahavah* 2:237.

31   See *Shaar Ha'ayin* 18:6; *Teshuvos V'Hanhagos* 3:76; *Yechaveh Daas* 4:16. They explain that an

dispute among the authorities whether one recites the *berachah* when seeing a great Jewish scholar of secular knowledge.[32]

atheist cannot be a truly wise person, as Hashem's existence is the foundation of all knowledge; see *Rambam, Mishneh Torah, Yesodei HaTorah* 1:1.

32   See discussion in *Shaar Ha'ayin*, chap. 18, note 10; *Ahaleich B'Amitecha* 14:1; *Chayei Adam* 63:8 (*l'basar v'dam*). See further discussion in *Mishnah Berurah* (*Oz V'Hadar*) 224:59, concerning the correct *berachah*, as well as whether any *berachah* is actually necessary. See also *Pachad Yitzchak*, Chanukah, 9:2–6, who suggests that no *berachah* may be necessary.

Chapter Seven

Children and Dear Friends

The Rabbis instituted various berachos upon seeing children, grandchildren, and other dear friends that bring much joy to the viewer.

A. CHILDREN

1. Birth of a Son

The *Shulchan Aruch* writes that when one's wife gives birth to a son, one recites the *berachah* of *Ha'tov v'ha'meitiv*—Hashem is good and does good. Many parents thus have the custom to recite the *berachah* when **seeing** their newly born son.[1] The meaning of the *berachah* is that the birth of the son is "good" to the parent who is blessing and also "does good" to the other parent.[2] The *berachah* may be recited by each

---

1   *Shulchan Aruch OC* 223; *Mishnah Berurah* 223:3; *Igros Moshe OC* 5:43:5; Rav Yaakov Kamenetsky, *Emes L'Yaakov* 223; *Aruch Hashulchan OC* 223:2 reports that others do not recite the *berachah*. Many Sephardim, *Kaf Hachaim OC* 223:6 and *Yalkut Yosef* 223:5, generally do not recite it because they rely on the *She'hecheyanu* they will recite at the child's *bris*, as is their custom. *Kaf Hachaim OC* 223:6, *Yalkut Yosef* 223:5, and *Ohr L'Tzion* 2:14:47 recommend having this *berachah* in mind when reciting the *berachah* of *Ha'tov v'ha'meitiv* in *Birkas Hamazon*.

2   *Ha'tov v'ha'meitiv* is generally recited when at least two people benefit from an item. See *Teshuvos HaRashba* (1:245, 4:77) and *L'Fa'eir U'L'vareich*, p. 40. The Talmud compares the birth of a son to acquiring "a cane in his hand and a shovel to bury him," meaning that the father feels assured that a son will support him in later life. These practical benefits also apply to the mother. The reason we do not recite *Ha'tov v'ha'meitiv* at the birth of a daughter is because girls were historically married off at a young age and were bound more to their husbands than their parents. *Shaarei Berachah* 22:66 cites the *Netziv*, who suggests that

parent separately or one may be *motzi* the other.[3] One may recite the *berachah* as soon as he hears the news; one need not wait until he sees the child. The *berachah* is recited even if the parents are not so happy; for example, they were hoping for a daughter.[4] The *berachah* may be recited even a long time after the baby is born as long as the parents feel much happiness.[5]

2. Birth of a Daughter

In many communities, it is customary for parents[6] to recite the *berachah* of *She'hecheyanu* when seeing[7] their newly born daughter.[8]

---

perhaps nowadays, when girls get married much later, one should be able to recite *Ha'tov v'ha'meitiv*, as it is "comparable" to acquiring a new item, i.e., there are practical benefits to having children. Perhaps an additional reason for the *berachah* of *Ha'tov v'ha'meitiv* is that the father has a feeling of continuity from a son, as a son will inherit him and keep the family name alive, as it says, "*Bra karah de'avua.*" See *Eruvin* 70b.

3   *V'Zos Haberachah*, p. 169. I.e., one makes the *berachah* with the other in mind and he/she says "Amen."

4   *Mishnah Berurah* 223:3; *Aruch Hashulchan*, *OC* 223:1; *L'Fa'eir U'L'vareich*, p. 82.

5   *Mishnah Berurah* ad loc.; *Shaarei Berachah* 22:62. *Shaar Ha'ayin* 21:4.

6   *Mishnah Berurah* 223:2; *Yad L'Yoledes*, p. 295; *Igros Moshe OC* 5:43:5; *Beis Avi* 4:56; *L'Fa'eir U'L'vareich*, p. 111; *Tzitz Eliezer* 4:21:22. There are also opinions that only the father recites the *berachah* (*Yad L'Yoledes*, p. 295) and other opinions that no *berachah* is recited; see *Aruch Hashulchan* 223:1.

7   *L'Fa'eir U'L'vareich*, p. 87, writes in the name of Rav Chaim Kanievsky that this is true even if the baby is no longer present and one still feels the joy. According to the *Netziv* (see next note), the *berachah* may be recited when one hears about the birth. *Chut Shani, Birkas Hodaah*, p. 179, says that if one did not recite the *berachah* the first time one saw the child, he may recite it the next time one sees her.

8   *Mishnah Berurah* 223:2; *Shaar Hatziyun* 223:3. The *Mishnah Berurah* says that seeing a daughter for the first time is no less significant than seeing a very close friend after a long absence. Rav Moshe Feinstein (*Igros Moshe OC* 5:43) encourages people to recite this *berachah*. *Tzitz Eliezer* 8:14:21, 13:20, writes that the *berachah* refers to seeing one's healthy child and wife. Cf. *Halichos Shlomo* 23:10, note 43, who questions the practice of reciting this *berachah*. *Aruch Hashulchan OC* 223:1 asks how one can recite a *berachah* on a child that one never saw before. Cf. *Har Tzvi OC*115 states that one may recite the *berachah* if one never saw the person before. See *Shaar Ha'ayin*, pp. 152–54) for further discussion. In a related subject, *L'Fa'eir U'L'vareich*, p. 99, reports that Rav Yosef Shalom Elyashiv says that one who did not have a child for ten years may say *Ha'tov v'ha'meitiv* on the birth of a girl. See *Shaar Hatziyun* 223:3 for more. Many Sephardim do not recite the *berachah* at all. See *Piskei Teshuvos* 223:2 for further discussion.

3. Twins

Upon hearing the birth of twin boys or upon seeing them, one should recite one *berachah* of *Ha'tov v'ha'meitiv*.[9] One *berachah* of *She'hecheyanu* is recited for twin girls unless one sees them at different times.[10]

Some authorities rule that only *Ha'tov v'ha'meitiv* is recited upon the birth of male and female twins as it is the more inclusive *berachah*.[11] Others rule that because of the birth of the girl *She'hecheyanu* should be recited as well.[12]

4. Premature Babies and Other Medical Issues

Some authorities suggest that one should wait thirty days before reciting the *berachah* on the birth of a premature baby.[13] Others rule that one may recite the *berachah* immediately if the doctors say that the baby is expected to be fine.[14]

There is a difference of opinion whether the *berachah* is recited if the baby does not look healthy or has other serious medical challenges, such as a baby born with Down syndrome.[15] Similarly, there are different opinions whether the *berachah* should be recited on the birth of a child who is missing a body part. This is somewhat dependent on the parents' level of happiness.[16]

---

9   *Mishna Berurah* 222:22.
10   Ibid.; *Yad L'Yoledes*, p. 295.
11   *Shaar Hatziyun* 225:6; *Toras Hayoledes*, p. 176, quotes the view of Rav Moshe Feinstein and Rav Chaim Pinchas Scheinberg.
12   *L'Fa'eir U'L'vareich*, p. 91, citing Rav Chaim Kanievsky. He explains that since *Ha'tov v'ha'meitiv* was not instituted for the birth of a girl, a separate *berachah* is required.
13   *Piskei Teshuvos* 223:4.
14   *L'Fa'eir U'L'vareich*, p. 78, quoting the view of Rav Chaim Kanievsky.
15   *Toras Hayoledes* 37:7, quoting Rav Chaim Pinchas Scheinberg that a *berachah* may be in place if parents are happy. He also rules that one fulfills the mitzvah of *peru u'revu* (procreation) if one has a child (or children) with Down syndrome. See fascinating suggestion there that by bringing these souls into the world, one is bringing the world closer to the coming of the Mashiach. However, Rav Elyashiv seems to opine that a *berachah* is not necessary.
16   *L'Fa'eir U'L'vareich*, p. 80. See *Toras Hayoledes*, p. 177. The Talmud tells us that even a blind person can become a *gadol b'Yisrael*, like the blind Talmudic sage Rav Yosef.

5. Grandparents

Some say that grandparents who are exceptionally happy upon the birth of their grandchild may recite the *berachah* of *She'hecheyanu* (or *Ha'tov v'ha'meitiv*) when they see the baby for the first time.[17]

6. General Halachos

- These *berachos* are recited even if the baby is not the first child.[18]
- If the nurse showed the wrong baby girl to the parents, and they made a *berachah*, a new *berachah* must be recited when they see their own child.[19]
- If one mistakenly recited *She'hecheyanu* instead of *Ha'tov v'ha'meitiv*, or vice versa, one should not make the correct *berachah* afterward.[20]
- These *berachos* may be recited during the "Nine Days" and the *sefirah* period, and also by a mourner.[21]

7. Naming a Daughter

There are various customs regarding when to name a daughter. In some communities, girls are named at the earliest opportunity, which is at the first Torah reading after her birth. The authorities write that the naming brings the holiness of Jewish status—*Kedushas Yisrael*—upon the child.[22] In other communities, the name is given on the Shabbos after the birth. There is also a custom to wait five days before naming a girl unless Shabbos arrives first.[23]

---

17   I heard from Rav Yehoshua Neuwirth that one may recite *She'hecheyanu* in full. See *Nishmas Avraham*, p. 181. *Ketzos Hashulchan* 64:10 and *Shulchan Aruch Harav, Seder Birkas Hanehenin* 12:7, rule that one may even recite *Ha'tov v'ha'meitiv* when one hears very good news about a friend. See *Biur Halachah* 223, s.v. *Yaldah*, based on *Sefer Hachassidim*. *Piskei Teshuvos* 223:1, note 15, rules that one will not lose out by reciting this *berachah*. See *V'Dibarta Bam* 1:53 for the opinion of Rav David Feinstein.

18   *Shaarei Berachah* 22:66.

19   *Shevet Halevi* 8:35:1; *Shaarei Berachah* ad loc.; *Tzitz Eliezer* 12:20. Since the *berachah* for a baby girl is on "seeing" her, in contrast to the *berachah* on "hearing" of the birth of a baby boy.

20   *Shaarei Berachah* ad loc.; *Toras Hayoledes* 37:3; *L'Fa'eir U'L'vareich*, pp. 119, 127.

21   *Yad L'Yoledes*, p. 311.

22   *Kaf Hachaim OC* 223:6. See also *Tzitz Eliezer* 13:20 and *Yad L'Yoledes*, pp. 182–85, for an exploration of the various opinions.

23   *Minchas Yitzchak* 4:107. See also *Halichos Beisah*, p. 117, and *Yad L'Yoledes*, p. 183, note 15,

There is a custom that one should make a meal or *Kiddush* either on the day a baby girl is given a name or at some point afterward.[24] Sephardic custom is to name a baby girl at a ceremony called *Zeved Ha'bat*. These ceremonies are expressions of thanking Hashem for the birth of the child.

C. DEAR FRIENDS

1. After Thirty Days

The *Shulchan Aruch* rules that one who has not seen a very dear friend for thirty days, and feels especially happy when seeing him again, should recite the *berachah* of *She'hecheyanu*.

Nowadays, the general custom is not to say the full *berachah* with Hashem's name. There are various explanations for this:

- Some explain that it is difficult to evaluate the necessary level of joy that this *berachah* requires.[25]
- Others explain that we are afraid that many people might only recite the *berachah* out of respect so as not to embarrass or insult others, but not out of a true feeling of love. It would therefore be a *berachah* in vain.[26]
- Similarly, some opine that we are concerned that people may recite the blessing as a form of flattery rather than out of a sincere feeling of joy.[27]
- Many authorities point out that, with modern communication, we promptly find out if something unusual has happened to a

---

for an explanation of this custom. For the various wordings of the *Mi she'beirach* recited at the naming, see *Yad L'Yoledes*, p. 185, especially note 23. See *Igros Moshe OC* 4:67, where Rav Moshe Feinstein suggests that one make a *Mi she'beirach* for the naming of the child first, before the *Mi she'beirach* for the mother's recovery. Alternatively, one may use the special version suggested by Rav Moshe Feinstein that combines the two blessings. There are also those who suggest using the words *"L'Torah u'l'ven Torah."*

24   *Yad L'Yoledes*, p. 186, especially note 26.
25   *Halichos Shlomo* 23:12.
26   *V'Zos Haberachah*, p. 170; *Shaar Ha'ayin* 20:11.
27   *Chessed L'Alafim* 225:15.

person, and this dampens the degree of excitement and *chavivus* (special fondness) required for the *berachah*.[28]

That being said, several authorities rule that one may still recite the full *berachah* in the following cases:

- When seeing a very close relative (e.g., parents, children, spouses, brother, or sister) after an extended period of absence[29]
- Dear friends or relatives who see soldiers coming back from the front during wartime[30]
- Seeing a very dear friend who has totally recovered from a very serious operation[31]

2. After Twelve Months

One who has not seen a friend for twelve months should recite the *berachah* of *Mechayei ha'meisim*:

בָּרוּךְ...מְחַיֵּה הַמֵּתִים.

Baruch...mechayeh ha'meisim—Blessed...Who revives the dead.[32]

---

28 Cited in the name of Rav Yosef Shalom Elyashiv and the Steipler Gaon. Rav Mordechai Eliyahu rules that Sephardim should not recite this *berachah*. However, the *Ben Ish Chai* (*Re'eh* 5) says that one should think the *berachah* in one's mind or recite it without including Hashem's name (*V'Zos Haberachah*, p. 168). *Aruch Hashulchan OC* 225:3 and *Har Tzvi* 1:115 rule that if one is very happy, one may recite the *berachah*, especially on close relatives.

29 I heard from Rav Avraham Cohen that Rav Shlomo Zalman Auerbach recited the *berachah* upon seeing his sister whom he had not seen in a long time. See also *Halichos Beisah*, p. 122.

30 *Shaarei Berachah* 12:24.

31 *Mishnah Berurah* 225:2, *Shaar Hatziyun* 225:3. See also *Yechaveh Daas* 3:17 and *Ahaleich B'Amitecha* 15:7.

32 See *Shaar Ha'ayin* 20:1, based on *Berachos* 58b. *Maharsha* points out that since people are judged for life or death on Rosh Hashanah and Yom Kippur, seeing the person is a sign that he was written for life. See *Halichos Shlomo* 23, note 47, and *Shaar Ha'ayin* 20:2, and *Iyunim* (ibid.). One can also look at it from the perspective of the *Ritva*, *Taanis* 3b, who expands the concept of "revival" to include all types of recovery from "death-like" situations, such as waking up in the morning, the birth of a child, recovering from an illness, and the growth of vegetation. In the same sense, when one has not seen a person for twelve months, it is as if they have been "nonexistent." Rav Avraham Kook (*Olas Re'iyah*, p. 380, as brought in *Peninei Halachah*, *Berachos*, p. 387) explains that not seeing one's good friend for a year creates changes in one's soul. He describes how the external feelings of friendship get dimmer as they recede into the depths of one's psyche, and how they are revived when meeting the

Common custom nowadays, however, is not to recite this *berachah*.[33] Some authorities rule that one should say it to oneself,[34] while others suggest that one should merely say, "*Baruch Hashem*, I see that you are well!"[35]

3. Pen Pal

According to common custom, even if one feels very close to an individual with whom he has been corresponding but has never met, he does not recite the *berachah* when seeing him.[36]

---

friend again. The awakening of these hidden feelings resembles a sort of *techiyas ha'meisim*. The reunification of these two yearning souls is similar to *techiyas ha'meisim*, which will reunite souls with their loved ones. See also *Minhag Yisrael Torah*, vol. 1, p. 354, and *Maharal*, *Bava Kama* 9, for further discussion.

33   Some say that this *berachah* is only recited if one has no idea of the whereabouts of the person and whether he or she is still alive. However, nowadays, due to our advanced communication systems, we usually know the well-being of good friends and relatives.

34   *Kaf Hachaim OC* 225:6.

35   *Shaarei Berachah* 21:24; *Birkas Habayis* 24:1.

36   See *Shaarei Berachah* 21:11, note 25. The *Netziv* recited the *berachah* on people about whom he was very excited, even if he had never seen them before. See also *Har Tzvi OC* 115.

Chapter Eight

Birkas Ha'nissim—
the Berachah for Miracles

*Due to the various opinions on these matters, one should make sure to consult
with a rabbi for specific guidance. It is important to point out that Birkas
Ha'gomel should be recited after most of the following situations.*

A. INTRODUCTION

The Rabbis instituted a set of thanksgiving *berachos* when visiting places where certain types of miraculous salvations[1] occurred, either to individuals or to the entire Jewish nation. These miracles can be categorized into two categories:

1. "Supernatural" miracles: This category includes when people were saved from dangerous situations in which under normal conditions there would be no chance of survival.[2]

---

1 The definition of a miracle is complex. See *Aruch Hashulchan OC* 219:1–4. See *Michtav M'Eliyahu*, vol. 1, pp. 177–83, who discusses the various levels of miracles at great length. On the one hand, there are daily miracles. One of the meanings of the word *nes* is a "banner" or "mast" (like that of a boat). As such, any occurrence that shows the presence of Hashem in one's life can be categorized as a *nes*. Every day, we thank Hashem in the *Modim* prayer when we recite the words "*V'al nisecha she'b'chol yom imanu*." This refers to the many miracles of daily survival that include our health, sustenance, livelihood, weather, and the like. Jewish history is full of all types of miracles—from the daily miracles in the Beis Hamikdash (see *Pirkei Avos* 5:8) to the continued survival of the Jewish People. The focus of this *berachah* is on "miracles" that are exceptional—i.e., that seem to be supernatural—happenings. See *Mekor Chaim*, pp. 194–95, for more discussion.

2 In the words of the *Abudraham (Berachos)*: "*Nes mofsi yotzei mi'geder ha'olam*," i.e., something that everybody recognizes is clearly the hand of Hashem. *Piskei Teshuvos* 218, notes 58–60, 65; *Peninei Halachah*, p. 343; *Shevet Halevi* 7:28. While some authorities (*Yalkut Yosef* 218:4; *Birkas Hashem* 4:6:45) rule that the *berachah* is only recited on supernatural events, most authorities understand it to refer to any situation where the chances of survival are minimal.

2. "Natural" miracles: This category incudes people being saved from dangerously fatal situations in a natural way, when chances of survival are minimal or the fatal circumstance just missed him, as we will see below.

In the first category, a full *berachah* is warranted. In the second, as we will see, there are various opinions, and thus a shortened *berachah* may be in place.[3]

1. Which *Berachos*

Upon returning to the site of the miracle, one recites the following *berachah*:

בָּרוּךְ...שֶׁעָשָׂה לִי נֵס בְּמָקוֹם הַזֶּה.

Baruch...she'asah li neis b'makom ha'zeh—Blessed...Who made a miracle for me in this place.

If the miracle happened to one's family, one recites:

בָּרוּךְ...שֶׁעָשָׂה לָנוּ נֵס בְּמָקוֹם הַזֶּה.

Baruch...she'asah lanu neis b'makom ha'zeh—Blessed...Who made a miracle for us in this place.

This would explain the *yotzei mi'geder ha'olam* and not *yotzei mi'geder ha'teva*. In *Berachos* 54a, the following examples are given: (1) being saved from a lion; (2) being saved in a desert from thirst by the sudden appearance of a spring; and (3) being attacked by a wild camel. In these cases, all opinions agree that any salvation (*hatzalah*) is considered *she'lo k'derech ha'olam* and would require a *berachah*. See *Shaar Ha'ayin*, pp. 170–72, for further discussion.

3   There is an involved discussion in *Shulchan Aruch OC* 218:9 concerning whether one recites a *berachah* when saved *k'derech ha'olam* (natural means), such as one who is rescued from bandits by someone who shows up unexpectedly. The first opinion says that no *berachah* is recited, while the second opinion says that a full *berachah* must be recited. *Shulchan Aruch* concudes that one should recite the *berachah* without including Hashem's name. *Chayei Adam* 65:4 rules that one who is saved from a dangerous attack in what seems to be a natural manner should not recite the *berachah* in full; rather, it should be recited without *Shem u'malchus*. See *Mizmor L'Sodah*, p. 57, for a full discussion of various opinions and applications. See also *Piskei Teshuvos* 218, note 76, and *Peninei Halachah*, p. 343. *Mekor Chaim*, p. 198, opines that this is why the Sages focused on the Chanukah miracle of the oil and not on the victorious battles.

2. Various Halachos

One may only make this *berachah* if he has not seen the place within the past thirty days. However, if he is not reciting the full *berachah* (with *Shem u'malchus*), he may say it as often as he likes. **It is even considered praiseworthy to recite it as often as possible.**

When reciting the *berachah* for a personal miracle, it is appropriate to add all the other places where one experienced a personal miracle.[4]

B. MIRACLES EXPERIENCED BY INDIVIDUALS OR FAMILIES

1. When Saved Miraclously from Definite Mortal Danger

When an individual or family is saved in a miraculous (supernatural) way from an extremely dangerous situation that most people do not survive, a full *berachah* is to be recited.

Some examples include:

- Surviving the collapse of a building that killed most people[5]
- Surviving a fall from a very tall building[6]
- Surviving a bus explosion or a serious car accident where many people were killed[7]
- Some authorities include Holocaust survivors who survived terrible experiences[8]

---

4   See *Shulchan Aruch OC* 218:5; *Shaar Hatziyun* 218:12. This idea is derived from Yisro in *Shemos* 18:8. In addition, I heard from Rav Joseph B. Soloveitchik a similar thought concerning the idea that when one thanks Hashem, he should expand the thanks to other areas as well. For example, we find Chazal adding this inclusive thanks for all good things in *Birkas Hamazon* ("*V'al Ha'kol*"), in *Shemoneh Esreh* ("*V'al Kulam*"), and in the *Birkas Haftarah* ("*V'al Ha'kol*").

5   *Mishnah Berurah* 218:32; *Shaar Hatziyun* 218:28. Even though there are two opinions in the *Shulchan Aruch* concerning *nissim k'minhag ha'olam*, all agree that when one has survived *she'lo k'derech ha'olam*, he recites a *berachah* (*Chayei Adam* 65:4; *Mishnah Berurah* 218:32). See *Piskei Teshuvos* 218, note 58, who cites commentaries who say that the Purim story is considered *she'lo k'derech ha'olam*, either because the edict of the king was changed or because Achashveirosh killed eighty thousand of his own people because of his love for one woman.

6   *Shaar Hatziyun* 218:29; *Piskei Teshuvos* 218:10.

7   *Avnei Yashfe* 1:46 reports that Rav Shalom Elyashiv and Rav Vozner rule that the *berachah* should be recited in full. Of course, this may depend on how close one was to the explosion or crash.

8   *B'Tzeil Hachochmah* 5:62.

2. When Saved in a More Natural Way

One who returns to a place where he was saved (in a "more" natural way) from a very dangerous situation that is nearly impossible for anyone to survive should recite the shortened *berachah* without including Hashem's name. However, if one escaped from such danger by himself on his own, no *berachah* is recited.[9]

Some examples include:

- One who was saved from a fire by another person, such as a fireman, who arrived at the last minute.[10] However, no *berachah* should be recited if one escaped from the deadly smoke on his own.[11]
- One who was accosted by robbers or terrorists but saved at the last minute by the appearance of people or soldiers. However, if one ran away before being sighted, no *berachah* is recited.
- One who was injured—but not killed!—by gunfire.[12]
- One who was saved when in a car that swerved off the highway and fell into a ravine.

3. Close Calls

If the source of the danger just **missed** him, a shortened *berachah* (without *Shem u'malchus*) should be recited. For example:

- There was an explosion on a bus, and the person was not sitting so close to the **center** of the explosion.
- The person was shot at and the bullet missed him.[13]
- An item fell off the roof of a house and just missed the person.

---

9   *Piskei Teshuvos* 218, note 74.

10   To recite a full *berachah*, one must be saved in a "miraculous" way. Here the salvation came in a "natural" way.

11   *Piskei Teshuvos* 218, note 88. Being saved by other people is considered much more natural than surviving a fall from a high building, which is considerably more miraculous.

12   *Mishnah Berurah* 218:32; *Shaarei Berachah* 22:39; *Mekor Chaim*, p. 198.

13   See *Piskei Teshuvos* 218:10, notes 58 and 76, for full discussion about criteria necessary to recite a *berachah* when rocks are thrown upon a bus or car.

4. Parents and Grandparents

The descendants of survivors should also recite the following *berachah* when seeing a place where their relatives survived:[14]

For a father (or mother):

בָּרוּךְ...שֶׁעָשָׂה לְאָבִי (לְאִמִּי) נֵס בְּמָקוֹם הַזֶּה.

Baruch...she'asah l'avi (l'imi) neis b'makom ha'zeh—Blessed... Who made a miracle for my father (or mother) in this place.

For grandparents (and other previous generations):

בָּרוּךְ...שֶׁעָשָׂה לִזְקֵנַי (לַאֲבוֹתַי) נֵס בְּמָקוֹם הַזֶּה.

Baruch...she'asah l'zekeinai (l'avosai) neis b'makom ha'zeh—Blessed...Who made a miracle for my grandparents (or ancestors) in this place.[15]

5. Other Close Relatives

There is basis for one to recite the *berachah* without including Hashem's name on a miracle that happened to one's children.[16] However, it appears that no *berachah* is recited over the survival of a spouse, though it is definitely appropriate to say words of thanks to Hashem.

For example, if one's children (*chas v'shalom*) were in a bad accident, parents can recite the abridged *berachah* every time they pass the spot at which the accident occurred.

6. Concentration Camps

A number of authorities are of the opinion that one who survived the evils of the concentration camps should recite the full *berachah* when visiting them.[17] It is also appropriate for all descendants of Holocaust

---

14   *Mishnah Berurah* 218:16–17; *Shaar Ha'ayin* 13:17.

15   *Shulchan Aruch OC* 218:4, *Mishnah Berurah* 218:16. See *The Travelers Halachic Handbook*, p. 70, for various other wordings.

16   *Be'er Moshe* 2:13, 17. *Rabbeinu Yonah* and *Meiri* write that the *berachah* is based on the joy and appreciation of the benefit gained from the survival of a very dear person.

17   *B'Tzeil Hachochmah* 5:62. In addition, he suggests that the fact that the Nazis kept Jews alive at the end of the war and were not afraid of retribution from their superiors is a *neis gamur*. See further discussion in *Ahaleich B'Amitecha* 13:23, note 27. It would seem that this

survivors to recite the *berachah* (at least without including Hashem's name) when visiting the concentration camps where their parents or grandparents survived.[18] There are grounds to also recite the *berachah* of *Dayan ha'emes* without including Hashem's name. This is based on the halachah that *Dayan ha'emes* is recited when seeing the "Pillar of Lot's wife" because it is a place where terrible things happened, and one feels in pain.[19]

7. Seeing Holocaust Survivors

The *Shulchan Aruch* writes that one who sees a person who experienced a miracle that would warrant one of the *berachos* outlined above should recite the following *berachah* without including Hashem's name:

בָּרוּךְ...שֶׁעָשָׂה לְךָ נֵס בְּמָקוֹם הַזֶּה.

Baruch...she'asah lecha neis b'makom ha'zeh—Blessed...Who made a miracle for you in this place.[20]

---

ruling is based on the opinion of *Chayei Adam* (25:4, *Nishmas Adam* 1), who opines that one recites a full *berachah* even when he is saved in a natural way from a certain mortal danger. See *Nesivos Haberachah*, p. 446, note 111, who discusses how one can learn this out from the story of Purim. See also *Taz* 218:6, who says that an event that everyone admits is the hand of Hashem is deserving of a *berachah* (*ha'kol modeh etzba elokim hi*). See *Shaar Ha'ayin* 23:20 for a full discussion. I heard that Rav Yehoshua Neuwirth recited the *berachah* in full when visiting a place in Amsterdam where a special miracle happened to him (see the introduction to *Shemiras Shabbos K'Hilchasah*). I also heard from Rav Yossi Cohen that Rav Moshe Shapiro opined that the *berachah* should not be made in the "area of selection" but rather in the "bunkers." Cf. *Mishnah Berurah* 218:30, *Shaar Hatziyun* 26, who seems to hold that the *berachah* should be recited without Hashem's name. See *Shaar Ha'ayin* 23:20 for a full discussion. I heard from Rav David Cohen and other authorities that the *berachah* is said only when there was a full act of aggression inflicted upon the person from whom he was saved, but this was not always the case.

18   *Shulchan Aruch OC* 218:4; *Mishnah Berurah* 218:16–17; *Shaar Hatziyun* 218:10.

19   This was relayed to me in correspondence from Rav Asher Weiss. See *Shulchan Aruch OC* 218–8. See *Shaar Ha'ayin*, p. 169 (23:44). We don't say a *berachah* on Lot's wife because we don't know where the real pillar is located.

20   *Shulchan Aruch OC* 218:6; *Mishnah Berurah* 218:21,22; *Shaar Hatziyun* 218:17; *Shaar Ha'ayin* 23:15; *Kaf Hachaim OC* 218:27. An alternate version is *She'asah neis la'adam ha'zeh*. *Ahaleich B'Amitecha* 13:53 writes that the *berachah* is not recited a second time if one sees the person and then sees the place (or vice versa) within thirty days.

Based on this halachah, some *poskim* conclude that upon seeing one's parents or grandparents who miraculously survived the Holocaust, one recites the following *berachah* (if he has not seen them in thirty days):

> *Baruch...She'asah l'avi (l'imi / l'zikni) neis b'makom ha'zeh—*
> *Blessed...Who made a miracle for my father (or mother or grandparent/s) in this place.*

8. Seeing a Lion Cage

Some say that when seeing a lions' cage, one should recite the *berachah*:

בָּרוּךְ...שֶׁעָשָׂה נֵס לְצַדִּיקִים (כְּ)בְּמָקוֹם הַזֶּה.

Baruch...she'asah neis l'tzaddikim (k')b'makom ha'zeh—
Blessed...Who made a miracle for tzaddikim (like) in this place.

This is intended to remind us of the miracle of Daniel in the lions' den.[21]

9. Thanking Hashem in Other Ways

When special salvations occurred, even in cases where no *berachah* is to be recited, it is appropriate to thank Hashem in one of the following ways:

- To recite the *parashah* of *korban todah* (*Vayikra* 7:13–18), *Mizmor L'Sodah* (*Tehillim* 100), and the *Nishmas* prayer
- To have in mind one's gratitude for the miracle when reciting *Ha'gomel chassadim tovim* in the morning blessings, when reciting *Barchu* and *Baruch Hashem ha'mevorach* as one is called to the Torah in shul, or when reciting *Modim*[22]
- To involve oneself with public needs
- To publish a *sefer*
- To host a *seudas hodaah* and tell the people present about the miracle

---

21 *Shaar Ha'ayin* 23:14, note 41; *Maharshal,* based on the *Rambam,* cited in *Bach* 218; *Kaf Hachaim OC* 218:32.

22 *Mishnah Berurah* 218:32; *Piskei Teshuvos* 218:11.

C. MIRACLES THAT OCCURRED TO THE JEWISH PEOPLE

One who sees **places** where a miracle occurred to the Jewish People should recite the *berachah* of *She'asah neis l'avoseinu ba'makom ha'zeh.*[23] According to some opinions, this applies even nowadays, even though we may visit the general area and not know the specific spot.[24]

The *Kaf Hachaim* suggests that one can recite the *berachah* (without including Hashem's name) when seeing places such as the Red Sea, the Jordan River,[25] the city of Jericho (near the walls of Jericho),[26] or Mount Carmel.[27] In addition, the *Mishnah Berurah* quotes from *Kaftor V'Ferach* that one who sees any part of the Red Sea or Jordan River should remember the great kindness of Hashem and praise Him.

Even a convert should recite these *berachos.*[28]

---

23 *Shulchan Aruch OC* 218:1; *Mishnah Berurah* 218:10; *Shaar Ha'ayin* 23:13.

24 *Piskei Teshuvos* 218:3; *Kaf Hachaim OC* 218:4; *Ahaleich B'Amitecha* 13:2.

25 Especially a place that is called Quasr al Yahud, which is off the Kvish HaBika (Highway 90), or others point out a place called Nachal Tirtzah (Wadi Farah). *Mishnah Berurah* 218:2; *Biur Halachah* 218, s.v. *K'gon*; *Ohr L'Tzion* 2:14:40 says that if one sees only a part of the area, he should say the *berachah* without including Hashem's name. When seeing the entire area, such as by helicopter, the *berachah* is recited in full.

26 This can be seen from the Mitzpeh Yericho settlement along the highway to Jericho. One should also contemplate the conquering of Eretz Yisrael in the days of Yehoshua. See *Mizmor L'sodah*, p. 11, for a discussion in *Berachos* 54b whether the walls of Jericho fell or were swallowed up.

27 *Biur Halachah* ad loc. See also *Shaar Ha'ayin*, chap. 23, note 3. When we see the place where Eliyahu built an altar on Mount Carmel, we remember the great *kiddush Hashem* of the miraculous fire that descended from Hashem in front of the people and the false prophets, and how Eliyahu was thus saved from King Achav. Some identify the place today by what is known as Mukhraka at the southeastern peak of Mount Carmel.

28 *Shaar Ha'ayin* 23:14. *Chut Shani, Birkas Hodaah*, p. 398. See also *Shulchan Aruch OC* 59:19 and *Ahaleich B'Amitecha* 13:4. The concept of *"avoseinu"* applies to them as well. See *Mizmor L'sodah*, which says that this may be based on the verse, "I have made you a father of a multitude of nations" (*Bereishis* 6:17). See also *Nesivos Haberachah* 29:28.

Chapter Nine

Seeing Synagogues and Jewish Communities in Eretz Yisrael—Rebuilt or in Desolation

A. INTRODUCTION

ת״ר הרואה בתי ישראל בישובן אומר ברוך מציב גבול אלמנה
בחורבנן אומר ברוך דיין האמת.

The Sages taught: One who sees the houses of Israel inhabited recites, "Baruch...Matziv gevul almanah—Blessed...Who establishes the border of the widow." [One who sees them] in ruins recites, "Baruch...Dayan ha'emes—Blessed...the true Judge."

(Berachos 58b)

These *berachos* are to be recited upon seeing Jewish "homes" or communities in Eretz Yisrael that were destroyed and have been rebuilt or are still in a state of desolation. There is discussion among the authorities whether these "houses" refer to synagogues (*batei knesses*) or to actual beautiful "homes."[1]

---

1   *Shulchan Aruch OC* 224:10; *Mishnah Berurah* 224:14. There is a discussion in the *Mishnah Berurah* whether this *berachah* is to be recited upon seeing beautiful homes or beautiful synagogues. The *Eliyahu Rabbah* even suggests that this *berachah* may even apply to the Diaspora. The conclusion of the *Mishnah Berurah* is that the abridged version of the *bera-chah* **should** be said when seeing a beautiful rebuilt synagogue. The *Kaf Hachaim* 224:35

85

The verse in *Eichah* states that Eretz Yisrael in its desolation has become like an *almanah* (widow).[2] *Maharsha* explains that she is only "like" a widow because she can be compared to an unfaithful wife whose husband will return to her when she will return to him. So too, Israel is not really widowed; Hashem will return to Israel and the Jewish People when they do *teshuvah*.[3] That being said, the wording of "widow" helps us focus on our loss. The *berachah* of *Matziv gevul almanah* affirms our appreciation of one of the greatest miracles of our day, namely, the revival of Eretz Yisrael. Witnessing the resettling of the land and the ingathering of exiles should surely strengthen our faith.

Seeing the destruction of particularly well-known places in Eretz Yisrael should bring a certain sadness; hence the *berachah* of *Dayan ha'emes* is recited.

B. REBUILT SYNAGOGUES AND SETTLEMENTS

As mentioned above, there is a *machlokes* among the authorities concerning the applicability of this *berachah*.[4] The conclusion of the *Mishnah Berurah* is that one should recite *Baruch matziv gevul almanah* without Hashem's name (shortened *berachah*) when one visits[5] newly built beautiful synagogues[6] and is **inspired** by their sight.[7] Other authorities include seeing new settlements, or even new sections of older cities in Eretz Yisrael (especially if they have a synagogue).[8] There are

---

suggests that even in the Diaspora it should be said, but in the shortened form (without *Shem u'malchus*).

2   *Eichah* 1:1.

3   *Maharsha, Berachos* 58b.

4   In addition to the question of what is actually considered a "house," the authorities seem to disagree whether the "homes" need to be rebuilt in the "actual" places where they stood, or whether we can consider all of Eretz Yisrael "destroyed," and is now being rebuilt. (See further opinion of Rav Avigdor Nebenzahl.)

5   These *berachos* are especially applicable to visitors. Those who live in these areas do not recite them as it is assumed that they no longer experience the necessary degree of *simchah* and excitement.

6   *Berachos* 58b; *Shulchan Aruch OC* 224:10; *Mishnah Berurah* 224:14.

7   *Shulchan Aruch OC* 224:13; The *berachah* (even in the shortened form) would only be made if he has not seen the synagogue within thirty days.

8   *Shulchan Aruch OC* 224:10; *Mishnah Berurah* 224:14. The *Kaf Hachaim* 224:35 suggests that even in the Diaspora, it should be said, but in the shortened form (without *Shem u'malchus*).

various authorities who opine that there are times today when one can recite a full *berachah* (see notes).[9]

While some authorities rule that the *berachah* is only recited the **first** time one sees them, others rule that as long as they still look new and one is excited or inspired by the sights (as long as they have not been seen within thirty days), the *berachah* should be recited. This *berachah* is especially relevant to people touring around Eretz Yisrael (especially for the first time).

Examples of these sites include the following:

- Seeing the many newly built (or rebuilt) synagogues in Jerusalem, such as the Belz Synagogue, the Churvah Synagogue, and others.
- Visiting newly built settlements and cities (especially when seeing the beautiful synagogues) in Gush Etzion, Judea, and Samaria.
- Visiting new neighborhoods (especially when seeing the beautiful synagogues), such as Ramat Beit Shemesh or Givat Ze'ev or new sections in Yerushalayim.

C. DESOLATE SETTLEMENTS OR SYNAGOGUES

If one sees Jewish settlements or synagogues in their desolation in Eretz Yisrael, he should recite *Baruch Dayan ha'emes* without the name of Hashem.[10] These would include the remnants of old homes in Tzippori, Usha, and Katzrin.

See Piskei Teshuvos 224:9 who points out that there is basis to even say the full *berachah* today in Eretz Yisrael.

9   *Shulchan Aruch Harav* (*Birkas Hanehenin* 13:11). Rav Avigdor Nebenzahl stipulates that the *berachah* only applies to a new synagogue built in a place that was settled by Jews during an earlier period (e.g., the Second Temple or pre-State periods. This includes synagogues in the Old City of Jerusalem, Rachel's Tomb, the Cave of *Machpeilah*, and Gush Etzion). Under these conditions, he ruled that one may even recite a full *berachah*. It is reported that Rav Yosef Shalom Elyashiv recited the full *berachah* when seeing the Churvah Synagogue. Rav Shlomo Zalman Auerbach recited the *berachah* when seeing Elon Moreh, and Rav Reuven Feinstein recited the *berachah* in Chevron (Beit K'nesset Avraham Avinu). See *Peninei Halachah, Harchavos*, p. 249, and *Peninei Halachah, Berachos*, p. 337, for opinions that it may be recited even on new neighborhoods.

10   *Shulchan Aruch OC* 224:10; *Shaarei Berachah* 21:33.

Some authorities rule that this also applies to synagogues in the Diaspora that were taken over by churches or were made into warehouses or other types of buildings. This was very common in Eastern Europe as a result of the Holocaust, as well as in changing neighborhoods in the United States.

D. CHURCHES, MONASTERIES, MOSQUES, IDOLATRY

One who sees a church or a monastery[11] should recite the *berachah*:

בָּרוּךְ...שֶׁנָּתַן אֶרֶךְ אַפַּיִם לְעוֹבְרֵי רְצוֹנוֹ.

Baruch...she'nasan erech apayim l'ovrei retzono—Blessed...
Who has patience with those who transgress His will.[12]

Nevertheless, common custom is not to recite this *berachah*, even if one has not seen the place within thirty days. The *Rama* points out that this is because many Jews are used to seeing them, and thus no special feelings of discomfort are aroused.[13] However, it would appear that those who are not used to such sights should recite the *berachah* (at least without including Hashem's name). This might include people who live in Eretz Yisrael, or any Jew who sees altars or images of the Hindu or Buddhist religion, for most Jews rarely see these sights.[14]

---

11 *Shaar Ha'ayin* 27:2, note 4. See also *Rambam, Mishneh Torah, Maachalos Asuros* 11:7; *Piskei Teshuvos* 224:2; *Divrei Yatziv* 1:90. All authorities seem to agree that this *berachah* would not be recited upon seeing a mosque.

12 We can derive a lesson in *chizuk emunah* from this *berachah*: The reason Hashem allows the *avodah zarah* to remain is only because of His outstanding attribute of patience.

13 *Rama OC* 224:1 writes that we don't recite this *berachah* nowadays since we are so accustomed to seeing churches. Some suggest it is because a church may not be considered a place of idolatry.

14 *Kaf Hachaim* 224:4; *Shaar Ha'ayin*, p. 180; *Peninei Halachah, Harchavos, Berachos*, p. 239; *Shaarei Berachah* 21:15, note 36; *Birkas Hashem*, vol. 4, p. 313.

One who sees a church,[15] monastery, or mosque[16] should recite the verse: "*Beis gei'im yisach Hashem v'yatzeiv gevul almanah*—He will uproot the house of the arrogant and uphold the boundary of the widow."[17]

E. DESTROYED CHURCHES, CHURCHES TURNED INTO SYNAGOGUES

One who sees a destroyed church that is in ruins, or a church that was bought in order to turn it into a synagogue, should recite the verse: "*Keil nekamos Hashem, Keil nekamos hofia*—Hashem is God of vengeance, God of vengeance appeared."[18]

One who sees a place in Eretz Yisrael from where idolatry was removed, such as an old pagan temple that is now destroyed,[19] or a church that was turned into a synagogue, should recite the *berachah* (without including Hashem's name):

בָּרוּךְ...שֶׁעָקַר עֲבוֹדָה זָרָה מֵאַרְצֵנוּ.

Baruch...she'akar avodah zarah mei'artzeinu—Blessed...Who uproots idolatry from His land.

When seeing such a place in the Diaspora,[20] one recites the *berachah* (without including Hashe"'s name):

בָּרוּךְ...שֶׁעָקַר עֲבוֹדָה זָרָה מֵהַמָּקוֹם הַזֶּה.

Baruch...she'akar avodah zarah mei'ha'makom ha'zeh—Blessed...Who uproots idolatry from this place.

In both cases, after reciting the *berachah*, one should add the words:

---

15 See *Shaar Ha'ayin*, chap. 27, note 5, for a discussion on whether a building that has a cross on it is considered a place of idolatry. The question is whether a cross is simply an adornment or whether it is actually worshipped. See also *Shulchan Aruch YD* 141:1 and 150:3; *B'Tzeil Hachochmah* 2:84.

16 See *Shaar Ha'ayin* 26:6.

17 *Mishlei* 15:25; *Shulchan Aruch OC* 224:11.

18 *Tehillim* 94:1; *Shulchan Aruch OC* ad loc.

19 For example, Banias in the Golan Heights.

20 This is a common occurrence in the Diaspora, where because of neighborhood changes, churches are turned into synagogues.

"K'sheim she'akarta osah mei'ha'makom ha'zeh kein taakor osah mi'kol ha'mekomos v'hasheiv leiv ovdeihem l'ovdecha—In the same way that You uprooted it (the *avodah zarah*) from this place, may You also uproot it from all places, and may You bring back the hearts of those worshipping it to worship You."[21]

F. VISITING CHURCHES

Even though it is permitted to walk on the sidewalk in front of a church, one should try keep a distance of at least four *amos* (6–8 ft) from the entrance.[22] One is forbidden to enter the actual church room (where services take place) under any circumstances.[23] It is questionable whether one may visit and tour Vatican City.[24] When necessary, some authorities permit entering a church building (a separate hall) for voting or other purposes.[25] One should avoid looking at the religious pictures in these buildings or listening to church music.[26] It is permitted

---

21   *Shulchan Aruch OC* 224:2; *Berachos* 57b. *Rashi* writes that this phrase refers to Jewish sinners, whereas *Rashba* says it refers to the non-Jews.

22   *YD* 150:1; if there are no images, there may be leniency. See *Halachically Speaking*, vol. 1, p. 295.

23   According to many opinions (*Ritva, Avodah Zarah* 11b; *Shulchan Aruch YD* 150:1; *Shach, YD* 149:1), a church is considered to be a place of idolatry. (It would seem that even if it is not considered idolatry today for the non-Jews who believe in the Trinity, concerning Jews it is considered idolatry; I heard this from Rav David Feinstein and Rav Herschel Shechter). The *Rambam, Mishneh Torah, Avodah Zarah* 9:4 (uncensored edition); *Rambam, Peirush Hamishnayos* 1:4; *Shut Binyan Tzion* 1:63; *Shut Tzitz Eliezer* 14:91. However, see *Meiri, Bava Kama* 113b, who does not seem to consider it idolatry.

24   *Shulchan Aruch YD* 149:2 discusses whether it is forbidden to pass through the courtyard of a place of idolatry (where no religious services take place). *Igros Moshe YD* 3:129 and *Yechaveh Daas* 4:45 forbid doing so. Note: Even those who pass through such places are not allowed to enjoy any of the religious pictures.

25   *Teshuvos V'Hanhagos* 2:410; *Halachically Speaking*, vol. 1, p. 298. *She'arim Hametzuyanim B'Halachah* 167:9. There are various opinions among the *poskim* whether one may enter for athletic purposes, such as to exercise in a gym. Rav Moshe Feinstein in *Igros Moshe OC* 4:40:26 did not allow one to enter a YMCA or church, even for exercise. It is interesting to note that *Divrei Chachamim*, p. 191, reports that Rav Yosef Shalom Elyashiv permitted using the YMCA facilities in Eretz Yisrael since they were mostly used by Jews.

26   *Avnei Yashfe* 1:53:4, 5; *Igros Moshe YD* 2:56.

to attend a sale in a churchyard if the money is not going toward idolatry.[27] It is also permitted to look at a clock on the outside of a church.[28]

G. CROSSES

The *Rama* says that the crosses that the non-Jews wear around their neck are just a symbol of their idolatry, and not an actual object of idolatry.[29] One is permitted to wear clothing that has patterns in the shape of a cross.[30] One may also collect stamps and awards that have the image of a cross on them.[31] It is permitted to write a plus sign because its form has nothing to do with a cross.[32]

H. ENTERING A MOSQUE

The consensus of authorities is that the religion of Islam is not considered a form of idolatry. Therefore, it is permitted to enter a mosque when necessary.[33]

---

27   *Yaskil Avdi* 8:20:46; *Teshuvos V'Hanhagos* 1:463; *Halachically Speaking*, vol. 1, p. 296.

28   *Minchas Elazar* 2:73 and *Teshuvos V'Hanhagos* 2:412.

29   *Shulchan Aruch YD* 141:1.

30   *Avnei Yashfe* 1:152.

31   *Igros Moshe YD* 1:69.

32   Ibid.; *Halachically Speaking*, vol. 1, p. 300. In Eretz Yisrael, many have the custom to alter the form of the plus sign.

33   *Avnei Yashfe* 1:153. See also *Hegyonei Haparashah*, vol. 1, p. 112, for additional authorities who permit it. Interestingly, *Tzitz Eliezer* 14:91:4 considers Islam to be *avodah zarah* and thus forbids entering a mosque.

Chapter Ten

Seeing Multitudes of People—Chacham Ha'razim

The *berachah* of *Chacham ha'razim* (He Who knows all secrets) is recited when seeing 600,000 Jews together in one place, corresponding to the number of Jewish men (from the age of twenty to sixty) who were present at *Matan Torah*. Such an occasion is considered significant because, despite the many different facial appearances and varying opinions and mindsets, there is still one "Greater Mind" above them all.[1] A number of authorities rule that it is not necessary to see all 600,000 Jews at the same time.[2]

One who sees 600,000 idolators should recite the verse: "*Bosha imchem me'od, chofrah yoladatchem; hinei acharis goyim midbar tziyah v'aravah*—Your mother is very shamed, the one who bore you is embarrassed; behold, the final outcome of the nations is as a wilderness, a wasteland, and a desert."[3]

---

1   *Berachos* 58a; *Shulchan Aruch OC* 224:5. It is interesting to note that the *Kaf Hachaim* (*OC* 224:15) rules that the *berachah* is only recited in Eretz Yisrael. *Mekor Chaim*, p. 217, states that 600,000 was the prerequisite number of people necessary to enable Hashem to rest his *Shechinah* upon the Jewish People at the time of *Matan Torah*; see *Kuzari* 2:14.

2   *Imrei Meir*, p. 26, quotes Rav Azriel Auerbach who holds that one must actually see all 600,000 people. On the other hand, Rav Chaim Kanievsky and Rav Nissim Karelitz (*Chut Hashani, Birchos Hodaah*, p. 189) hold that it is enough to simply see a massive gathering. Rav Yitzchak Zilberstein rules that a police report of 600,000 in attendance is sufficient grounds to recite the *berachah*. *L'maaseh*, Rav Baruch Ezrachi recited it a recent gathering in Yerushalayim.

3   *Yirmiyahu* 50:12; *Shulchan Aruch OC* 224:5.

Chapter Eleven
Holy Places

A. CITIES OF YEHUDAH

One who sees the cities in Judea (or in the land of Binyamin[1]) in their desolation should recite the following verse and rend his garment.[2]

עָרֵי קָדְשְׁךָ הָיוּ מִדְבָּר.

Arei kodshecha hayu midbar—Your holy cities have become a desert.

(Yeshayahu 64:9)

Most authorities write that the above procedure is not observed nowadays because many of the cities are under the control of a Jewish government and thus are not considered desolate.[3]

---

1   *Tel Talpiyos*, p. 53; *Mishnas Yavetz* 48:1.

2   *Shulchan Aruch OC* 561:1. Such cities would include Jericho, Bethlehem, Gaza, Beer Sheva, and others. Concerning Chevron, see *Shaarei Teshuvah* 561:1 and *Tel Talpiyos*, p. 53. The *Mishnah Berurah* 561:2 points out that these cities are still considered desolate if they are under the rule of gentile authority, even though Jews are living there. There is an interesting discussion regarding cities under Jewish control where only Arabs live. The question revolves around the criteria to be used for the city to be considered "desolate." Some authorities (*Zichron Betzalel*, p. 142) opine that if it is under Jewish control, it is not considered desolate. *Kaftor V'Ferach* requires that the city must also have a substantial Jewish presence. *Levush* maintains that until the Beis Hamikdash is rebuilt, all the cities of Yehudah are considered desolate. See discussion in *Bach OC* 561 and *Beis Yosef OC* 561. Regarding the status of cities under the Palestinian Authority where the Israeli Army are entitled to enter, see *Kum His'haleich B'Aretz*, pp. 76–78) who cites Rav Bakshi Doron (*Binyan Av* 4:30) and Rav Shlomo Zalman Auerbach as saying that there is basis to require these procedures in these areas. See also *Peninas Hamikdash*, p. 301.

3   *Igros Moshe* 4:70:11 and 5:37:1. Cf. *Peninas Hamikdash*, pp. 317–18, and *Mo'adim U'Z'manim* 4:348 in the note. *Be'er Moshe*, vol. 7, *Kuntres Dinei B'nei Eretz Yisrael*, writes that even if Israel was under a religious government, we would still be obligated to follow these procedures.

Additionally, in many cases we do not know the exact location of the ancient city.[4]

B. JERUSALEM

One who sees the Old City of Jerusalem in its desolation[5] should cry, wail, recite the following verse, and rend his garment:[6]

צִיּוֹן מִדְבָּר הָיָתָה יְרוּשָׁלַ͏ִם שְׁמָמָה.

Tzion midbar hayasah, Yerushalayim shemamah—Tzion has become a desert, Jerusalem a desolation.[7]

(Yeshayahu 64:9)

Contemporary authorities debate whether nowadays Jerusalem is considered a desolate city:

- Rav Moshe Feinstein rules that since Jerusalem is under Jewish control, it is no longer desolate, and thus there is no need to rend one's garments and recite the verse.[8]
- In contrast, Rav Moshe Shternbuch writes that it will only be considered rebuilt when the *Beis Hamikdash* is rebuilt. In addition, Rav Shlomo Zalman Auerbach suggests that the continued presence of places of worship and cemeteries of other religions in our holy city demonstrates that it is not truly under Jewish

---

4   *Ir Hakodesh V'Hamikdash* 17:2.

5   According to some authorities (*Yerushalayim B'Mo'adeha*, p. 244), this refers to the borders of the Old City in the days of the first Beis Hamikdash. For a discussion regarding the extent of those borders at that time, see *Tel Talpiyos*, p. 56, and *Peninas Hamikdash*, p. 500. Other authorities opine that these laws apply to seeing any part of the Old City. *Mishnah Berurah* (*Dirshu*) 561, note 3, reports that *Chazon Ish* and the Steipler Gaon performed *keriah* at the entrance of today's Old City.

6   See *Tel Talpiyos*, p. 57; *Minchas Shlomo* 1:73; *Be'er Moshe*, vol. 7.

7   *Shaarei Nechamah*, p. 144, notes that in over 650 places in Tanach (with only five exceptions), Yerushalayim is written without a *yud*. Tosafos (*Taanis* 16b, s.v. *har Har she'yatze'ah*) explains that the word *Yerushalayim* is a combination of the name *Shalem*, given to it by Shem ben Noach ("*Malkitzedek melech Shalem*" [*Bereishis* 14:18]) and the name *Yireh* given by Avraham ("*B'har Hashem Yireh*" [ibid., 22:14]), and therefore no *yud* is necessary. Although it is written without a *yud*, it is pronounced with a *yud* (the plural form) in order to hint that the physical "Yerushalayim of Below" is connected to the "Yerushalayim of Above," which is destined to descend (*Taanis* 5a).

8   *Igros Moshe OC* 4:70:11 and 5:37:1.

control.[9] In this context, Rav Yisrael Yaakov Kanievsky, the *Kehillas Yaakov*, is reported to have said, "The Americans are running the show." According to these authorities one is required to tear and recite the verse.

C. TEMPLE MOUNT GATES

Upon seeing one of the original gates around the Temple Mount, a special verse is to be recited:

טָבְעוּ בָאָרֶץ שְׁעָרֶיהָ אִבַּד וְשִׁבַּר בְּרִיחֶיהָ מַלְכָּה וְשָׂרֶיהָ בַגּוֹיִם אֵין תּוֹרָה גַּם נְבִיאֶיהָ לֹא מָצְאוּ חָזוֹן מֵה'.

Tavu va'aretz she'areha ibad v'shibar bericheha malkah v'sareha va'goyim ein Torah gam nevieha lo matzu chazon mei'Hashem—Her gates are sunk into the ground; He has destroyed and broken her bars; her king and her officers are among the nations; there is no Torah; her prophets too find no vision from Hashem.

(Eichah 2:9)[10]

The list of gates include:

- The two sealed gates on the eastern side of the Temple Mount, known as the *Shaarei Rachamim*—Gates of Mercy (*Bab Al Rachma* in Arabic). Some authorities point out that this gate is referred to in the Mishnah as the Shushan Gate.[11]

---

9   *Mo'adim U'Z'manim* 4:348; *Minchas Shlomo* 1:73.

10 *Bach* 561. See *Eretz Hatzvi*, p. 43; *Sefer Eretz Yisrael* 22:6; Rav Avraham Danzig, *Shaarei Tzedek, Mishpatei Eretz Yisrael* 11:7.

11 *Bach* ad loc.; Mishnah, *Middos* 1:3. See *Sefer Eretz Yisrael* ad loc.; *Tel Talpiyos*, p. 89; *Peninas Hamikdash*, p. 302. The Sages (*Sofrim* 19) relate that one door of the gate was for *chassanim* and one was for *aveilim*, who would be greeted as they passed through them. *Kaftor V'Ferach* 6; *Pe'as Hashulchan* 3:2; *Tzitz Eliezer* 10:1; *Ir Hakodesh*, p. 216. It is said that the cemetery now in front of these gates was placed there by the Arabs in the belief that this would prevent the arrival of Eliyahu HaNavi, who, as a Kohen, would be forbidden to walk among the graves. See *Zechariah* 14:4. Rav Ovadia MiBartenura (*Middos* 1:3, from *Menachos* 98a) writes that the Persians demanded that an engraving depicting the city of Shushan be placed on the gate in order to remind the Jews to still feel fear of their empire. Others say this was in fulfillment of Yirmiyahu's directive (*Yirmiyahu* 16:14–15; 23:7–8) to remember the *geulah*

- There are two gates on the southern side known as the *Shaarei Chuldah*.[12]
- There are those who recite this verse when seeing the *Kosel*, the western side of the Temple Mount, because of an ancient gate, known as *Shaar Kipunus*, located below the visible part of the *Kosel*, even though it is no longer fully recognizable today (see note).[13]

D. *MAKOM HAMIKDASH*—THE TEMPLE MOUNT

If one has not seen the Temple Mount for at least thirty days, one who sees the place where the Beis Hamikdash once stood should recite the verse:

בֵּית קָדְשֵׁנוּ וְתִפְאַרְתֵּנוּ אֲשֶׁר הִלְלוּךְ אֲבֹתֵינוּ הָיָה לִשְׂרֵפַת אֵשׁ וְכָל מַחֲמַדֵּינוּ הָיָה לְחָרְבָּה.

Beis kodesheinu v'sifarteinu asher hilelucha avoseinu hayah li'sereifas eish v'chol machamadeinu hayah l'chorbah—Our holy and beautiful house where our fathers praised You has been burned by fire, and all our precious things have become a ruin."

(Yeshayahu 64:10)

---

from Persia, similar to why we use the Persian names for the months (*Ramban, Bereishis* 12:2, s.v. *Ha'chodesh ha'zeh lachem*).

12   Many people used to enter the Beis Hamikdash from the southern gates. *Tiferes Yisrael* (*Middos* 1:3, *Yachin* 24) explains that it was called by this name because Chuldah the prophetess used to deliver her prophecies from this place. Others explain that its name comes from the fact that it ascended from below up to the floor level, like a mole's tunnel; such entranceways were indeed found on the south side.

13   *Middos* 3:1. There is much discussion among archaeological scholars concerning the position of this gate. Some identify this gate as the one below the *Shaar Hamugrabim* used nowadays to access the Temple Mount. *Tosafos Yom Tov* and *Tiferes Yisrael* (*Yachin* 25) write that this gate was located behind the *Kodesh Hakodashim* and contained a beautiful rose garden. *Kipunus* means "the product of the garden" in Greek. According to the archeological authorities, there are remnants of additional gates around the Temple Mount from the period of the Beis Hamikdash.

Some also recite:

בֵּית גֵּאִים יִסַּח ה' וְיַצֵּב גְּבוּל אַלְמָנָה.

Beis gei'im yisach Hashem v'yatzeiv gevul almanah—Hashem will destroy the house of the proud, but he will establish the border of the widow.

(Mishlei 15:25)

One bows toward the site of the Beis Hamikdash, **rends his garment,** and recites the *berachah* of *Baruch Dayan ha'emes* (without *Shem u'malchus*).[14] He should then mourn over the destruction of the Beis Hamikdash and offer a prayer that it be speedily rebuilt.

He then continues with the *Tzidduk Hadin* prayer and recites *Tehillim* 79, which bemoans the destruction of the Beis Hamikdash.[15]

What Must Be Seen

There are various opinions regarding which part of the Beis Hamikdash site must be seen:

- Some say that one must actually see the floor of where the Beis Hamikdash stood. This can only be seen from a few places, such as Mount Scopus, Mount of Olives, the Jerusalem promenade ("the *Tayelet*"), or the rooftops of the Moslem quarter.[16]
- Others say that one may perform *keriah* even if he only sees the Dome of the Rock or the *Kosel*.[17]

---

14   *Mishnah Berurah* 561:6; *Pe'as Hashulchan* 3:2. See *Tel Talpiyos*, p. 58; *Shaarei Nechamah*, p. 121; *Tzitz Eliezer* 10:1:88. *Igros Moshe YD* 3:129 writes that *Mishnah Berurah* would agree that there is nothing wrong with saying: "*Baruch atah melech ha'olam,*" as long as he leaves out the names of Hashem.

15   *Mishnah Berurah* 561:6; *Pe'as Hashulchan* 3:2. See *Tel Talpiyos*, p. 58; *Shaarei Nechamah*, p. 121; *Tzitz Eliezer* 10:1:88.

16   *Sefer Eretz Yisrael* 22:5; *Tel Talpiyos*, p. 60. *Teshuvos V'Hanhagos* 1:331 writes that this is the ideal practice.

17   *Igros Moshe OC* 4:70:11. *Teshuvos V'Hanhagos* ad loc. and *Tel Talpiyos* ad loc. write that this is the *minhag* of Yerushalayim. *Peninas Hamikdash*, p. 308, writes that the whole Har Habayis is considered part of the Beis Hamikdash in this context.

E. PERFORMING *KERIAH* TODAY

The great majority of authorities concur that upon seeing the *Makom Hamikdash*, *keriah* is obligatory even today. However, there are some who do not perform it in our times.[18] Some explain that this latter custom is based on the observation that most people don't genuinely feel the pain of the *Churban* nowadays.[19]

There is a custom that residents of Jerusalem do not perform *keriah*. Nevertheless, it is proper for everyone to try and fulfill this mitzvah at least once in their life.[20]

F. HOW TO PERFORM *KERIAH*

The custom is to rend only one item of clothing, such as a shirt or suit jacket.[21] However, even according to this view, some write that it is acceptable to remove the outer garment for a moment and perform *keriah* on the shirt.[22]

Women ideally should have an extra garment available in order to perform *keriah*. However, when necessary, they may rip the lower part of a garment (which is obviously not seen).[23]

---

18   According to the opinions cited above, seeing the *Kosel* may not qualify as seeing the *Makom Hamikdash*.

19   *Tel Talpiyos*, p. 83; *Mo'adim U'Z'manim* 7:257 writes that this applies especially to people who live in Eretz Yisrael and are faced with constant reminders of the desolation of the "King's Palace." If it is without meaning, there is no point to the *keriah* and may even be *baal tashchis*. *Peninas Hamikdash*, pp. 329–30; *Shaarei Nechamah*, p. 124; *Mishneh Halachos* 6:106. See also *Chasam Sofer YD* 233:4.

20   *Magen Avraham* 561:4; *Mo'adim U'Z'manim* ad loc. writes that this only applies to residents of the Old City, but other authorities extend it to include residents of modern-day Jerusalem. Rav Shlomo Zalman Auerbach (*Halichos Shlomo*, *Tefillah* 23, note 116) says that the custom may be based on the assumption that residents of Jerusalem who can easily visit the *Kosel* more than once in thirty days and do not do so obviously do not feel the pain of the *Churban* sufficiently and are therefore exempt from *keriah*. Rav Auerbach himself and also Rav Moshe Feinstein (*Igros Moshe OC* 3:85) disagree with this custom and rule that even residents of Jerusalem should perform *keriah*. See *Mishnah Berurah* (*Dirshu*) 561, notes 7 and 9; *Yerushalayim B'Mo'adeha*, p. 248. Some even extend this exemption to anyone living in Eretz Yisrael. See *Peninas Hamikdash*, p. 330.

21   *Tel Talpiyos*, pp. 67–68, note 92; *Minchas Shlomo* 1:73:1.

22   *Teshuvos V'Hanhagos* 1:331.

23   *Peninas Hamikdash*, p. 339:58, note 93; see *Shulchan Aruch YD* 340:2.

One then takes hold of the garment and rips it downward a *tefach* (handbreadth: 8–10 cm) while standing.[24] According to the *Mishnah Berurah* and other *poskim*, one tears on the left side of the garment as one would do upon the death of a parent.[25] Although they write that the tear must be done by hand, if this is difficult, it is acceptable to start the tear with an instrument.[26]

In contrast, several contemporary authorities write that the prevailing custom in Jerusalem is to tear on the right side as one does upon the death of relatives other than parents. They also write that one may even use an instrument for the entire tear.[27]

One may use the same garment more than once by ripping a further *tefach* into the same tear or by ripping another tear three fingerbreadths away from the first.[28] One may remove the garment immediately after performing *keriah*.[29]

G. WHEN *KERIAH* IS NOT DONE

There is a custom not to perform *keriah* whenever *Tachanun* is not recited. As such, some do not perform *keriah* on the afternoon of Erev Shabbos or Erev Yom Tov,[30] Motzaei Shabbos,[31] Chol Hamoed,[32] Chanukah, Purim (both days), and Rosh Chodesh.

---

24 *Tel Talpiyos*, p. 70; *Zichron Betzalel*, p. 148.

25 *Mishnah Berurah* 561:12–13, citing *Magen Avraham* 561:4; *Aruch Hashulchan* 561:2; *Teshuvos V'Hanhagos* 1:331.

26 *Shaarei Nechamah,* p. 122; *Yerushalayim B'Mo'adeha* 310.

27 *Minchas Shlomo* 1:73:1; *Zichron Betzalel*, p. 148; *Tel Talpiyos*, pp. 67–68; *Sefer Eretz Yisrael* 22:4.

28 *Tel Talpiyos*, p. 72, note 128; *Shaarei Nechamah*, p. 123.

29 *Tel Talpiyos*, p. 73. Rav Yosef Shalom Elyashiv is cited as ruling that one should continue to wear the garment as long as one is still at the site.

30 See *Tel Talpiyos*, p. 76. *Teshuvos V'Hanhagos* (1:334) rules that this is only true if one is wearing one's Shabbos clothes. There is some discussion on the purpose of this *keriah*. *Ir Hakodesh V'Hamikdash* (3:17:10) suggests that the purpose of *keriah* is to arouse emotions of pain, while *Igros Moshe* (*OC* 5:37:2) writes that it may be an act of respect in memory of the destruction of the Beis Hamikdash. Rav Moshe Feinstein conjectures that the *minhag* not to rip *keriah* on Erev Shabbos may be because this might cause pain to be aroused on Shabbos itself. He rules that if this is truly the *minhag* one may follow it, but he personally holds that one should perform *keriah*.

31 *Yerushalayim B'Mo'adeha*, p. 245. See *Halichos Shlomo*, p. 190.

32 *Tel Talpiyos*, p. 76; *Minchas Shlomo* 1:73; *Ir Hakodesh V'Hamikdash* 3:17:4.

Other authorities are more stringent and require one to do *keriah* on these days, as well as on any other days on which *Tachanun* is not recited except Chol Hamoed.[33]

Even on days when *keriah* is not performed, one still says "*Baruch Dayan ha'emes*," but does not recite the other passages.[34]

One does not perform these procedures if he has seen the Kosel within the last thirty days.[35] Even if one visited the *Kosel* on Shabbos or Yom Tov and did not tear, and then he visits it again within thirty days, some rule that *keriah* is not required.[36] Others write that *keriah* must still be performed in such situations.[37]

If one visited the *Kosel* and did not perform *keriah*, and then one visits the *Kosel* again within thirty days, many authorities opine that *keriah* need not be done.[38]

Children under bar or bas mitzvah do not need to do *keriah*.[39]

A bride and groom do not perform *keriah* on their wedding day or during the week following their marriage.[40]

An *onein* and others tending to the deceased may only be required to perform *keriah* after the burial. This would apply to one who sees the Temple Mount during a funeral on the Mount of Olives.[41]

H. AVOIDING *KERIAH*

Although it is proper to perform the mitzvah of *keriah*, if necessary, one may avoid doing so in one of the following ways:

---

33 *Tel Talpiyos*, p. 78; *Shaarei Nechamah*, p. 124, citing Rav Elyashiv and Steipler Rav; *Teshuvos V'Hanhagos* 1:334, citing Chazon Ish; *Igros Moshe YD* 3:52 and *OC* 5:37:2. See also *Peninas Hamikdash*, p. 368.

34 *Shaarei Nechamah*, p. 124.

35 *Rema OC* 561:5.

36 *Minchas Shlomo* 1:73; *Ir Hakodesh V'Hamikdash* 3:17:4.

37 *Igros Moshe YD* 3:52:4.

38 *Tel Talpiyos*, p. 82, but see the opinion of *Igros Moshe YD* ad loc. Based on his understanding of *keriah*, one would require it still to be done.

39 *Shaarei Nechamah*, p. 133.

40 *Yerushalayim B'Mo'adeha*, p. 247.

41 Ibid.

Note: Whenever possible, it would be better to rip a lower part of one's garment (shirt), even in a place where it may not be obviously seen, than not to perform any *keriah*.[42]

- **Transferring ownership of one's garment to another person**: This can be accomplished by *"kinyan chalifin,"* where the other person gives an object (e.g., a pen or a handkerchief) to the wearer and thereby acquires the garment.[43]
- **Borrowing**: Some authorities rule that there is no obligation to perform *keriah* on borrowed clothes.[44]
- **Renouncing Ownership (*Hefker*)**: Some authorities rule that one who renounces ownership of his garment in front of three people has no obligation to do *keriah* on it.[45]

In any case, the authorities point out that everyone should at least do the mitzvah of *keriah* once in their lifetime.[46]

I. PRAYER AT THE *KOSEL*

It is considered very auspicious to pray at the *Kosel*. The midrash teaches, "Hashem's Presence never departed from the *Kosel*."[47] There is also a *segulah* to pray at the *Kosel* for forty consecutive days.[48]

---

42   I heard this from various *poskim*.

43   Thus the the person wearing the garment is exempt from rending it, as it does not belong to him. See *Tel Talpiyos*, p. 85. *Avnei Yashfe* 3:59 and *Peninas Hamikdash*, p. 333, record that Rav Yosef Shalom Elyashiv stipulated that the lender must state that he does not want the borrower to rip the garment. Rav Shlomo Zalman Auerbach considered this procedure a form of deception.

44   *Tel Talpiyos* (p. 86) discusses whether a person still has an obligation to tear later on during the day when he puts on his own garment.

45   Ibid. *Avnei Yashfe* 3:59:1 writes that a great contemporary authority agreed with him in principle that the *hefker* declaration is only effective when it is made before three people.

46   *Peninei Hamikdash*, p. 331.

47   *Midrash Rabbah, Shemos* 2:2. *Kli Yakar, Bereishis* 13:17; *Tel Talpiyos*, p. 32; note 57.

48   *Tel Talpiyos*, p. 35. Some attribute this idea to *Arizal*. *Zohar Chadash* points out that any proper behavior that a person repeats for forty days in a row will have great spiritual effect (e.g., Moshe davening for forty days to be allowed entry into Eretz Yisrael); see *Midrash Rabbah, Va'eschanan*.

The prayer area in front of the *Kosel* has the status and sanctity of a synagogue. Authorities debate whether this designation also applies to the larger plaza area where tourists gather.[49]

There are those who say that it is better to pray in the inside covered area of the *Kosel* rather than in the open plaza.[50]

While many have the custom to pray directly facing the *Kosel*, there are some authorities who suggest praying at an angle, facing the Dome of the Rock, which was the site of the Holy of Holies.[51]

Most authorities rule that it is permitted to touch and kiss the *Kosel*, to put notes in the *Kosel*, and even to lean on it when reciting *Tachanun*.[52] Others forbid touching the stones in any way.[53] According to all, it is also forbidden to remove stones from the *Kosel*.[54] In any case, most *poskim* are of the opinion that it is forbidden to walk on the Temple Mount (Har Habayis) today.[55]

---

49 See *Shaarei Tzion*, p. 27. This would have an effect on the permissibility of eating there or using the area as a shortcut.

50 *Tel Talpiyos*, p. 34.

51 *Tel Talpiyos*, p. 32, note 59. Rav Avigdor Nebenzahl (*Yerushalayim B'Mo'adeha*, p. 250) considers the mosque to be an object of idolatry, and thus he questions how one can pray toward it.

52 *Tzitz Eliezer* 10:1:61–65; *Tel Talpiyos*, p. 27, citing Rav Shlomo Zalman Auerbach; *Shaar Tzion* 1.

53 *Tel Talpiyos*, p. 27, note 37, quoting *Chazon Ish* and Maharil Diskin. This seems to also be the opinion of Rav Avigdor Nebenzahl (*Yerushalayim B'Mo'adeha*, p. 249) He also writes that there is no point putting notes in the *Kosel* because Hashem does not need letters.

54 *Tel Talpiyos*, p. 28, note 43. This is tantamount to destroying a synagogue; *Ohr L'Tzion* 2:45:58.

55 In special circumstances, such as Israeli security personnel who are engaged in lifesaving activities, several halachic preparations should be undertaken: Mikvah preparations and immersion, with particular stringincies, are necessary. Leather shoes are not allowed, and unnecessary clothing, including *tallis katan*, should be removed. One must also shave and trim all unkempt or unnecessary hair. However, under normal circumstances, many authorities forbid one to walk in that area because: (a) it is not so clear where the actual ground of the Beis Hamikdash begins, and treading upon the ground of Beis Hamikdash can transgress an *issur kares*; (b) it may lead other people who are not properly prepared, i.e., *tamei* without proper mikvah and other preparations, to very serious transgressions. See also *Berachos* 54b; *Ohr L'Tzion* 3:30:4; *Mishnah Berurah* (Dirshu) 561:5; *Shaarei* Nechamah, p. 142; *Tzitz Eliezer* 10:1:53, 62, 92; *Minchas Yitzchak* 5:1:8; *Tel Talpiyos*, p. 19.

There are several personal customs regarding prayer at the *Kosel*:

- When leaving the *Kosel*, some people kiss its stones and step away backward so as not to turn their backs to it.[56]
- There are those who are particular to refer to it as the *"Kosel Ha'maaravi,"* and not merely the *"Kosel,"* as a sign of respect.[57]
- Some people try to fulfill the special mitzvah of *vidui maaser* at the *Kosel* on the last day of Pesach during the fourth and seventh years of the *shemittah* cycle.[58]
- One should endeavour to recite the following chapters of *Tehillim* at the *Kosel*: 30, 32, 84, 87, 125, 126, 127, 132, 134, 137.[59]

J. OTHER RELEVANT HALACHOS

At times, one may hear different minyanim praying at the same time. Preference should be given to answering *Kaddish* rather than *Kedushah*.[60] One who is praying in one minyan is not required to answer *Kaddish*, *Kedushah*, or *Barchu* from a different minyan.[61]

One who has already recited *Maariv* before sunset on Friday afternoon (and thus has accepted Shabbos) may still answer *Kaddish* and *Kedushah* when hearing it recited in a *Minchah* minyan nearby. Similarly, one who is about to recite the weekday *Minchah* may respond to *Barchu* when hearing it recited in a *Maariv* minyan and then continue with *Minchah*.[62]

A number of authorities rule that a woman may be driven in a taxi to the *Kosel* after lighting her Shabbos candles, as long as she makes a condition as she lights that she does not thereby accept upon herself the laws of Shabbos at that time.[63] She must then make sure to accept

---

56　See *Radvaz* 2:548; *Tel Talpiyos*, p. 30:51, wher he discusses kissing the *Kosel*).

57　*Tel Talpiyos*, p. 31, note 56; *Shaarei Tzion*, p. 23.

58　*Tel Talpiyos*, p. 34. This is the "Confession of the Tithes" described in *Devarim* 26:12–15.

59　See additional prayers in *Tel Talpiyos*, p. 32.

60　*Tel Talpiyos*, p. 40:12; *Orach Yisrael* 2:8.

61　*Tzitz Eliezer* 11:3; *Tel Talpiyos* 38:5. Similarly, one who is reciting *Shemoneh Esreh* and hears *Kedushah* does not respond but rather pauses and listens to the *chazzan*. *Mishnah Berurah* 104:7; *Dirshu* #39.

62　*Shemiras Shabbos K'Hilchasah* 46, note 59.

63　Generally speaking, a woman automatically accepts Shabbos upon herself by lighting candles.

Shabbos upon arrival at the *Kosel*.[64] Other authorities recommend against following this procedure.[65]

One should not pass in front of people who are reciting *Shemoneh Esreh*,[66] though one may do so if necessary,[67] preferably along their side.[68] One who needs to take three steps back at the conclusion of *Shemoneh Esreh* when the person behind is still praying should take the three steps back in a diagonal form, if necessary.[69]

One should not sit within four *amos* of one who is reciting *Shemoneh Esreh*.[70] However, one may be lenient in any of the following cases:

- He feels weak.[71]

- He is occupied with prayer, including merely listening to the repetition of the *Shemoneh Esreh*.[72]

---

64   *Tzitz Eliezer* 3:5, 10:19, 11:21:2; *Chayei Adam* 21:2, *Shabbos* 5:16; see *Piskei Teshuvos* 264, note 304, and *Ohr L'Tzion* 2:18:9.

65   *Shemiras Shabbos K'Hilchasah* 43, note 137, reports that Rav Shlomo Zalman Auerbach was not in favor of this practice.

66   *Shulchan Aruch OC* 102:4, *Mishnah Berurah* 102:15, and *Aruch Hashulchan OC* 102:13, 146:1, explain that walking in front of a person disturbs his concentration. *Chayei Adam* 26:4 writes that this is considered coming between between a man in prayer and the *Shechinah* that stands in front of him. Some authorities say that this applies to one who is reciting *k'rias Shema* and *Kaddish*, as well. *Biur Halachah* 102, s.v., *Assur*; *Mishnah Berurah* (*Dirshu*), note24.

67   *Ishei Yisrael* 19, note 52, quotes the *Eshel Avraham* who says that this applies for any mitzvah; *Halichos Shlomo* 8:33; *Shaarei Tzion*, p. 302. This is especially true in extenuating circumstances, such as for the sake of a mitzvah, to hear a *devar she'b'kedushah* or *Birkas Kohanim*, or if one needs to go to the bathroom. Additional reasons for leniency include the following: (1) the fact that nowadays most people don't pray with proper *kavanah* (see *Piskei Teshuvos* 102:3:3); (2) perhaps the person completed the main body of *Shemoneh Esreh* and is now in the *Elokai Netzor* paragraph; (3) sometimes the person is praying in a way that obstructs the public, such as in an aisle; (4) if there is a *mechitzah* at least ten *tefachim* high in front of the person (*Chayei Adam* 26:4). Some are lenient if the person behind you is covering his head with a *tallis* (based on the reasoning of the *Mishnah Berurah*). There is a difference of opinion whether these halachos apply to minors; *Tzitz Eliezer* 9:8 and *Halichos Shlomo* 8:33 are lenient with minors, while *Ishei Yisrael* 29:29, *Chazon Ish*, and Rav Chaim Kanievsky are strict. See also *Piskei Teshuvos* 102:1.

68   *Mishnah Berurah* 102:19; *Aruch Hashulchan OC* 102:11; *Tel Talpiyos*, p. 39.

69   See *Mishnah Berurah* (*Dirshu*) 102:18–19, note 26.

70   *Shulchan Aruch OC* 102:1; *Aruch Hashulchan* 102:4; the four *amos* around the person praying is considered "holy ground."

71   On Yom Kippur, all are considered to be weak. See *Piskei Teshuvos* 102:2, note 39.

72   *Rivevos Ephraim* 1:73.

- He is engaged in Torah study.
- He was sitting there first.[73]

It is forbidden to take a bus card to the *Kosel* on Shabbos in order to use it on the way home.[74]

It is very commendable, and possibly even a mitzvah, to visit the *Kosel* on Yom Tov.[75] Although the ideal time for this visit is the first day of Yom Tov, several authorities write that it is also a mitzvah to visit on Chol Hamoed, the last day of Yom Tov, and during the six days that follow Shavuos.[76]

Some have the custom to shake a lulav and esrog at the *Kosel* on Sukkos, even if they already fulfilled the mitzvah at home.[77]

---

73   One who was already sitting is not obligated to stand if someone starts to pray in his area, though it is commendable to do so. See *Shulchan Aruch OC* 102:3.

74   *Tzitz Eliezer* 14:37.

75   *Tzitz Eliezer* 10:1:93; *Sdei Chemed*, vol. 5, *Eretz Yisrael*, 1.

76   *Tel Talpiyos*, p. 45; *Kum His'halech B'Aretz*, p. 137; *Yechaveh Daas* 1:25, 2:48; *Tzitz Eliezer* 10:1:93; *Mo'adim U'Z'manim* 7:141:1; *V'Aleihu Lo Yibol*, p. 183.

77   *Tel Talpiyos*, p. 48. This is in accordance with the opinion that there is a Torah mitzvah to shake a lulav and esrog every day of Sukkos in the Old City. Cf. *Tzitz Eliezer* 10:2:10.

Chapter Twelve
The Berachah at a Cemetery— Beis Ha'chaim[1]

A. INTRODUCTION

When seeing a Jewish cemetery, one recites a special *berachah*:

בָּרוּךְ...אֲשֶׁר יָצַר אֶתְכֶם בַּדִּין וְזָן וְכִלְכֵּל אֶתְכֶם בַּדִּין, וְהֵמִית אֶתְכֶם בַּדִּין, וְיוֹדֵעַ מִסְפַּר כֻּלְּכֶם בַּדִּין, וְהוּא עָתִיד לְהַחֲיוֹתְכֶם וּלְקַיֵּם אֶתְכֶם בַּדִּין. בָּרוּךְ...מְחַיֵּה הַמֵּתִים.

Blessed...Who formed you in judgment, nourished and sustained you in judgment, [took your soul] in judgment, knows your number in judgment, and in the future will restore you to life and sustain you in judgment. Blessed...Who revives the dead.

He then recites the second *berachah* of the *Shemoneh Esreh* (*Mechalkel chaim b'chessed...*). In Eretz Yisrael, some insert the words *morid ha'tal*, even in the winter.

Gesher Hachaim explains that the purpose of this *berachah* is to arouse us to do *teshuvah* by reminding us of our mortality. It also serves to acknowledge Hashem's judgment (*tzidduk ha'din*). Others explain that it also reminds us of *techiyas ha'meisim* (revival of the dead), which is one of the thirteen fundamental principles of Judaism.[2]

---

1   The traditional names for cemeteries, such as *beis olam* (or *almin*) and *beis ha'chaim*, all represent the ongoing life of the *neshamah*, in contrast to the common name, *beis ha'kevaros*.

2   *Gesher Hachaim* 2:28:6; *Asra Kadisha*, p. 13. The words *morid ha'tal* allude also to the spiritual "dew" connected to *techiyas ha'meisim*; *Yeshayahu* 26:19; *Shabbos* 86b.

One who sees a non-Jewish cemetery recites the following verse:

בּוֹשָׁה אִמְּכֶם מְאֹד חָפְרָה יוֹלַדְתְּכֶם הִנֵּה אַחֲרִית גּוֹיִם מִדְבָּר צִיָּה
וַעֲרָבָה.

Bosha imchem me'od, chofrah yoladetchem, hinei acharis goyim midbar tziyah v'aravah—Your mother will be greatly ashamed; the one who bore you is embarrassed; behold, the final outcome of the nations is as a wilderness, a wasteland, and a desert.[3]

B. WHEN TO RECITE THE *BERACHAH*

Many authorities recommend that (ideally) one should recite the *berachah* as one walks into the cemetery. Some even suggest that it should preferably be within four *amos* (about 7.5 ft) of a grave.[4] Nevertheless, it may even be recited from a distance as long as one can clearly see the graves.[5] As such, a Kohen is able to recite this *berachah*.

One only recites the *berachah* if one can see the ground above the grave, or at least see a headstone that is very close to the ground.[6] One may recite the *berachah* as long as one knows there is a grave, even if grass has grown over it. There are various opinions whether it is sufficient to simply see mausoleum buildings or caves filled with graves.[7]

One may recite the *berachah* as long as one is still in the cemetery. If one left without reciting *berachah*, it may no longer be recited.

---

3   *Yirmiyahu* 50:12; *Shulchan Aruch OC* 224:12; *Shaar Ha'ayin*, p. 134. Rav Serayah Deblitski points out that one may recite it even if one saw the cemetery within thirty days.

4   *Aruch Hashulchan, OC* 224:8; *Gesher Hachaim* 5:2:4; *Chazon Ovadiah*, p. 420, rules that one may only recite the *berachah* inside the cemetery. However, see *Yesodei Semachos*, p. 48, who opines that it should not be recited within the *arba amos* of a grave.

5   *Shaar Ha'ayin* 16:4.

6   *Aruch HaShulchan, OC* 224:8; *Shaar Ha'ayin* 16:4; *Shaarei Teshuvah OC* 224:4.

7   *Igros Moshe OC* 5:37:10. Cf. *Shaar Ha'ayin* 16:13, note 22, who reports that Rav Yosef Shalom Elyashiv considers a mausoleum to be a proper *kever*.

Passing a Cemetery

If one passed a cemetery without really taking notice of it, many authorities allow reciting the *berachah* within thirty days,[8] while others forbid it.[9]

C. VISITING DIFFERENT CEMETERIES

- A *berachah* is not generally recited on the same cemetery within thirty days of the first visit.[10]
- However, there is a *machlokes* among the authorities whether one who sees a different cemetery within the thirty days can still recite a *berachah*. While many authorities rule that one should recite the *berachah*,[11] others hold that one should not. Thus when visiting two different cemeteries, for example, Har Menuchos and Har Hazeisim in Jerusalem, there is basis for one to recite two separate *berachos*.

1. Traveling to Different Cemeteries of *Gedolim, Tzaddikim, Tanna'im, Amora'im*—"*Kever* Hopping"

Today, it has become common for people to visit various *kivrei tzaddikim* in Eastern Europe or the *kevarim* of *Tanna'im* and *Amora'im* in the Galil in Eretz Yisrael.

If one is planning to visit a number of *kevaros* on one day, while many authorities would say that one may recite individual *berachos* on each cemetery, others recommend that one should have in mind when

---

8   See *Igros Moshe OC* 5:37:10.

9   *Shaar Ha'ayin* 16:5.

10   *Shaarei Teshuvah* 224:9; *Shaar Ha'ayin* 16:11; *Birkas Hashem*, p. 317. Some authorities rule that if there are new graves there, one is allowed to recite a new *berachah*.

11   *Be'er Heitev OC* 224:9; *Radvaz* 1:296:7; *Kitzur Shulchan Aruch* 60:12; *Aruch Hashulchan OC* 224:8; *Shaar Ha'ayin* 16:17; *Halichos Shlomo* 23, note 52; *Yabia Omer* 5:7; *Yesodei Semachos*, p. 48. Rav Ephraim Kirschenbaum reports that this is also the view of Rav Isser Zalman Meltzer, also heard in the name of Rav David Feinstein. Some *poskim* related to me that even if, in general, one follows the opinion not to make *berachos re'iyah* upon seeing the same type of sight within less than thirty days because there is not enough *hispaalus*, the *berachah* on *kevarim* has a different message (see before), and might apply even in this case.

making the *berachah* at the first cemetery to include all the others that he will visit that day.[12]

Other authorities are unsure whether one may make a *berachah* on a second cemetery within thirty days (as mentioned above); therefore, they recommend that one recite the *berachah* without including Hashem's name.[13]

Common custom is not to recite the *berachah* in the following situations:

- At the entrance of an ancient burial tomb, such as the Cave of the Patriarchs (*Me'aras Hamachpelah*) and Rachel's Tomb[14]
- On a building or cave that houses the dead, i.e., Meron (*Rashbi*)[15] or Kever Shimon HaTzaddik in Yerushalayim
- There are different opinions concerning the graves of the Mishnaic or Talmudic sages in Northern Israel. While there is basis to recite the *berachah* on these *kevaros* (must be more than one *kever* (see further),[16] other authorities recommend reciting the *berachah* without including Hashem's name.[17]

---

12   *Birkos Eliyahu*, p. 303; *Ahaleich B'Amitecha* 18:9; *B'Tzeil Hachochmah* 5:84.

13   *Mishnah Berurah* 224:17; for full discussion on this subject, see *Shaar Ha'ayin*, pp. 43, 130–31, 447.

14   *Shaar Ha'ayin* 16:27; *Yesodei Semachos*, p. 48, note 12. Rav Moshe Feinstein is quoted that the words of the *berachah* do not apply to the Avos.

15   *Shaar Ha'ayin* 16:14. Rav Chaim Kanievsky is of the opinion that we need to know the exact spot where the deceased is buried.

16   *Shaar Ha'ayin* 16:14. I heard from Rav Yisrael Ganz and Rav Avigdor Nebenzahl that the *berachah* applies to these *kevarim*; I also heard that this is the opinion of Rav David Feinstein (see also previous note). In Tiveria, there are two fascinating cemeteries. The first is the cemetery of the *Rambam*, which also includes *Tanna'im* such as Rav Yochanan ben Zakkai, *Amora'im* such as Ravina and Rav Ashi, other Rishonim, and early early Acharonim like the *Shelah Hakadosh*. The second cemetery up the hill includes Rabbi Akiva and Rav Moshe Chaim Luzzatto, (the *Ramchal*).

17   *Shaar Ha'ayin* 16:14, *B'Tzeil Hachochmah* 5:84. There is an additional question if the person needs to be buried within four *amos* or ten *tefachim* of the *kever*.

2. Other Halachos

Most authorities rule that a single grave does not constitute a cemetery.[18] However, a mass grave *is* considered to be one.[19]

Most authorities rule that the *berachah* may be recited on Shabbos and Yom Tov.[20]

There are different customs as to whether those attending a burial at a cemetery are required to recite the *berachah*. While several authorities opine that this *berachah* may be recited even on the way to the burial (if it does not interfere with the burial),[21] other authorities say that it should definitely be recited afterward.[22] An *onein* is exempt from the *berachah*, even after the burial.[23]

A number of authorities rule that one who lives next to a cemetery, or passes by one every day, does not recite the *berachah*, even if he never looks at it and has not seen it within thirty days.[24] However, if he lives in another part of the city, he would be clearly obligated to recite the *berachah*.

D. LAWS AND CUSTOMS WHEN VISITING A CEMETERY

1. *Kivrei Avos* and *Kivrei Tzaddikim*

There is an ancient custom to visit the burial places of one's ancestors (*kivrei avos*) and of great *tzaddikim*, and to recite various prayers

---

18   *Mishnah Berurah* 224:16 notes that the *berachah* is worded in the plural ("*eschem*"). *Gesher Hachaim* 1:29 writes that the *berachah* should be recited without including Hashem's name.

19   *Ahaleich B'Amitecha* 18:5, 8.

20   *Shaar Ha'ayin* 16:8; *Maharsham* 224:12; *Kol Bo* 63:1; *Halichos Shlomo* 23:32.

21   This is based on the principle, "*ha'osek b'mitzvah patur min ha'mitzvah*—if one is preoccupied with one mitzvah, he is exempt from another mitzvah" (*Sukkah* 25a), i.e., one is exempt from the blessing because he is involved in the mitzvah of accompanying the deceased.

22   *Shaar Ha'ayin* 16:12, note 22. According to *Minchas Shlomo* 91:25:6 and *B'Tzeil Hachochmah* 5:27, the *berachah* should be recited afterward. *Eishel Avraham* 224 opines that one is no longer obligated afterward since he has already seen (the graves) within thirty days. For a full treatment of this subject in English, see *Mourning in Halachah*, p. 132, with notes 45–48.

23   *Mourning in Halachah*, p. 132, note 48, quoting Rabbi Shlomo Zalman Auerbach; *Yesodei Semachos*, p. 48.

24   For full discussion, see *Shaar Ha'ayin* 1:16 and *Iyunim* 12; *Mishnah Berurah* 224:3; *Halichos Shlomo* 23:28. See *Piskei Teshuvos* 224:11, but if he is away for thirty days, he would recite a *berachah*.

there.[25] The Sages teach that a cemetery is a holy place and prayers are more readily accepted there.[26] Additionally, praying at a cemetery strengthens our connection with past generations. However, based on Kabbalah, there are those who refrain from visiting cemeteries.[27]

There are also different ways of understanding how one should pray at *kevarim*:

- Some explain that it is not appropriate to address our prayers to the souls of the departed; rather, we must beseech Hashem that He should answer us in the merit of the *tzaddikim*.
- Others opine that it is permitted to ask the deceased to intercede on our behalf before the Divine throne.[28]
- Some have the custom not to pray at a cemetery at all.

2. Kohanim

It is forbidden for a Kohen to visit a Jewish cemetery or to otherwise be in close proximity of a dead body. A Kohen may only enter a cemetery if he stays at least four *amos* (8 ft/2.5 m) from the graves or if there is a partition (*mechitzah*) of at least ten *tefachim* (40 in/100 cm) high separating him from the graves.[29]

The only exception to this rule is when the deceased is one of the Kohen's seven closest relatives, which includes his father, mother, wife, son, daughter, brother, and unmarried sister (see *Vayikra* 21:2–4). Once the relative is interred and his grave is minimally covered, the Kohen

---

25   *Midrash Bereishis* 48:7; *Rama OC* 581:4; *Mishnah Berurah* 559:41; *Chayei Adam* 138:5; *Minchas Yitzchak* 8:53. See *Halachically Speaking* (vol. 2, p. 322) for more sources. See *Mekor Hachaim* (pp. 222–25) regarding the power of *tefillah* at the graves of *tzaddikim*. Rav Chaim Kanievsky is quoted as saying that it does not make a difference whether the *tzaddikim* are from a recent or an older generation. I heard that when Rav Shlomo Zalman Auerbach was asked by his students where to find *kivrei tzaddikim*, he told them to go to the Har Hertzl military cemetery in Jerusalem. *Sefer Chassidim* is quoted to say that the *meisim* love the fact that people come to visit and daven at their graves.

26   *Mishnah Berurah* 581:27.

27   This seems to be the opinion of the *Gra* (heard from Rabbi Yisroel Ber Kaplan) because of the impurity (*tumah*) associated with the cemetery. See *Mishnah Berurah* (*Dirshu*) 559:41, §49, for treatment of this subject; see also *Magen Avraham* §15.

28   *P'nei Baruch*, p. 431.

29   This is why Kohanim are buried at the edges of cemetery rows.

must then distance himself from the grave and from all other graves or dead bodies.

Kohanim must be aware that there are neighborhoods and roads, such as the Mount of Olives Road near the Intercontinental Hotel, that have been built over old cemeteries.

Some authorities allow a Kohen to enter a non-Jewish cemetery as long as he has no physical contact with the dead.

3. When to Visit a Cemetery

It is customary to a visit cemetery on Tishah B'Av, during the month of Elul, Erev Rosh Hashanah,[30] and Erev Yom Kippur.

It is customary *not* to visit cemeteries on Shabbos, Yom Tov, Chol Hamoed, and Purim.[31]

There are different customs[32] concerning visiting cemeteries on Erev Shabbos, Chanukah, Rosh Chodesh, and during the month of Nissan.[33] However, there are customs that permit visiting *kivrei tzaddikim* even during these times.[34]

Some have the custom to visit the graves of relatives at the end of the *shivah* and the *sheloshim* periods, and on the day of the yahrzeit.[35] There is a custom that children do not visit their parents' graves during the first year of their passing, except for at the aforementioned times.[36]

Some authorities say that one should avoid going to a cemetery alone.[37]

There is a custom not to visit the same *kever* twice in the same day.[38] However, some say that this does not apply to *kivrei tzaddikim*.[39]

---

30   *Mishnah Berurah* 581:27; *Piskei Teshuvos* 581:21.
31   *Gesher Hachaim* 1:29:15; *P'nei Baruch* 37:14.
32   *Gesher Hachaim* 1:29.
33   Ibid., §5.
34   *Minchas Elazar* 3:37.
35   *Gesher Hachaim* 1:29:1.
36   See *Gesher Hachaim* 1:29:2; *Yesodei Semachos*, p. 49.
37   *Kaf Hachaim, OC* 605:31; *Halachically Speaking*, vol. 2, p. 327.
38   *Mishnah Berurah* 581:27.
39   *Tzavaas R' Yehudah Hachassid* 12; *Magen Avraham OC* 581:16; *Mourning in Halachah* 42:3; see note 6, where he says that this custom may be based on the fact that we do not want to give the impression that he suspects the deceased of not praying for him the first time, implying that he considers him uncompassionate; *Halachically Speaking*, vol. 2, p. 324.

4. Women at Cemeteries

Authorities record that while some women have the custom not to visit a cemetery when they are in their *niddah* state, others do not have this custom and visit cemeteries without restriction, especially on a yahrzeit and the like.[40] Some say that a woman who is a *niddah* should try to keep a distance of at least four *amos* (6–8 ft) from a grave. Some authorities rule that this does not apply to *kivrei tzaddikim*.[41]

While there are different customs regarding whether a pregnant woman should visit a cemetery,[42] several authorities state that a woman may be lenient in the case of a yahrzeit or other special circumstances. This is especially true if she keeps a distance of at least four *amos* (6–8 ft) from graves.[43] Many authorities are lenient when it comes to a woman visiting *kivrei tzaddikim*.[44]

5. Washing Hands Afterward

The custom is that one should pour water over one's hands three times from a utensil after visiting a cemetery.[45] When necessary, it is sufficient to use any amount of water, even once without a utensil. There are different opinions whether one needs to wash one's hands after visiting the *kever* of a *tzaddik*.[46]

Some people observe the following practices:

- To empty out any remaining water in the cup after one has finished washing
- To place the cup upside down and not to hand it to another person[47]

---

40 See *Shulchan Aruch OC* 88:1; *Mishnah Berurah* 88:7.

41 *Piskei Teshuvos* 88:9; *Halichos Bas Yisrael* 13:3:10; *Halachically Speaking*, vol. 2, pp. 325–26.

42 *Halachically Speaking* ad loc. Among those who permit it are Rav Yisroel Belsky and Rav Chaim Pinchas Scheinberg.

43 See *Halachically Speaking* ibid.; *Shevet Hakehasi* 3:296.

44 *Asra Kadisha*, p. 87; *Nitei Gavriel, Aveilus*, vol. 2, p. 648.

45 Because of a level of *ruach raah* and *tumah*. *Mishnah Berurah* 4:42; *Shaarei Teshuvah* 4:20. Note, however, that none of the normal restrictions that apply before *netilas yadayim* in the morning apply here. Thus, one may touch food, recite any *devarim she'b'kedushah*, etc.; *Piskei Teshuvos* 4:18.

46 *Halachically Speaking*, vol. 2, p. 327; *Shevet Hakehasi* 5:71.

47 Some explain that this and the previous bullet point are in order to avoid the appearance of passing a distressful thing on to a friend.

- To not dry the hands[48] (However, if it is cold outside, it is permitted to dry one's hands.)
- To not enter a home before washing[49]

6. Visiting a Grave

Some people observe the following practices:

- To place one's left hand on the grave[50]
- To not touch the grave at all
- To light candles
- To set aside money for *tzedakah*
- To place a stone or piece of grass on the grave[51]
- To circle the *kever* when visiting the *kever* of a *tzaddik*[52]

7. Showing Respect to the Deceased or Graves

- One should not eat or drink in the presence of graves.
- One should avoid walking on a grave unless it is the only way to get to another grave.[53] Some say that if this is done, one should ask for forgiveness from the deceased.[54]
- One should not sit or lean on a grave.[55]
- One should not greet a person with the word "*Shalom*" in the presence of the deceased or within the proximity of four to six feet from the grave.[56]
- One should not pray or say words of Torah in the presence of the dead or the proximity of the grave unless the prayers or Torah

---

48 *Shulchan Aruch YD* 376:4. This is a gesture of showing that one is not removing his attention from the mourning.
49 *Yesodei Semachos*, pp. 49, 58; *Shulchan Aruch YD* 376:4. When necessary, one may enter the home or public place to wash hands.
50 *Mourning in Halachah* 42:20.
51 *Be'er Heitev OC* 224:8 to show that one has visited the grave.
52 *Mishnah Berurah* 581:27. This is a sign of endearment.
53 *Kitzur Shulchan Aruch* 199:14.
54 *P'nei Baruch* 37:28.
55 *Shulchan Aruch YD* 364:1.
56 Ibid., 343:2; *Nitei Gavriel, Aveilus* 86:7.

study are in honor of the deceased.[57] However, there are those who allow praying and studying Torah at *kivrei tzaddikim*.[58]

- One should cover one's tzitzis when entering a cemetery.[59]
- *Berachos* on lightning and thunder are not recited in a cemetery in the proximity (four *amos* [6–8 ft]) of a grave.[60]

8. Reading a Tombstone

There are differing opinions concerning the permissibility of reading the lettering on a tombstone. Most authorities are lenient if one does not verbalize the words or if the words are engraved.[61]

---

57   *Shulchan Aruch YD* 344:17. This is in order not to mock the deceased (*lo'eig la'rash*) who are exempt from mitzvos.

58   *Tzitz Eliezer* 10:1; *Sh'eilas Rav* 1:2:12.

59   *Shulchan Aruch OC* 23:1.

60   There is an aspect of *lo'eg la'rash* (ridiculing the helpless), as if mocking the deceased for no longer being capable of perfoming mitzvos; *Shulchan Aruch OC* 23:2; *Chut Shani, Birkos Hodaah*, p. 184.

61   The Sages (*Horayos* 13b) state that reading a tombstone could lead to forgetting one's Torah knowledge. *Kitzur Shulchan Aruch* 128:13; *Mishnah Berurah* (*Dirshu*) 2:2, note 7.

Chapter Thirteen

Tefillas Ha'derech— the Traveler's Prayer

A. INTRODUCTION

The Sages instituted that a person who embarks upon a journey should ask Hashem for protection from the various perils of the road.[1] Today, perils may include wild deer on the highway, terrorists, car accidents, dangerous taxi and bus drivers, etc.

Tefillas Ha'derech is recited for a trip of at least one *parsah* (2.5 miles/3.8 km) beyond the city limits.[2] In this context, the "city limits" generally

---

1 See *Mishnah Berurah* 110:24, who writes that one is obligated to say it. See *Semak* 1:11, who considers it a *mitzvah d'Rabbanan*. See *Maharal, Nesivos Olam, Nesiv Avodah* 13. Those who do not recite *Tefillas Ha'derech* today point out that our roads are much safer than in the times of Chazal, there is a lot more police enforcement, and there are many cars on the road. (In halachic terms, they would say that the road is defined as a "*shayara*" [caravan], and thus one may not be considered "leaving the city" when traveling on the highway). However, most authorities seem to disagree with this thinking.

2 *Biur Halachah* ad loc., s.v., *V'ein*, discusses the question of the conditions necessary to calculate the distance of the first *parsah* necessary to obligate one in *Tefillas Ha'derech*. Is the first *parsah* of the route calculated from the **city limit** or from the **edge of the first parsah outside that limit** (i.e., 5 miles/7.4 km)? The reason behind the "two *parsah*" opinion is the understanding that the proximity to any city offers a "protection" from the various dangers of the road, such as wild animals and enemies, etc. Thus this would eliminate the need for *Tefillas Ha'derech*. According to this understanding, when one travels on a highway nowadays, he would need to ascertain at the beginning of his trip whether any part of the road is outside of two *parsah* from a city, for only then would he be obligated to recite the *tefillah*. The *Mishnah Berurah* leaves this question unresolved. This was the view of Rav Shlomo Zalman Auerbach, and as such he did not recite *Tefillas Ha'derech* when driving between B'nei Brak and Jerusalem (*Halichos Shlomo* 21, note 12). However, the more common approach is that the *parsah* is measured after leaving the city limits, as long as the trip will be at least a distance of a *parsah*. This view is based on the following points:

refers to the last houses at the edge of the city.[3] However, if the roads one is traveling on are considered to be dangerous, such as in Judea and Samaria, one may recite the prayer even for a shorter trip.[4] One must recite *Tefillas Ha'derech* even if he will be returning the same day.

Many Sephardic authorities hold that *Tefillas Ha'derech* is only required for a trip of at least seventy-two minutes (see note),[5] unless it is a clearly dangerous road.[6]

B. WHEN TO RECITE

Ideally, one should recite *Tefillas Ha'derech* is as soon as he passes the city limits (150 ft/45 m beyond the last house),[7] and within the first *parsah* (2.5 miles/3.8 km) of the trip.[8] There are also opinions that *Tefillas Ha'derech* may be recited when one is about to leave one's home,[9]

- *Chazon Ish* suggests that the possibility of "car accidents" also qualifies as a dangerous situation (*sakanas derachim*). Because of this factor, he entertains the possibility of saying it even within the city—surely after the first *parsah*.
- Rav Yaakov Kamenetsky rules that since *Tefillas Ha'derech* may be categorized as a *tefillah*, rather than a formal "*berachah*" (see further), one may recite it even when its obligation is doubtful.
- Rav Yosef Shalom Elyashiv rules that in the case of *tefillos* that are requests (*bakashos*), one may recite the concluding blessing in full, even in doubtful situations (based on *P'nei Yehoshua, Berachos* 29).
- Some authorities define a highway as a distinct entity and considered "out of the city," especially if it is difficult to get help if one gets stuck there (*Kitzur Tefillas Haderech*, p. 83, citing Rav Shmuel Kamenetsky). I personally heard this *sevarah* from Rav Tzvi Rosen.

This opinion is reportedly the view of *Chazon Ish*, the Steipler, Rav Chaim Kanievsky, Rav Shach, Rav Elyashiv, and Rav Yaakov Kamenetsky (*Kuntres Tefillas Haderech*, pp. 51–62). It is interesting to note that Rav Chaim Pinchas Scheinberg recited *Tefillas Ha'derech* as soon as he passed Telzstone and was out of city limits. Similarly, Rav Moshe Feinstein and Rav Yaakov Kamenetsky used to say recite *Tefillas Ha'derech* when traveling in the Catskill Mountains. For further discussion, see *Kuntres Tefillas Haderech*, pp. 48–65.

3   *Shulchan Aruch OC* 110:7:2. See further for a clearer definition of city limits.

4   *Halichos Shlomo Tefillah* 21:1.

5   Even if one only gets to seventy-two minutes by combining the time needed for both going to one's destination and coming back.

6   *Yalkut Yosef*, vol. 3, p. 579; *Ohr L'Tzion* 2:7:27 says to say it when there is sparse traffic or at night. On trips less than seventy-two minutes, he recommends saying the concluding *berachah* without the name of Hashem.

7   *Mishnah Berurah* 110:29; Cf. *Kitzur Shulchan Aruch* 68:1.

8   *Kitzur Shulchan Aruch* 68:2.

9   *Mishnah Berurah* 110:29 (quoting the opinion of the *Taz*); *Aruch Hashulchan OC* 110:13. It

or as one is about to enter the highway. If one is uneasy about reciting it when already on the road, one may rely upon these opinions.

One may recite *Tefillas Ha'derech* as long as one has not reached the last *parsah* of one's destination. Some authorities rule that a person flying on an airplane may recite it as long as the plane has not landed.[10] If one is beyond this point, one should recite it without including Hashem's name in the concluding *berachah*:

בָּרוּךְ אַתָּה שׁוֹמֵעַ תְּפִלָּה.

Baruch Atah shomei'a tefillah—Blessed are You Who hears prayer."[11]

C. CALCULATING CITY LIMITS

The *Mishnah Berurah* points out that once a traveler no longer encounters houses every seventy *amos* (150 ft/45 m), he has passed the city limits.[12] However, various authorities point out that today, a number of additional criteria should also be considered.

In Talmudic times, people who lived in cities lived much closer to each other than they do today. Thus, contemporary authorities opine that in order to consider the cities as two distinct entities, there must be more of a **substantial gap** of open space between them (three-fifths to one mile). Rav Shmuel Kamenetsky suggests that they must be thought of as "distinct" places in the popular mind.[13]

---

is interesting to note that the *Zohar* (*Bereishis* 49:2) writes that the best place to recite it is while one is still in the city. See also *Teshuvos V'Hanhagos* 5:46.

10 *Piskei Teshuvos* 110:3; *Doleh U'Mashkeh*, p. 74.

11 *Shulchan Aruch OC* 110: 7.

12 *Mishnah Berurah* 110:29.

13 Rabbi Baruch Stauber, *Kuntres Tefillas Haderech*, pp. 83, 110. Perhaps this is connected to the common expression: "We are leaving the city." He also quotes Rav Forchheimer, who opines that a person entering the highway can be said to have "left the city" when he can no longer easily call for help. Areas that are considered part of the same municipality, such as all the boroughs of New York City, or areas that are considered attached to the city, such as Westchester, Nassau, and Suffolk Counties, may still be considered as part of the city. This may explain the practice of Rav Moshe Feinstein, who reportedly recited *Tefillas Ha'derech* when he would pass over the George Washington Bridge to New Jersey, but not when he would go over the Manhattan, Brooklyn, or Verrazano Bridges. Rav Chaim Kanievsky

C. AIR TRAVEL

One should recite *Tefillas Ha'derech* as the aircraft is taxiing on the runway[14] or taking off from the ground.[15] If the airport is outside of the city limits, one should recite it on the way to the airport (as soon as he leaves the city limits). The Rogatchover Gaon reportedly held, however, that traveling by air travel is not considered going on a *"derech"* and therefore *Tefillas Ha'derech* is not recited.[16]

D. BOAT CRUISES AND HIKING

Tefillas Ha'derech is also recited when traveling by boat and when traveling by train.[17] If one is taking a boat cruise or going fishing on the ocean (a trip of at least 2.5 miles/3.8 km, which is at least 150 ft/46 m away from the shore) the *tefillah* should be recited as you would on a regular road, assuming one has fulfilled the necessary prerequisites as listed above.

Authorities hold that one may recite *Tefillas Ha'derech* when hiking outside the city (a trip of at least 2.5 miles/3.8 km), as per the criteria listed above.[18]

E. CONTINUOUS TRAVEL ON THE SAME DAY

As a general rule, one does not recite *Tefillas Ha'derech* more than once a day. This is because one recitation covers all the travel that one will do that day, including the night that follows, even if one will make a number of stops.[19] However, if at the time of the recitation one had in mind to conclude his journey at a particular destination, and later

---

reportedly rules that Gush Dan is considered to be one big "city," even though there are open areas between the settlements in the middle. *Doleh U'Mashkeh*, p. 73; *Kuntres Tefillas Haderech*, pp. 110–15.

14   *Emes L'Yaakov*; p. 65; *Be'er Moshe* 7:170. Rav Chaim Pinchas Scheinberg reportedly ruled that once the plane is on the runway, it is already considered to be in a place of *sakanah*.

15   See *Halichos Shlomo* 21:4.

16   *Ishim V'Shitos*, p. 149; *Shut Chelkas Yaakov* 2:9, based on *Chullin* 139b.

17   *Mishnah Berurah* 110:30.

18   Cf. *Ketzos Hashulchan* 67:3; *Doleh U'Mashkeh*, p. 73, who suggests that it is not usually done.

19   *Mishnah Berurah* 110:24, 26; *Biur Halachah*, s.v. *Tzarich…lailah holeich achar ha'yom*.

decided to resume the trip or to return home, *Tefillas Ha'derech* should be recited again.[20]

F. CONTINUOUS TRAVEL ON DIFFERENT DAYS

If one embarks on a trip that will cover more than one day, the following halachos are applicable:[21]

1. With Sleepover Stops

If one has stopped traveling that day and remains (sleeps) in that place overnight, *Tefillas Ha'derech* is recited again the next day.[22] For example, one who travels from Israel to New York with an overnight stop in London must say a new *berachah* as he takes off from London.

2. Without Sleepover Stops

If one continues traveling throughout the night and does not stop to have a normal sleeping place (or continues on route without stopping at all), no new *tefillah* is necessary. Examples of this are one flying overnight from Israel to New York, or riding on a cross-country bus ride; in those cases, one need not recite *Tefillas Ha'derech* a second time.[23]

However, many authorities recommend that one should insert the words of *Tefillas Ha'derech* before the conclusion of the *berachah* of *Shema Koleinu* in *Shemoneh Esreh* the next morning.[24]

---

20 *Shulchan Aruch OC* 110:5.
21 There is an interesting *machlokes* among the *poskim* concerning this matter: (a) *Bach/Taz* 110:5 opine that every day (morning) a new *tefillah* should be recited, similar to the obligation to recite the *Shmoneh Esreh* every day; (b) *Radvaz*, brought in *Shaarei Teshuvah* 110, in the name of the *Birkei Yosef*, says that if one sleeps a normal sleep (*keva*), he recites a new *berachah*. However, if it is a temporay sleep or short nap (or no sleep), no new *berachah* is necessary. There is an interesting discussion concerning one who sleeps outdoors. According to Rav Shlomo Zalman Auerbach, this would be considered a fixed sleep, but according to *Kitzur Shulchan Aruch* 68:5, it would not be considered a proper sleep; (c) *Pri Chadash* 110:5 and *Shulchan Aruch Harav*: One only recites *Tefillas Ha'derech* one time upon embarking upon a trip, even if he sleeps overnight in a hotel. The *Mishnah Berurah* 110:26 seems to follow the opinion of the *Radvaz*. See full discussion in *Piskei Teshuvos* 110:6.
22 *Mishnah Berurah (Dirshu)* 110:24; *Kitzur Shulchan Aruch* 68:5.
23 *Ohr L'Tzion* 2:7:28.
24 *Mishnah Berurah* 110:24, 26; this is in deference to the opinions that every "day" a new *berachah* should be recited; *Halichos Shlomo Tefillah* 21:6.

Alternatively, one should recite *Tefillas Ha'derech* without including Hashem's name in the concluding *berachah*: "*Baruch atah shomei'a tefillah.*"[25]

3. Boat Trips or Cruises

Many opinions state that one who takes a boat cruise (a trip of more than one day) should recite the full *tefillah* only the first day, and from the second day onward should either include the words of *Tefillas Ha'derech* before the conclusion of the *berachah* of *Shema Koleinu* in *Shemoneh Esreh*, or recite *Tefillas Ha'derech* without including Hashem's name in the concluding *berachah*.[26]

G. *TEFILLAH* OR *BERACHAH*?

The authorities debate whether *Tefillas Ha'derech* is considered a form of *tefillah* or a *berachah*. There are a number of halachic ramifications arising from this debate:

- If it is a *tefillah*, the concept of *berachah ha'semuchah la'chaveirtah* (adjoining *berachah*) would not apply. (See further.)
- If it is a *tefillah*, it can be recited in situations when its obligation is doubtful, as the rule of "*safeik berachos l'hakeil*" would not apply.
- If it is a *tefillah*, some hold that one can add personal requests to its texts, and one who is without a siddur can make up a personal petition in his own words; whereas a *berachah* must be recited in its exact wording.[27] (See next section.)

It is interesting that Rav Joseph B. Soloveitchik reportedly ruled that one must feel anxious or distressed about the trip in order to recite *Tefillas Ha'derech*.[28] As such, one who travels a particular route very often and does not feel any fear is therefore exempt from *Tefillas Ha'derech*.

---

25   *Shaarei Teshuvah* 110:8; *Mishnah Berurah* 110:26; *Halichos Shlomo* 21:2.
26   *Mishnah Berurah* 110:24 seems to opine that one should say full *berachah* every day, but see *Halichos Shlomo* 21:2; *Mishnah Berurah* (*Dirshu*) 110:25 says that since a boat is in constant motion, it is not called a *kevius*; see *Ishei Yisrael* 50, note 13.
27   *Kuntres Tefillas Haderech*, p. 39. It is interesting to note that the *Shulchan Aruch OC* 110 includes the halachos of *Tefillas Ha'derech* in the section dealing with the laws of *tefillah*.
28   *Nefesh HaRav*, p. 149. The obligation for *tefillah* is based on the concept of *eis tzarah*.

H. TEXT OF THE *TEFILLAH*

Even a person who is traveling by himself recites *Tefillas Ha'derech* in the plural form. The Sages explain that this is so because an individual's prayer is more effective when he includes others.[29]

Many have the custom to add the words, "*V'sachazireinu l'veiseinu l'shalom*—Return us to our home in peace," only if one is planning to return on the same day.[30] Some rule that one should include these words even if he is returning home on another day.[31]

Some authorities rule that one may add his own specific requests in *Tefillas Ha'derech* in accordance with his particular situation. For example, one who is driving in a car can add, "*V'satzileinu mi'tenuos derachim*—Save us from traffic accidents," and one who is afraid of a terroist attack can add: "*V'satzileinu mi'mokshim u'mechablim*—Save us from traps and terrorists."[32]

Some have the custom to recite a number of verses after reciting *Tefillas Ha'derech* that invoke Hashem's protection. There are different opinions whether these additions may be recited on Tishah B'Av.[33]

---

29   The Sages (*Berachos* 30a; *Bereishis Rabbah* 91:9) teach that in the merit of the community, one's prayers are more acceptable. *Mishnah Berurah* (*Dirshu*) 110:18, 19, and note 16. See *Magen Avraham* 565:1. Some explain that when we ask Hashem to grant us favor in the eyes of all who see us, we are also referring to the angels who accompany us on our journey.

30   See *Siddur Harav* (*Baal Hatanya*), who says that we only add it if we are returning that day. This seems to be *minhag ha'olam*. See *Kuntres Tefillas Haderech*, p. 31.

31   *Piskei Teshuvos* 110:3, note 18. See *Ahaleich B'Amitecha* 9:15, who quotes opinions that one may say it even if one will not be returning the same day, arguing that it was part of some of the original sources. This seems to be the opinion of the *Griz* and Rav Yaakov Kamenetsky. Others never insert it. See *Kaf Hachaim* 110:13, who suggests that this is because it is included in the word "*v'sagi'einu*." See *Kuntres Tefillas Haderech*, pp. 30–31.

32   *Halichos Shlomo* 21:1; *Piskei Teshuvos* 110:3, *Ishei Yisrael* 50:4; *Kuntres Tefillas Haderech*, p. 39. According to those who rule that *Tefillas Ha'derech* is a form of "prayer" (see further), it would be permitted to make such additions. However, according to those who rule it has the status of a *berachah*, it is questionable whether one can make additions, because *berachos* have an established form. See *Kuntres Tefillas Haderech*, p. 38, for more on this matter. It is interesting to note that the Gemara (*Berachos* 29b) does not include the addition of *listim v'chayos ra'os*.

33   See *Ishei Yisrael* 50:4 and *Ahaleich B'Amitecha* 9:10 for more on this.

There are different opinions regarding whether it is appropriate to recite a recently composed prayer that is found in various siddurim meant to be recited before airplane travel.[34]

One who does not have the text of *Tefillas Ha'derech* before him may say a prayer of his own that resembles its wording to the best of his ability, as long as it includes some kind of request for a safe journey. One may even conclude this prayer with Hashem's name like the regular *berachah*.[35] If one does not have any text, one should simply say a prayer in one's own words and language without the concluding *berachah*. To avoid this situation, it is advisable to learn *Tefillas Ha'derech* by heart.[36]

I. ON BEHALF OF OTHERS

Since many authorities define *Tefillas Ha'derech* as a personal petition, it is preferable for each person to recite it on his own; one may also say it quietly along with someone who is saying it aloud.[37] When possible, it is better to avoid hearing it over a microphone.[38]

It is questionable whether one who has already recited *Tefillas Ha'derech* may recite it again on behalf of others.[39]

J. BODILY NEEDS

One who needs to relieve oneself and feels that he would not be able to hold back for seventy-two minutes should preferably hear *Tefillas Ha'derech* from another person rather than recite it himself.[40]

---

34 See *Kuntres Tefillas Haderech*, p. 38; *Emes L'Yaakov* 110, note 139. Rav Shmuel Kamenetsky rules that one should not add any *tefillos*.

35 *Ahaleich B'Amitecha* 9:18; *Piskei Teshuvos* 110:3. See *Kuntres Tefillas Haderech*, p. 40.

36 For similar reasons, it is a good idea to know "*Berich Shmei*" and "*Modim d'Rabbanan*" by heart.

37 *Shulchan Aruch OC* 59:4; *Mishnah Berurah* 59:15, 193:5; *Rivevos Ephraim* 6:32. As mentioned earlier, according to those who define *Tefillas Ha'derech* as a prayer and not a *berachah*, it is better to recite it.

38 *Shut Minchas Yitzchak* 3:38:16; *Minchas Shlomo* 1:9:1; *Igros Moshe OC* 2:108.

39 *Halichos Shlomo* 21:5; *Ishei Yisrael* 50:1; *Piskei Teshuvos* 110:3.

40 *Mishnah Berurah* 92:5, 227:10. See *Biur Halachah* 104, s.v. *V'yihiyeh*. See the opinion of *Eliyahu Rabbah*.

K. STANDING OR SITTING

It is preferable to recite *Tefillas Ha'derech* while standing. Nevertheless, it may be recited while sitting if doing so will allow one to feel more relaxed and to concentrate better.[41]

One who is driving and is uncomfortable stopping the car along the side of the road in order to recite *Tefillas Ha'derech* may recite it while driving or before leaving on their trip,[42] as discussed above.[43] Other authorities recommend that in such a situation, it is best that one of the other passengers should recite it for him.

L. ADJOINING *TEFILLAS HA'DERECH* TO ANOTHER *BERACHAH*

Because *Tefillas Ha'derech* does not begin with the words, "Baruch Atah Hashem," some authorities suggest that it should follow on from a *berachah* that does.

This can be done in one of the following ways:[44]

- After eating some food, one recites a *berachah acharonah* and then continues immediately with *Tefillas Ha'derech*.[45]
- One makes a *berachah rishonah* on some food, swallows a bit of it, and then continues immediately with *Tefillas Ha'derech*.[46]
- However, there are those who argue that this may not be necessary for *Tefillas Ha'derech* for the following reasons:

---

41   *Shulchan Aruch OC* 110:22; *Taz* §4. See *Ra'ah, Berachos* 30a, who suggest that the prayer was instituted for one who is in the process of traveling.

42   See *Piskei Teshuvos* 110, note 30. See *Kuntres Tefillas Haderech*, pp. 93–94, for further discussion. Rav Moshe Feinstein permitted a driver to recite the *tefillah* while driving if he can concentrate on its words. Obviously, this would only apply when there was no safety consideration, as driving in some situations is an automatic activity that does not require any special concentration.

43   *Tefillah K'Hilchasah*, p. 520, note 80, quoting Rav Chaim Pinchas Scheinberg.

44   *Shulchan Aruch OC* 110:6. This is in order to "strengthen" a *berachah* that does not start with "Baruch." This concept is known as "*berachah ha'semuchah la'chaveirtah*."

45   *Kitzur Shulchan Aruch* 68:3. This approach generally refers to a food requiring the "*mei'ein shalosh*" *berachah*, which concludes with "Baruch Atah Hashem," though some authorities include a food requiring *Borei nefashos* as well.

46   *Halichos Shlomo* 21:11; *Ishei Yisrael* 14. I heard from Rav Moshe Rubin that Rav Moshe Feinstein used to say the verse, "Baruch atah Hashem lamdeini chukecha" before *Tefillas Ha'derech*.

- The *Tur* points out that this rule applies only to *berachos*, but *Tefillas Ha'derech* is a *tefillah*.[47] (See further discussion.)
- *Beis Yosef*, citing *Rabbeinu Yonah* (*Berachos*), points out that since this *tefillah* was originally instituted as part of *Shema Koleinu* in *Shemoneh Esreh*, it is considered a *berachah chashuvah*, worthy of standing on its own.[48]

M. SPECIAL CIRCUMSTANCES

One who must travel on Shabbos, such as in an emergency, should recite *Tefillas Ha'derech*.[49] On Tishah B'Av, *Tefillas Ha'derech* is recited, however, there are different opinions concerning reciting the additional verses on Tishah B'Av for those who recite them.

An *onein* may also recite *Tefillas Ha'derech*, but not in the presence of the deceased.[50]

N. BEFORE LEAVING ON A TRIP

Before departing on a trip, it is customary to perform one or more of the following activities:

- *Tzedakah*—To set aside some money for tzedakah. This is based on the verse in *Tehilim*: "Righteousness [*tzedakah*] shall go before Him and shall make His footsteps a way."[51]
- *Berachah*—To receive a *berachah* from a great rabbi[52] or other people.[53]

---

47   This view is supported by the fact that *Tefillas Ha'derech* is codified in the *Shulchan Aruch* in *hilchos tefillah* rather than in *hilchos berachos*.

48   It is reported that Rav Yaakov Kamenetsky, Rav Moshe Feinstein, and *Chazon Ish* followed this later opinion.

49   *Ahaleich B'Amitecha* 9:7; *Kuntres Tefillas Haderech*, p. 42. But see *Mishnah Berurah* (*Dirshu*) OC 110:10, which brings the opinion of Rav Elyashiv that on Shabbos one does not recite the *tefillah* because we do not make personal requests.

50   *Shemiras Shabbos K'Hilchasah* 64, note 75, says that this is a matter of protection from danger and is thus permitted; see *Ahaleich B'Amitecha* 9:9; *Piskei Teshuvos* 110:3; *Shevet Halevi* 11:262; but see *Mishnah Berurah* (*Dirshu*) ad loc., which recommends, if possible, having somebody be *motzi* him.

51   *Shelah, Chullin, perek Ner Mitzvah; Tehillim* 85:14.

52   *Mishnah Berurah* 110:28.

53   *Shalom Rav* 7:4.

- Torah—To bring along a *sefer* or something to learn Torah from each day.[54]
- *Tefillah*—To pack one's tallis, tefillin, siddur, and to take some food along (*tzeidah la'derech*), regardless of the length of the journey.[55]

The following is also widely practiced:

- To appoint the traveler as his agent to perform a mitzvah at his destination. This can be accomplished by giving the traveler some money to give to *tzedakah* upon the completion of his journey.[56]
- To say to one departing on a trip: *"L'chaim u'l'shalom"* or *"Leich l'shalom."* One should be carefull not to say *"Leich b'shalom,"* as this expression is said to the deceased at a funeral when he has reached his final resting place.[57]
- To escort the traveler for at least four *amos* (8 ft/3 m) as he departs.[58]

---

54 This is also a fulfillment of *"u'v'lechtecha va'derech,"* to learn Hashem's words as we go on the road. It is also taught that the merit of Torah learning offers protection when on a trip. See *Kovetz Halachos, Country,* p. 33.

55 *Pesachim* 113b; *Mishnah Berurah* 110:20; *Aruch Hashulchan OC* 110:15; *Piskei Teshuvos* 110:9.

56 This is based on the concept of *sheluchei mitzvah einam nizokim* (*Pesachim* 8b), meaning that one who is engaged in performing a mitzvah is granted Divine protection. If someone is on his way to Eretz Yisrael, this practice may not be necessary, as the trip itself is considered to be a mitzvah.

57 *Berachos* 64a; *Mishnah Berurah* 110:1; *Piskei Teshuvos* 110:9; *Shalom Rav* 7:1. These expressions are all considered to be a blessing. The term *Leich l'shalom* (go *toward* peace) is a blessing that the person should continue to grow and reach his potential. *Leich b'shalom* (go *into* peace), which is addressed to the deceased, expresses our prayer that he should enter into the perfection in the Next World that he has earned in this world.

58 *Sotah* 46b; *Rambam, Mishneh Torah, Aveil* 14:2, 3; *Shulchan Aruch CM* 427:11. There are various ways to understand the requirement of *leviah*. Some explain that it is a practical act of kindness to help one's guest find his way out of the city. Alternatively, it is a matter of showing respect to one's guest to escort him on his way. The Sages (*Sotah* 45b) suggest that escorting a person will protect him from physical danger: If robbers see that nobody cares about a person as he leaves a city, they might come out to kill and rob him (as we learn from the *parashah* of *eglah arufah*). *Maharsha* (ibid., 46b) explains that it provides a spiritual protection. Even if one accompanies the person only four *amos,* he will be protected for the entire journey. See also *Radak* (*Bereishis* 18:16), who discusses Avraham accompanying the angels.

The question of how far one must accompany a person is dependent on the various reasons for *leviah.* Although the *Kitzur Shulchan Aruch* 68:6 rules that one should wait until the

- To share words of Torah with the traveler before his journey.[59] The Sages say that in this manner people will remember each other.
- If something is forgotten at home, some have the custom to not go back for it themselves. Rather, they ask someone else to enter their home and get the item.[60]
- To receive an *aliyah* to the Torah before departing on their journey.[61]

O. GUESTS

When a guest arrives, one should say *"Shalom Aleichem"*[62] and/or *"Baruch Haba."* It is also appropriate to extend one's hand to him.[63]

A guest who returns to a city should lodge with his original host, even if he has multiple invitations from others.[64]

The Sages write that it is inappropriate for a guest to refuse his host's invitation to lead the *Birkas Hamazon.*

---

guest has disappeared from sight, today we are more lenient with this practice for various reasons. People do not expect it, and thus it is considered as if they have excused the host (*mechilah*). Also, roads are generally safe and well-marked. Moreover, many times people go in groups and thus accompany each other. See *Piskei Teshuvos* 110:9. The *Gra* once told a very hospitable person that the reason his house burned down was because he was not particular about this mitzvah. This mitzvah is described by some with the word *"eishel,"* an acronym for *"achilah, shesiyah, and leviah"* (eating, drinking, and accompanying). They note that without the *lamed* of *leviah*, we are left with *eish* (fire).

Semak 11. *Halichos Bein Adam L'Chaveiro*, p. 15, writes that in the merit of the mitzvah, even the one who accompanies the traveler will not be injured that day.

59   *Berachos* 31a; *Shalom Rav* 7:3. This can be either a well-known halachah, a *chiddush* in halachah along with the reasoning, a halachic question, or even an Aggadic teaching. An interesting question regards who should share with whom, and what the purpose of remembering each other is.

60   *Minhag Yisrael Torah* 110:2. However, one may return home for a mitzvah, to close a light inadvertently left on, or if the trip was delayed.

61   *Biur Halachah* 136, s.v. *B'Shabbos.*

62   The reason why both the greeting and the traditional response are phrased in plural is because speaking in plural is considered to be more respectful. Additionally, the greeting is intended to be directed to the angels accompanying the traveler as well. See *Piskei Teshuvos* 110:9; *Minhag Yisrael Torah* 110:3; *Kaf Hachaim CM* 426:41; *Shalom Rav*, p. 54, notes 101–4.

63   *Minhag Yisrael Torah* 110:3. Shaking hands is said to be a conduit for sharing blessings.

64   *Rashi, Bereishis* 13:3.

As part of the standard *Harachamans* in *Birkas Hamazon*, there is a *berachah* to bless the host. Many add an additional *berachah* (found in *Berachos* 46) to bless the host (known as *Birkas Ha'orei'ach*).[65]

---

65   *Shulchan Aruch OC* 201:1; *Mishnah Berurah* §5; *Aruch Hashulchan* 201:3. For more details and discussion see *Shaarei Haberachah*, p. 126, note 63, and *V'Zos Haberachah*, p. 143.

Chapter Fourteen

Summary Table: Birchos Re'iyah

OCEANS AND LAKES

Body of Water	Location	Berachah
Arctic Ocean		*She'asah es ha'yam ha'gadol*; some say: *Oseh maaseh vereishis*
Atlantic Ocean		*She'asah es ha'yam ha'gadol*; some say: *Oseh maaseh vereishis*
Baltic Sea	Europe	*Oseh maaseh vereishis*
Black Sea	Europe	*Oseh maaseh vereishis*
Caribbean Sea	North America	*She'asah es ha'yam ha'gadol*; some say: *Oseh maaseh vereishis*
Dams		No *berachah*
Dead Sea	Israel	*Oseh maaseh vereishis* (full *berachah*/short *berachah*/no *berachah*); see discussion in addendum
Gulf of Mexico		*She'asah es ha'yam ha'gadol*; some say: *Oseh maaseh vereishis*
Hoover Dam	USA	No *berachah*
Indian Ocean		*She'asah es ha'yam ha'gadol*; some say: *Oseh maaseh vereishis*

Body of Water	Location	Berachah
Lake Erie	USA	*Oseh maaseh vereishis*
Lake Geneva	Switzerland	*Oseh maaseh vereishis*
Lake Huron	Canada/USA	*Oseh maaseh vereishis*
Lake Jackson	Wyoming	*Oseh maaseh vereishis*
Lake Michigan	USA	*Oseh maaseh vereishis*
Lake Ontario	Canada/USA	*Oseh maaseh vereishis*
Lake Superior	Canada/USA	*Oseh maaseh vereishis*
Lakes of Florida	USA	No *berachah*
Lakes of Holland		No *berachah*
Long Island Sound	New York/New England	*She'asah es ha'yam ha'gadol;* some say: *Oseh maaseh vereishis*[1]
Mediterranean Sea		*Oseh maaseh vereishis;* some add: *She'asah es ha'yam ha'gadol.* Sephardim say only: *She'asah es ha'yam ha'gadol.*
North Sea	Europe/England	*She'asah es ha'yam ha'gadol;* some say: *Oseh maaseh vereishis*
Pacific Ocean		*She'asah es ha'yam ha'gadol;* some say: *Oseh maaseh vereishis*
Panama Canal		No *berachah*
Persian Gulf		*Oseh maaseh vereishis*
Red Sea		*Oseh maaseh vereishis;* some add: *She'asah es ha'yam ha'gadol;* some add *Birkas Ha'nissim* (short *berachah*)
Sea of Galilee (Kinneret)	Israel	*Oseh maaseh vereishis*

1   *Shaar Ha'ayin* 8:16 (p. 82, 481).

Body of Water	Location	Berachah
Straits of Gibraltar	Europe	If one sees the point where the two oceans meet, according to all opinions, say *She'asah es ha'yam ha'gadol*
Suez Canal		No *berachah*

RIVERS

River	Location	Berachah
Amazon River	South America	*Oseh maaseh vereishis;* some say short *berachah*[2]
Arkansas River	USA	*Oseh maaseh vereishis;* some say short *berachah*
Colorado River	USA	*Oseh maaseh vereishis;* some say short *berachah*
Danube River	Europe	*Oseh maaseh vereishis;* some say short *berachah*
Don River	Russia	*Oseh maaseh vereishis;* some say short *berachah*
European Channel		No *berachah*
Harlem River	New York	No *berachah*
Hudson River	New York	*Oseh maaseh vereishis;* some say short *berachah*[3]
Jordan River		No *berachah;* some say *Oseh maaseh vereishis.* If one sees the area where the Jews crossed, recite *Birkas Ha'nissim* (short *berachah*).[4]

---

2   Ibid., p. 481.

3   Ibid., 8:5, p. 481.

4   *Kum Hishaleich*, p. 238.

River	Location	Berachah
Mississippi River	USA	*Oseh maaseh vereishis;* some say short *berachah*
Murray River (1500 miles)	Australia	*Oseh maaseh vereishis;* some say short *berachah*
Nile River	Egypt, Africa	*Oseh maaseh vereishis*
Ohio River	USA	*Oseh maaseh vereishis;* some say short *berachah*
Rhine River	Europe	*Oseh maaseh vereishis;* some say short *berachah*
St. Lawrence River	Canada/USA	*Oseh maaseh vereishis;* some say short *berachah*
Volga River		*Oseh maaseh vereishis;* some say short *berachah*

MOUNTAINS

Mountain/Range	Location	Berachah
Alps	Europe	*Oseh maaseh vereishis*
Andes Mountains	South America	*Oseh maaseh vereishis*
Carpathian Mountains	Hungary/Russia	*Oseh maaseh vereishis*
Catskill Mountains	New York	*Oseh maaseh vereishis,* if inspired. Some say short *berachah*
Grand Teton	Wyoming	*Oseh maaseh vereishis*
High cliffs		*Oseh maaseh vereishis,* if it has an outstanding form or shape and one is inspired; some say short *berachah*
Himalayas	Southeast Asia	*Oseh maaseh vereishis*
Judean Desert—unusual, high cliffs (Masada)	Israel	*Oseh maaseh vereishis,* if inspired. Some say short *berachah*

Mountain/Range	Location	Berachah
Mt. Arbel	Israel	*Oseh maaseh vereishis*, if inspired. Some say short *berachah*[5]
Mt. Carmel	Israel	*Oseh maaseh vereishis*, if inspired. Some say short *berachah*.[6] Some add *Birkas Ha'nissim* (short *berachah*)
Mt. Hermon	Israel	*Oseh maaseh vereishis*
Mt. Everest	Nepal	*Oseh maaseh vereishis*
Mt. Katahdin	Maine	*Oseh maaseh vereishis*
Mt. Marcy (Adirondack)	New York	*Oseh maaseh vereishis*, if inspired. Some say short *berachah*.
Mt. Rainier	Washington	*Oseh maaseh vereishis*, if inspired. Some say short *berachah*.[7]
Mt. Sartaba	Israel	*Oseh maaseh vereishis*, if inspired. Some say short *berachah*.[8]
Mt. Shasta (Cascade Range)	California	*Oseh maaseh vereishis*
Mt. Sinai		No *berachah*. Some say *Birkas Ha'nissim* (short *berachah*).
Mt. Tavor	Israel	*Oseh maaseh vereishis*, if inspired. Some say short *berachah*.[9]
Mt. Washington	New Hampshire	*Oseh maaseh vereishis*
Mt. Whitney	California	*Oseh maaseh vereishis*

5   *Shaar Ha'ayin*, p. 483. *Kum Hishaleich*, pp. 49, 224.
6   *Shaar Ha'ayin*, p. 483.
7   *Kum Hishaleich*, p. 243
8   Ibid.
9   *Shaar Ha'ayin*, p. 481. *Kum Hishaleich*, p. 243.

Mountain/Range	Location	Berachah
Poconos	Pennsylvania	*Oseh maaseh vereishis*, if inspired. Some say short *berachah*
Rocky Mountains	Western USA	*Oseh maaseh vereishis*
Rosh Hanikra cliffs	Israel	*Oseh maaseh vereishis* (short *berachah*)[10]

DESERTS

Desert	Location	Berachah
Atacama	South America	*Oseh maaseh vereishis*
Chihuahuan	Mexico/ Southwest USA	*Oseh maaseh vereishis*
Colorado Desert (Plateau)	Southwest USA	*Oseh maaseh vereishis*
Great Sandy Desert	Australia	*Oseh maaseh vereishis*
Judean Desert	Israel	*Oseh maaseh vereishis*; some say short *berachah*
Mojave	Southwest USA	*Oseh maaseh vereishis*
Negev	Israel	*Oseh maaseh vereishis*
Sahara Desert	Africa	*Oseh maaseh vereishis*
Sinai Desert	Israel	*Oseh maaseh vereishis*

NATURAL WONDERS

Natural Wonder	Location	Berachah
Aurora Polaris (Polar/ North light)[11]	Manitoba Canada, Alaska, and Norway	*Oseh maaseh vereishis* (short *berachah*)
Comet (*cochav shavit*)		*Oseh maaseh vereishis*

---

10   *Shaar Ha'ayin*, p. 484.
11   *Aurora Polaris* (Polar/North light): An electrically charged wind brings particles to earth in form of various colors.

Natural Wonder	Location	Berachah
Coral Reefs		*She'kachah lo b'olamo* (short *berachah*)
Craters (*machteshim*)	Israel	*Oseh maaseh vereishis* (short *berachah*). Some say no *berachah* at all[12]
Earthquake[13]		*Oseh maaseh vereishis* or *She'kocho u'gevuraso malei olam*[14]
Erupting Volcano		*Oseh maaseh vereishis*; some say short *berachah*[15]
Fjords[16]		See *berachos* on seas and cliffs
Falling Stars		*Oseh maaseh vereishis*
Geyser		*Oseh maaseh vereishis*; some say short *berachah*
Glacier		Some say *Oseh maaseh vereishis* (short *berachah*)
Lightning		*Oseh maaseh vereishis*[17]
Lightning (result of heat)		No *berachah*; some say *Oseh maaseh vereishis*
Lunar Eclipse		No *berachah*; some say *Oseh maaseh vereishis* (short *berachah*)
Meteor		*Oseh maaseh vereishis*
Rainbow over Waterfall		*Oseh maaseh vereishis* (short *berachah*)[18]

12 *Shaar Ha'ayin*, p. 485.
13 Ibid., pp. 72, 486.
14 When the object moves, one may recite either of the *berachos*, but if the object is stationary, only *Oseh maaseh vereishis* is recited.
15 *Shaar Ha'ayin*, p. 485.
16 Ibid., p. 487.
17 If one says *Shekocho u'gevuraso malei olam*, he has fulfilled his obligation.
18 *Shaar Ha'ayin*, p. 487.

Natural Wonder	Location	Berachah
Solar Eclipse		No *berachah*; some say *Oseh maaseh vereishis* (short *berachah*)
Stalactite and Stalagmite Cave		*Oseh maaseh vereishis*; some say short *berachah*
Storm with Winds at Least 60 km (38 m)/h		*Oseh maaseh vereishis*
Thunder		*She'kocho u'gevuraso malei olam*[19]
Trees Changing Colors in Fall		*She'kachah lo b'olamo* (short *berachah*)
Tornado		*Oseh maaseh vereishis* or *She'kocho u'gevuraso malei olam*
Tsunami Waves		*Oseh maaseh vereishis*; some say short *berachah*.[20]
Typhoon		*Oseh maaseh vereishis* or *She'kocho u'gevuraso malei olam*
Waterfall (Major)		*Oseh maaseh vereishis*; some say short *berachah*[21]
Very Tall Trees (e.g., Eucalyptus, Redwood Trees)		*She'kachah lo b'olamo* (short *berachah*); some say full *berachah*
Outstandingly Beautiful Animals, Birds (e.g., Peacock or Parrot), Moths, and Fish		*She'kachah lo b'olamo* (short *berachah*); some say full *berachah*

---

19   If one says *Oseh maaseh vereishis*, he has fulfilled his obligation.
20   *Shaar Ha'ayin*, p. 485.
21   Ibid., p. 486.

SITES

Site	Location	Berachah
Adelsberg (Postojna) Caverns	Former Yugoslavia, Slovenia	On the stalagmites and stalactites: *Oseh maaseh vereishis*; some say short *berachah*
Banias Waterfall	Israel	*Oseh maaseh vereishis* (short *berachah*)
Blue Mountains	Australia	*Oseh maaseh vereishis*
Carlsbad Caverns	New Mexico, USA	On the stalagmites and stalactites, waterfalls, and lakes: *Oseh maaseh vereishis*; some say short *berachah*
Grand Canyon	Arizona, USA	On the craters: *Oseh maaseh vereishis*
Grand Teton National Park	Wyoming, USA	On the Grand Teton mountain: *Oseh maaseh vereishis*; on the waterfalls: *Oseh maaseh vereishis* (short *berachah*)
Great Australian Bight (outstanding rock formations/cliffs)	Australia	*Oseh maaseh vereishis*
Great Barrier Reef (beautiful fish)	Australia	*She'kachah lo b'olamo* (short *berachah*)
Karst Phenomena	Former Yugoslavia	On the stalactites: *Oseh maaseh vereishis*; some say short *berachah*
Niagara Falls	USA/Canada	*Oseh maaseh vereishis*
Plitvice National Park	Croatia	On the waterfalls and lakes: *Oseh maaseh vereishis* (short *berachah*)
Rose Valley	Bulgaria	*She'kachah lo b'olamo* (short *berachah*)

Site	Location	Berachah
Sequoia National Park	California, USA	On the tall Sequoia trees: *She'kachah lo b'olamo* (short *berachah*)
Stalagmites (Me'arat Hanetifim)	Israel	*Oseh maaseh vereishis*; some say short *berachah*
Triglav Mountain (cliff)	Yugoslavia	*Oseh maaseh vereishis*
Uluru (outstanding rock formation)	Central Australia	*Oseh maaseh vereishis*
Yellowstone National Park	USA	On the lake, cliffs, and geysers: *Oseh maaseh vereishis*; on the waterfalls, and river: short *berachah*
Yosemite National Park	California, USA	On the strange-shaped cliffs (such as the Half Dome and El Capitan) and on the lakes: *Oseh maaseh vereishis*; on the waterfalls: short *berachah*; On the Sequoia groves: *She'kachah lo b'olamo* (short *berachah*)

KINGS

Category	Location	Berachah
Dictators—Very Wicked Gentile Kings	Anywhere, but especially African and Middle-Eastern absolute monarchs	*She'nasan mi'kevodo l'vasar v'dam*; some say no *berachah*[22]

---

22   *Shaar Ha'ayin*, p. 358; *Peninei Halachah*, p. 331; *Chazon Ovadiah*, p. 412 (short *berachah*).

Category	Location	Berachah
European Limited Monarchs	E.g., Denmark, Sweden, Netherlands	*She'nasan mi'kevodo l'vasar v'dam*; some say short *berachah*
Governors/Mayors		*She'nasan mi'kevodo l'vasar v'dam* (short *berachah*)
Honorary President		No *berachah*
Jewish Kings		*She'chalak mi'kevodo li'rei'av*
President of Israel		No *berachah*
Prime Minister		*She'nasan mi'kevodo l'vasar v'dam* (short *berachah*); some say no *berachah*
Queen of England		*She'nasan mi'kevodo l'vasar v'dam*; some say short *berachah*
US Elected President		*She'nasan mi'kevodo l'vasar v'dam*; some say short *berachah*

BIRKAS HA'NISSIM

Neis	Location	Berachah
Jordan River—Where Jews Crossed	See note[23]	*She'asah nissim l'avoseinu ba'makom ha'azeh* (short *berachah*); give praise and express gratitude to Hashem[24]
Lion's Cage	Zoos, Circuses	*She'asah neis l'tzaddikim (k')ba'makom ha'zeh* (short *berachah*)

---

23 Kessar Eliyahu Beit Aravah, which is off the Kvish HaBika (Route 90), or others point out a place called Nachal Tirtzah (Wadi Farah), also known as Quasr al Yehud. One could say the *berachah* (without Hashem's name) in either place.

24 *Shaar Ha'ayin*, p. 490.

Neis	Location	Berachah
Lot's Wife (if known)		*Zocheir ha'tzaddikim* and *Dayan ha'emes*
Mt. Carmel		*She'asah nissim l'avoseinu ba'makom ha'azeh* (short *berachah*)[25]
Red Sea		*She'asah nissim l'avoseinu ba'makom ha'azeh* (short *berachah*);[26] give praise and express gratitude to Hashem (even not in the spot where the Jews crossed)
Walls of Jericho[27]		*She'asah nissim l'avoseinu ba'makom ha'zeh* (short *berachah*)

DEFORMITIES IN PEOPLE

Deformity	Berachah
Abnormally Long or Short Hands	*Meshaneh ha'berios*; some say short *berachah*
Albino	*Meshaneh ha'berios*; some say short *berachah*
Blue person	*Meshaneh ha'berios*; some say short *berachah*
Blind	From birth (in both eyes): *Meshaneh ha'berios*; some say short *berachah* Not from birth (even in one eye): *Dayan ha'emes* (if the observer feels pain)
Giant	*Meshaneh ha'berios*;[28] some say short *berachah*
Midget	*Meshaneh ha'berios*

---

25   See *Kum Hishaleich*, p. 227, for discussion.
26   *Shaar Ha'ayin*, p. 490.
27   *Kum Hishaleich*, p. 227, for discussion
28   *Shaar Ha'ayin*, p. 492.

Deformity	Berachah
Missing or Additional Fingers	Meshaneh ha'berios (if from birth)
Person without Hand/s	From birth: Meshaneh ha'berios; some say short berachah Not from birth: Dayan ha'emes (short berachah) if the observer feels pain
Person without Leg/s	From birth: Meshaneh ha'berios; some say short berachah Not from birth: Dayan ha'emes (short berachah) if the observer feels pain
Siamese Twins	Meshaneh ha'berios

ABNORMAL ANIMALS/DEFORMITIES IN ANIMALS

Animal/Deformity	Berachah
Deformed Animals (from Birth)	Meshaneh ha'berios[29]
Elephant (all species)	Meshaneh ha'berios;[30] some say short berachah
Giraffe	Meshaneh ha'berios; some say short berachah
Kangaroo	Meshaneh ha'berios; some say short berachah
Monkey (all species)	Meshaneh ha'berios; some say short berachah
Owl	Meshaneh ha'berios;[31] some say short berachah
Unusual-Looking Fish, Crocodiles, Alligators	Some say Meshaneh ha'berios; (short berachah); if beautiful: She'kachah lo be'olamo (short berachah)

---

29   Shaar Ha'ayin, p. 122.
30   Some recommend reciting one berachah when entering a zoo, while others recommend separate berachos on the elephant and monkey.
31   Heard from Rav David Feinstein.

TREES—*BIRKAS HA'ILANOS*

Tree Type	Berachah
Grafted Trees	Some say full *berachah*; some say no *berachah*
Fruit Tree That Grows from a Grafted Tree	Full *berachah*
Tree of Orlah	Short *berachah* (best to make on regular tree)

GRAVES

Type of Grave	Berachah
Gentile graves	*Boshah imchem me'od*, etc.[32]
Jewish graves	*Asher yatzer eschem ba'din*, etc.
Kever Rashbi	No *berachah*
Me'aras Hamachpelah	No *berachah*
One grave	No *berachah*

OTHER BERACHOS

Event/Sight	Location	Berachah
600,000 non-Jews		*Boshah imchem me'od*
600,000 Jews		*Chacham Ha'razim*
Blessing of the sun (every twenty-eight years)		*Oseh maaseh vereishis*
Church (especially with a cross)		*Beis gei'im yisach Hashem*[33]
Church "sold" to be a synagogue		*Keil nekamos Hashem*
Destroyed church		*Keil nekamos Hashem*

---

32 *Yirmiyahu* 50:12.
33 Some Sephardic authorities opine that the *berachah* of *She'nasan erech apayim* (short) should be recited.

Event/Sight	Location	Berachah
Destroyed temples	E.g., Banias, Israel	*She'akar avodah zarah mei'artzeinu* (short *berachah*)[34]
Destroyed Jewish homes	E.g., Katzrin, Israel	*Dayan ha'emes* (short *berachah*)
Destroyed mosque		*Keil nekamos Hashem*
First rain of season in Eretz Yisrael		The *berachah* for rain (short *berachah*)[35]
First rain outside Eretz Yisrael		No *berachah*
Non-Jewish or Jewish scholars (secular)		*She'nasan mei'chochmaso l'vasar v'dam* (short *berachah*)
Hearing about a new son		*Ha'tov v'ha'meitiv*
Idols (images)	e.g., India and China	*She'nasan erech apayim l'ovrei retzono*
Idols (temple)		*Beis gei'im yisach Hashem*
Jewish scholars (*Gedolei Hador*)		*She'chalak mei'chochmaso li'rei'av*; some say no *berachah*
Mosque		*Beis gei'im yisach Hashem*
Newly established Jewish communities, cities, neighborhoods, or beautiful synagogues in Eretz Yisrael		*Matziv gevul almanah* (short *berachah*)
Non-Jewish destroyed homes		*Keil nekamos Hashem*

---

34   *Peninei Halachah*, p. 326.
35   *Mishnah Berurah* 221:1.

Event/Sight	Location	Berachah
Non-Jewish rebuilt homes or cities of Jewish enemies		*Beis gei'im yisach Hashem*
Rain after drought (Eretz Yisrael and abroad)		The *berachah* for rain (short *berachah*)[36]
Rainbow		*Zocheir ha'bris v'ne'eman bi'veriso v'kayam b'ma'amaro*
Rebuilt Jewish homes or synagogues		*Matziv gevul almanah* (short *berachah*)
Seeing one's very good friend (overjoyed)—more than thirty days		*She'hecheyanu* (short *berachah*/no *berachah*)
Seeing a very close relative after a long period		*She'hecheyanu*
Seeing one's new daughter		*She'hecheyanu*; some say no *berachah*
Seeing one's good friend who has recuperated from a very serious operation (overjoyed)		*She'hecheyanu* (if very happy)
Seeing one's new son		*Ha'tov v'ha'meitiv*
Synagogue turned into a church (CV)		*Dayan ha'emes* (short *berachah*)

---

36   See *Shulchan Aruch O.C.* 221.

Birchos Shevach V'Hodaah

Chapter Fifteen
Birkas Ha'gomel

A. INTRODUCTION

In the days of the Beis Hamikdash, one who survived a potentially life-threatening situation would bring a *korban todah* (thanksgiving offering) to express gratitude to Hashem. Nowadays, we recite *Birkas Ha'gomel* as an expression of this thanksgiving.

The *berachah* recited is:

בָּרוּךְ...הַגּוֹמֵל לַחַיָּבִים טוֹבוֹת שֶׁגְּמָלַנִי כָּל טוֹב.

Baruch...ha'gomel l'chayavim tovos she'gemalani (kol) tov—Blessed...Who bestows good things upon the unworthy [guilty] who has bestowed upon me much [every] goodness."[1]

Those who hear the *berachah* should respond:

אָמֵן, מִי שֶׁגְּמָלְךָ טוֹב, הוּא יִגְמָלְךָ כָּל טוֹב סֶלָה.

Amen, mi she'gemalcha tov, hu yigmalcha kol tov, selah—May He Who has bestowed [much] goodness upon you continue to bestow every goodness upon you forever, selah.[2]

---

1   See *Shulchan Aruch OC* 219:2; *Mishnah Berurah* 219:4; *Shaarei Berachah* 22:1. One explanation for the word "*l'chayavim*" is that we are thanking Hashem for giving good life even to people who are deserving of punishment. Another explanation is that we are thanking Hashem for taking care of people who should have a tremendous debt of gratitude to Hashem for so many good things (*Toras Chaim*, p. 230). See *Halichos Shlomo* 23:7, where he questions the use of word "*kol*" in the *berachah*, even when it should be included in the response. See *Peninei Halachah, Harchavos, Berachos*, p. 259, and *Toras Chaim*, p. 230 for additional interpretations.

2   *Toras Chaim*, p. 232. He explains why it is not enough to just answer "*Amen*." The additional response is to indicate that the salvation should not come at the expense of using up one's merits. Some suggest that the *mevarech* should respond by saying, "*Amen, ken yehi ratzon*" (*Ben Ish Chai*, Eikev 1).

If one was saved from danger in a truly miraculous way (see below for details), one might also be obligated to say an additional *berachah, Birkas Ha'nissim,* when seeing the actual place where the miracle occurred.[3]

These are the four classic circumstances after which one is obligated to recite *Ha'gomel*:

1. *Chavush* (חבוש)—Being released from prison
2. *Yam* (ים)—Crossing an ocean
3. *Yissurim* (יסורים)—Recovering from illness
4. *Midbar* (מדבר)—Traveling through a desert

(The mnemonic to remember this is the verse, "*V'chol* **ha'chaim** *yoducha selah*—And all the living will praise You"; the letters of the word חיים—*chaim* represent *chavush, yam, yissurim,* and **midbar**.[4])

1. Prison

There is a dispute among the authorities regarding the conditions of one's imprisonment, and the length of time one must be imprisoned, in order to be obligated to recite *Ha'gomel* upon release.[5] For more details, see note.

2. Crossing an Ocean

Ashkenazic authorities rule that only one who takes at least a one- or two-day trip over the ocean recites *Ha'gomel*. On a shorter trip or cruise, one would not recite *Ha'gomel*, unless they experienced a dangerous

---

3   See *Shulchan Aruch OC* 218:4–9 for details.

4   *Ben Ish Chai, Eikev* (*hakdamah*), points out that there is an added urgency to thank Hashem in these four specific cases. It is explained that, in general, people rely on human resources to survive these four events. For example, on a boat, one relies on the captain; for release from jail, one relies on ransom money or the influence of certain people, and so on. By thanking Hashem, we remember that He is the one who saves us from all danger. In some of these cases, one may not have been in actual danger, but since he found himself in a place or situation where it is common to encounter danger, the *berachah* is recited.

5   *Mishnah Berurah* 219:3; *Biur Halachah,* s.v. *Chavush; Shaarei Berachah* 22:4. See *Binyan Av* 1:6, where he says that modern-day prisons may have a different status than prisons in ancient times. As such, he recommends reciting *Ha'gomel* without including Hashem's name. There are also differences of opinion, for example, whether one must be handcuffed during one's imprisonment, whether it applies to short sentences, and whether it applies to monetary matters. See *Shaarei Berachah* 24, note 14, and *Piskei Teshuvos* 219:6 for more details.

situation, such as a fisherman going far out to sea,[6] or one who nearly drowns and is saved. Sephardic authorities opine that as long as one takes a seventy-two-minute trip that takes one beyond sight of the shore, one must recite *Ha'gomel*.[7]

3. Traveling through a Desert

The authorities point out that the deserts referred to are those that are naturally dangerous places, such as where wild beasts or marauders are found, specifically when it is difficult to call for help. If one travels by train (or car) through a desert,[8] the Ashkenazic custom is not to recite *Ha'gomel*, while Sephardic practice is to recite it.[9]

a. Flying in an Airplane

There is much discussion among contemporary authorities regarding the question of whether one who travels by plane must recite *Ha'gomel*:

• Many authorities rule that all air travel requires the recitation of *Ha'gomel*.[10]

• Some rule that one is only obligated to recite *Ha'gomel* if one flies over an ocean or desert, but not on routine local flights.[11]

• There are also those who rule that nowadays we do not recite *Ha'gomel* in any of these situations.[12]

---

6   See *Ohr L'Tzion* 2:14, who says that if one can no longer see the shore, one must recite *Ha'gomel*.

7   *Shaarei Berachah* 22:15.

8   See *Ketzos Hashulchan* 65:2; *Shaarei Berachah* 22:17; *Piskei Teshuvos* 219:2; *Peninei Halachah, Berachos*, p. 356. An interesting application would be someone taking a hike in a desert area, i.e., Vadi Kelt in Eretz Yisrael.

9   *Birkas Hashem* 4:6:26.

10   *Igros Moshe OC* 2:59 (it is impossible to stay alive when suspended in mid-air); *Halichos Shlomo* 23:5; *Be'er Moshe* 7:68–69; *Avnei Yashfe* 1:46; *Shaarei Berachah* 22:18; *Rivevos Ephraim* 1:155. See also *Ohr L'Tzion* 2:14, 43, regarding private planes. See *Yechaveh Daas* 2:26, where he writes that any seventy-two-minute trip will require *Ha'gomel*.

11   *Orchos Rabbeinu*, p. 91; *Teshuvos V'Hanhagos* 1:193, 2:148; *Piskei Teshuvos* 219:16; *Halachically Speaking*, vol. 2. This is the view of *Chazon Ish*, the Satmar Rebbe, Rav Chaim Kanievsky, the Lubavitcher Rebbe, and Rav Chaim Pinchas Scheinberg. Rav Yisroel Belsky says that common custom is not to recite *Ha'gomel* for flights within the United States. See *Tzitz Eliezer* 11:14 regarding three-hour flights.

12   See *Minchas Yitzchak* 2:47, who writes that it is only recited if a person feels *tzarah*—great distress because of the danger involved; if flying was really considered a real danger today, we

Note: If there is an incident that endangers the lives of the passengers, all agree that *Ha'gomel* should be recited.

b. Business/Vacation Trips with Numerous Destinations

One who is traveling and stops briefly, even overnight, but intends to continue traveling, such as one who is traveling to Eretz Yisrael from the US with a stopover in London, does not recite *Ha'gomel* until reaching their final destination.[13] However, if they consider the current place as one of their destinations, such as in order to visit museums, *kevarim*, or for a business meeting, there are different opinions regarding what they should do:

- Many authorities rule that one should recite *Ha'gomel*.[14]
- Some rule that one only recites *Ha'gomel* if he will remain at the current destination for three or more days.[15]
- Some rule that one recites *Ha'gomel* without including Hashem's name at the stop, but recites the full *berachah* when returning home.[16]

c. Trips out of Town/Dangerous Roads

There are different customs regarding a short trip out of the city that lasts more than seventy-two minutes, or when driving on very dangerous roads, such as in Judea and Samaria. While most Ashkenazim do not recite *Ha'gomel* in these instances, many Sephardim do recite it.[17]

---

wouldn't be allowed to do it! According to this approach, going on a plane or boat nowadays may be comparable to driving in a car, in which case *Ha'gomel* should not be recited. As such, some recommend reciting it without including Hashem's name; see *Libun B'Halachah*, p. 404.

13   *Shulchan Aruch OC* 219:1.

14   See *Halichos Shlomo* 23:4; *Chazon Ovadiah*, p. 369; *Piskei Teshuvos* 219:29, note 32; *B'Tzeil Hachochmah* 1:21. This is the view of Rav Chaim Pinchas Scheinberg, as quoted in *Hegyonei Haparashah, Vayikra*, p. 111.

15   *Kaf Hachaim OC* 219:5. See *Hegyonei Haparashah*, who quotes the opinion of Rabbi Moshe Feinstein, and *Ashrei Ha'ish*, p. 269 (Rav Elyashiv), that this only applies if one will remain in this place for more than thirty days.

16   *Piskei Teshuvos* 219, note 31; *Ashrei Ha'ish* 40:16–17.

17   *Shulchan Aruch OC* 219:7; *Yabia Omer* 1:13; *Yechaveh Daas* 2:26. This is as long as the entire trip back and forth is more than seventy-two minutes. See *Ohr L'Tzion* 2:14:42.

4. Recovery from Illness

One who recovers from a life-threatening or potentially life-threatening illness recites *Ha'gomel*.[18] This includes major injuries, operations with full anaesthesia, any procedure that affects internal organs,[19] a heart attack, heart surgery, as well as procedures to insert stents and balloons.[20] This might also include serious bronchitis or pneumonia (especially if one required hospitalization),[21] hepatitis and cellulitis (where there are complications), loss of consciousness,[22] poisonous snake bites, and ingesting poison. Some include kidney donations.[23]

There are also some minor procedures to individual organs that may require *Ha'gomel*. For example, eye operations; removal of a cataract;[24] prostate or hernia surgery or other **invasive** procedures, even if they only require local anasthesia;[25] and at times, a fracture or a serious cut that requires stitches (if there was serious possibility of infection). Common custom, however, is not to recite *Ha'gomel* for cosmetic procedures or teeth surgeries.[26]

---

18   Either a complete recovery or, if one will never totally recover, when one is well enough to walk or otherwise function as normally as possible; *Shevet Halevi* 4:152:3

19   *Beis Avi* 3:79; *Chazon Ovadiah, Berachos*, p. 372; *Birkas Hashem* 4:6:11.

20   *Tzitz Eliezer* 12:18.

21   See *Toras Chaim*, p. 19, who says that *Ha'gomel* is recited upon being cured from any sickness that could have been potentially deadly. The definition of a sickness that requires *Ha'gomel* seems to be disputed. Rabbi Dr. Avraham Abraham feels that one who recovers from an illness that could be deadly (pneumonia, bronchitis, etc.) should recite *Ha'gomel*. However, others, such as Rav Chaim Kanievsky and Rav Nissim Karelitz, rule that if a cure is easily available, or if most people don't consider it very dangerous, one does not recite *Ha'gomel*. See *Toras Chaim*, p. 17.

22   *Piskei Teshuvos* 219:20; *Tzitz Eliezer* 12:18. This is because it could affect internal organs. See *Beis Avi* 3:79.

23   *Birkas Eliyahu*, p. 306. See *Yechaveh Daas* 3:84, and *Chazon Ovadiah, Berachos*, p. 378, for a discussion about donating organs.

24   *Piskei Teshuvos* 219:105; *Shaarei Berachah* 22:7; *Nishmas Avraham*, p. 180; *Halichos Shlomo* 23:2; *Tzitz Eliezer* 12:18. See *Shaarei Berachah* 22:7 and *Har Tzvi* 113.

25   *Masores Moshe* 2, p. 49.

26   *Piskei Teshuvos* 219:11, note 54.

Many Sephardim recite *Ha'gomel* for any illness that caused one to be bedridden for three days e.g., flu or virus.[27] However, Ashkenazic custom is not to recite it under these conditions.[28]

5. Potentially Hazardous Situations

In addition to the four primary cases, Ashkenazic and Yemenite practice is to recite *Ha'gomel* when one is saved from any life-threatening situation,[29] such as car accidents or fires (if one was directly affected). There is a basis for Sephardim to do so as well.[30]

6. Close Calls

There are various levels of "close calls" where one might have missed a dangerous situation. In most such situations, *Ha'gomel* should not be recited. As a general rule, to recite *Ha'gomel*, one must have been in a state of danger (*matzav sakanah*) or in a place of danger (*makom sakanah*) and been saved. At times, this may be difficult to evaluate. See notes and examples below. In any case, it is still appropriate to say prayers of thanksgiving (see further).[31] In certain circumstances, some authorities recommend reciting *Ha'gomel* without including Hashem's name.

Below is a list of some examples. Due to the differing circumstances of such situations, **a rabbi should be consulted regarding individual cases**.

27   See *Ohr L'Tzion* 2:14:44; *Ben Ish Chai, Eikev*; *Chazon Ovadiah*, p. 372, says even one day.

28   It is not considered *he'ala l'gardum* (fatal), especially when medicines are available.

29   *Shulchan Aruch OC* 219:9. The question is whether *Ha'gomel* is only to be recited on the four primary situations or for any situation that resembles them. See *Igros Moshe OC* 2:59 regarding situations that are inherently dangerous, such as air travel.

30   See *Peninei Halachah, Berachos*, p. 267; *Chazon Ovadiah, Berachos*, p. 279, says to recite it without *Shem u'malchus*.

31   *Mishnah Berurah* 218:32; *Piskei Teshuvos* 218, note 84. *Chayei Adam* 65:4 rules that if a stone fell near where one was standing, and one's life would have been in danger if one would have been hit, one should recite *Ha'gomel*. *Maharal, Nesivos Olam, Nesiv Ha'avodah* 13, rules that one must actually be hit by the stone in order to recite *Ha'gomel*. For a full discussion concerning this *machlokes*, see *Toras Chaim*, pp. 218–20, and *Piskei Teshuvos*, note 58. At times, it may make a difference if the dangerous item was intentionally thrown.

a. Falling from a Ladder—Falling Objects

One who falls from a high-standing ladder or from the first floor of a building should recite *Ha'gomel*.[32] If an object fell from a roof and hit a person, he should recite the *berachah*. If it barely missed him, no *berachah* is necessary.[33]

b. Fire/Near Drowning/Gas Leak

One who was in a fire and was saved, one who was drowning and was saved, or one who was awakened due to a gas leak in one's home should recite *Ha'gomel*. However, one who escaped a fire, **saved oneself** from a near drowning, or became aware of a gas leak on their own does not recite *Ha'gomel*.[34]

c. Car/Bus Accidents

One who was in a car accident that could have been fatal (i.e., a high-impact collision,[35] the car skidding on ice while traveling at high speed, or a car that turned over and fell off the road) should recite *Ha'gomel*. *Ha'gomel* is not recited for a minor collision, a sudden swerve, or a last-minute stop.

One who survived being struck by a bus must recite *Ha'gomel*, and perhaps even *Birkas Ha'nissim*. However, *Ha'gomel* is not recited if a bus missed a person, albeit barely. This is true even if the bus brushed him.

One who missed or got off a bus just before it was in a fatal accident does not recite *Ha'gomel*.[36]

One who is traveling in a car that hits a large animal, such as a deer, should recite *Ha'gomel*, but not for a near-miss.[37] One who fell asleep while driving should recite *Ha'gomel*.[38]

---

32 *Shaar Hatziyun* 218:29.
33 Based on *Piskei Teshuvos* 218, note 58; *Halichos Shlomo* 23:1. However, to fulfill the opinion of the *Chayei Adam* 65:4, it would be a good idea to recite the shortened *berachah*.
34 *Toras Chaim*, p. 70. *Piskei Teshuvos* 10:4 says that this is considered as if he just missed a *matzav sakanah*.
35 *Shulchan Aruch OC* 219:9; *Mishnah Berurah* 219:31; *Avnei Yashfe* 1:46; *Piskei Teshuvos* 218:84. See also *Tzitz Eliezer* 18:22 and *Halichos Shlomo* 23:1.
36 Since one was never in a *matzav sakanah*.
37 Heard from Rav Zvi Rosen.
38 *Toras Chaim*, p. 68; *Masores Moshe* 3, p. 49.

d. Holdups

One who was held up by a thug or mugger might be required to recite *Ha'gomel*. However, *Ha'gomel* is not recited if the potential mugger(s) saw someone approaching and ran off.[39]

e. Rocks

Most authorities rule that one does not recite *Ha'gomel* for traveling on roads in dangerous areas, such as in Judea and Samaria. Many authorities rule that for any vehicular attack, especially if large rocks or fire bombs are thrown, everybody in the vehicle, and perhaps even those in nearby vehicles, must recite *Ha'gomel*.[40] However, other authorities rule that only if one's vehicle was stoned and caused a window to shatter, and one was hit by pieces of glass, should they recite *Ha'gomel*. If one is not hit by the glass, or the rocks miss the vehicle entirely, *Ha'gomel* is not recited (although some suggest reciting it without including Hashem's name).[41]

f. Explosive Rockets

If an explosive rocket hits and damages a building, everyone inside the building should recite *Ha'gomel*; if it didn't explode, *Birkas Ha'nissim* may also be warranted.[42] If one left the building before the rocket attack, *Ha'gomel* is not recited. However, there is basis to recite *Ha'gomel* if the rocket narrowly missed the building.[43]

---

39 *Mishnah Berurah* 219:29; *Toras Chaim*, p. 65 (especially if the attacker is holding a weapon). *Piskei Teshuvos* 218:71 says that it depends if the thief was holding a weapon in his hand. *Sefer Mizmor L'Sodah*, p. 58, quoting Rav Kushelevsky, notes that most criminals are on drugs and are therefore very dangerous.

40 See *Piskei Teshuvos* 218:10:72. See *Shevet Halevi* 9:45, who rules that if the area is considered a *makom sakanah*, all cars in the area may be included. See also *Peninei Halachah, Berachos*, p. 356; *Techumim* 24.

41 *Halichos Shlomo* 23:1, but see *Libun B'Halachah*, p. 399–401, for his understanding of *Halichos Shlomo*.

42 *Mizmor L'Sodah*, p. 58, s.v. *Matzav sakanah*.

43 This is based on the opinion of the *Chayei Adam* (65:4) and *Mishnah Berurah*, and especially in this case where there was intent to kill (*Toras Chaim*, p. 66, note 59; see above).

g. Explosives on a Bus

One who was on a bus where a bomb was discovered before it exploded, or one who experienced a bombing but wasn't hurt, should recite *Ha'gomel*. Some authorities also require one to recite *Ha'gomel* if one got off the bus just before the bomb exploded.[44] However, *Ha'gomel* is not recited if one missed the bus entirely.

h. Soldiers Returning from Battle—Other Dangerous Actions

A soldier who escapes from a terrorist attack,[45] or who completes a parachuting course[46] should recite *Ha'gomel*. Soldiers who are in combat on the battlefront who return home—even temporarily—recite *Ha'gomel*, even if they plan to return to the front.[47]

i. Dangerous Trips/Self-Imposed Dangers

One who endangered oneself by taking a dangerous trip, such as after speeding on a highway or engaging in other dangerous forms of recreation, and was miraculously saved, may recite *Ha'gomel*.[48] One who donates an organ (when permitted according to halachah) is permitted to recite *Ha'gomel*.[49] However, there are different opinions whether *Ha'gomel* may be recited after elective surgery, such as cosmetic or plastic surgery, even if it was dangerous.[50]

7. General Note

It is always appropriate to give *tzedakah* and to say prayers of thanksgiving whenever one goes through a traumatic experience. These might include *Mizmor L'Sodah* and *Nishmas* (and *Mizmor shir l'yom haShabbos*

---

44 One who got off after the bomb was already on the bus or was neutralized recites *Ha'gomel*, as it is considered a *makom sakanah*; *Avnei Yashfe* 1:46:4; *Toras Chaim*, p. 63 and 72.

45 *Shevet Halevi* 5:24:2; 9:65.

46 *Peninei Halachah, Harchavos, Berachos*, p. 357.

47 *Shevet Halevi* 9:45.

48 *Toras Chaim*, p. 51, 72. See the important discussion about people putting themselves into danger on p. 329–32; see also *Libun B'Halachah*, p. 405.

49 *Yechaveh Daas* 3:4; *Chazon Ovadiah, Berachos*, p. 374, who writes that there is an obligation to recite the *berachah*.

50 *Kaf Hachaim OC* 219:48 rules that it is recited, while *Chazon Ovadiah*, p. 374, rules that it is not. See *Piskei Teshuvah* 219:11, note 54.

on Shabbos).[51] One should also have his rescue in mind during the recitation of *Modim*.

B. SPECIAL CASES

1. Women

There are different customs regarding women reciting *Ha'gomel*:

With the exception of a woman after birth, Ashkenazic custom is that a woman does not recite *Ha'gomel*. This is because *Ha'gomel* should ideally be recited in front of ten men, and it is considered a breach of modesty for a woman to appear in front of so many men. However, women should say other prayers of thanksgiving (see below).[52]

Other customs include:

- For a woman to recite *Ha'gomel* from the *ezras nashim* or in her home;[53] this is common among the Sephardic community.
- For a husband to have his wife's situation in mind when receiving an *aliyah* and reciting the words, *"Barchu es Hashem ha'mevorach,"* to thank Hashem on his wife's behalf.[54]
- For a husband to recite *Ha'gomel* on his wife's behalf. According to this approach, he recites, *"she'gemaleich kol tov,"* if she is present, or *"she'gamal l'ishti kol tov"* if she is not present.[55]
- For a woman to have in mind her thanks to Hashem when hearing someone recite *Barchu*.[56]

---

51   *Teshuvos V'Hanhagos* 1:175.

52   *Mishnah Berurah* 219:3; *Be'er Heiteiv* 219:1.

53   *Piskei Teshuvos* 219:10. See *Mishnah Berurah* 219:3, who permits a woman saying it even if there are (including her) nine women and one man. This is also the view of Rav Elyashiv. The *Aruch Hashulchan OC* 219:9 disagrees. See *Igros Moshe OC* 5:14, where he wrote that *Ha'gomel* can be recited when necessary even in front of one person (a man or a woman).

54   Some say that she does not need to be present. *She'arim Metzuyanim B'halachah* 61:1.

55   *Mishnah Berurah* 219:17. Other customs include: (1) To say it in front of one man or woman. This can be her husband if she is married (*Igros Moshe, OC* 14:2); (2) To have it in mind when reciting the morning *berachah* of *Ha'gomel chasadim tovim l'amo Yisrael* (*Halichos Shlomo* 23:8, note 10).

56   *Shaarei Berachah* 22:20; *B'Tzeil Hachochmah* 6:78. Some say that any *Barchu* is sufficient.

- Many Sephardim have the custom to recite the *berachah* whenever the men recite the *berachah*.[57]

2. *Yoledes*—After Giving Birth

Recently it has become more common for women to recite *Ha'gomel* in a minyan in a family setting, such as at the *bris* or *kiddush*.[58] Some women have the custom to follow one of the procedures mentioned above. *Ha'gomel* is not recited after a miscarriage.[59]

3. Minors

A minor is not obligated to say *Ha'gomel* (see note).[60] It is proper for either the father or the son to have the event in mind during the morning *berachah* of *Ha'gomel chasadim tovim*. Some Sephardic authorities rule that a minor should recite *Ha'gomel*.[61]

4. *Hiddurim*

Ha'gomel should ideally be recited in front of ten men.[62] It is ideal for two of the ten to be Torah scholars.[63]

Many have the custom is to recite *Ha'gomel* during *k'rias haTorah*, even if it is more than three days after the event (see further).[64] One who

57 *Kaf Hachaim* 219:7.

58 It is noted that in the time of the Beis Hamikdash, a woman is obligated to bring a *korban yoledes* (the sacrifice after giving birth), so there is even more reason to recite *Ha'gomel*. The *Magen Avraham* 282 and *Biur Halachah* 126 point out that there is a custom for the husband to receive an *aliyah* on the first Shabbos that his wife is well enough to go to shul, or if she is not well enough, then on the fortieth day after the birth for a boy or the eightieth day after birth for a girl. For more details, see *Halichos Beisah*, p. 116 and *Halichos Shlomo* 23:3. *Minhag Yerushalayim* is to recite it in the house with a minyan at the *bris*, or seven days after giving birth to a girl, but not before (*Kaf Hachaim OC* 219:7).

59 *Peninei Halachah*, *Berachos*, p. 351. This is due to *kavod ha'bri'os* (to avoid any discomfort the woman might feel about this becoming public knowledge).

60 Since the word *chayav* can mean either "obligated" or "guilty" (see above), neither of which apply to a minor; *Toras Chaim*, p. 371.

61 See *Ben Ish Chai, Eikev* 4.

62 *Shulchan Aruch OC* 219:3; *Aruch Hashulchan OC* 219:6.

63 This is based on the verse, "*Yeromemuhu b'kehal am u'v'moshav zekeinim yehaleluhu*—Let them exalt Him in the assembly of people and praise Him in the presence of the Elders" (*Tehillim* 107:32). "Elders" is often synonymous with "Torah scholars." Perhaps this makes it into a more meaningful act.

64 *Shulchan Aruch* ad loc. It is a good opportunity to publicize the miracle. See *Chasam Sofer* 51,

must recite *Ha'gomel* should receive an *aliyah*⁶⁵ or another honor, such as *hagbah* or *gelilah*, if possible.⁶⁶ It is preferable to recite it during the day.⁶⁷

C. TIME LIMIT

It is preferable to recite *Ha'gomel* within three days of the event.⁶⁸ However, if necessary, one may recite it as long as they still remember the incident and feel moved by it. A woman who has given birth does not usually recite *Ha'gomel* before seven days have passed.

1. When It Can Be Recited

Ha'gomel may be recited on any day, including Tishah B'Av⁶⁹ (preferably at *Minchah* on Tishah B'Av). A mourner (within *shivah*) may recite it without receiving an *aliyah*.⁷⁰

2. Groups

If a whole group becomes obligated in *Ha'gomel*, such as if they travel together, it is best if everyone recites their own *berachah*.⁷¹ If necessary, however, one person may recite it on behalf of many. If this is done, the one reciting it should say (in plural), "*she'gemalanu kol tov*," and the response should be "*mi she'gemalchem kol tov*."⁷²

---

who compares receiving an *aliyah* or *kavod* (or just going up to the *shulchan*) to going up to the *Mizbei'ach* to bring a *korban todah*, thus reenacting the service in the Beis Hamikdash. See *Biur Halachah* 219, s.v. *B'Shabbos*; *Piskei Teshuvos* 219:73; *Minhag Yisrael Torah* 219; *Shaarei Berachah* 22:22 for more.

65   Nevertheless, this is considered a low-level priority. For a list of priorities regarding *aliyos*, see *Biur Halachah* 137, s.v. *B'Shabbos*.

66   In this case, *Ha'gomel* should be recited before the *hagbah* or *gelilah*; *Shaarei Ephraim* 4:27.

67   *Korbanos* were only brought during the day.

68   *Mishnah Berurah* 219:20; *Aruch Hashulchan OC* 219:7. This is true even if there is no Torah present. However, see *Teshuvos V'Hanhagos* 1:197, where it is noted that the custom is to wait for a *k'rias haTorah*.

69   *Ahaleich B'Amitecha* 23:35.

70   *Piskei Teshuvos* 219:18.

71   Especially *berachos* in the category of *hodaah*. It is interesting to note that this concept can be demonstrated through the recitation of *Modim d'Rabbanan* **by all** during *chazaras ha'shatz*. One cannot have another express thanksgiving on his behalf, for it is very personal feeling.

72   *Shulchan Aruch OC* 219:5; *Piskei Teshuvos* 219:17, note 89; *Ahaleich B'Amitecha* 23:35. However, see *Halichos Shlomo* 23, note 26, who says that the *berachah* can still be recited in singular.

3. Doubts

If one is in doubt whether one is obligated to recite *Ha'gomel*, one should have one's thanksgiving in mind when reciting the morning *berachah* of *Ha'gomel chasadim tovim*.[73] Alternatively, when he gets an *aliyah* to the Torah, he should have it in mind when reciting *Barchu*.

---

73   See *Halichos Shlomo* 23:8.

Chapter Sixteen

Birkas Hodaas Geshamim— Appreciation for Rain

A. INTRODUCTION

Water is one of the most important commodities of life. The lack of rain can affect the world in many negative ways. The Sages therefore instituted a special set of thanksgiving *berachos* that should be recited when it begins to rain[1] after a serious drought.[2]

Today, we are (generally) not as sensitive as we should be to the possible repercussions of not having enough rain. As such, these *berachos* are generally not recited.[3] Nevertheless, there are still situations when they should be recited, such as by those involved in agriculture who are directly affected by a lack of rain. Some authorities rule that everyone in Eretz Yisrael should recite these *berachos* upon the first serious rainfall

---

1   *Berachos* 59b; *Shulchan Aruch OC* 221:1. The amount of rain that must fall in order to recite the *berachah* must be enough that it brings joy to people. In fact, the Talmud describes the abundance of water that falls and flows in bubbling streams to the joy of a groom going out to meet his bride. See also the opinion of *Rambam, Mishneh Torah, Berachos* 10:5, and *Aruch Hashulchan* 221:2.

2   I.e., including famine, inflated food prices, and unhealthy air that could lead to sickness. See *Shaar Ha'ayin* 22:6, note 13, and *Peninei Halachah, Harchavos, Berachos*, p. 221. Many authorities rule that these *berachos* should even be recited in *chutz la'aretz*; *Mishnah Berurah* 221:2; *Chayei Adam* 65:7.

3   See *Shulchan Aruch OC* 221:1. This is due to the fact that we always have water in our homes, regardless of the national water levels, through desalination. Ocean water is becoming more popular, and water is can be shipped from other countries when needed.

of the rainy season.[4] It is definitely proper to at least recite these *berachos* without including Hashem's name.[5]

B. WHICH *BERACHOS*?

One who does not own a field should say, *"Modim...v'eilu finu..."* (from the *Nishmas* prayer), and conclude with the words: *Baruch Atah, Kel rov ha'hoda'os.*

One who is the sole owner of a field should also recite the *She'hecheyanu.* If the field is jointly owned, or one supports one's family with the field, one should recite *Ha'tov v'ha'meitiv.*[6]

---

4   *Shulchan Aruch OC* 221:1; *Mishnah Berurah* 221:1; *Shaar Ha'ayin* 22:1, quoting Rav Sraya Deblitzki and Rav Moshe Shternbuch. See also *Birkas Hashem*, vol. 4, p. 211.

5   *Biur Halachah* 221.

6   *Shulchan Aruch OC* 222:2; *Kaf Hachaim OC* 222:12; *Piskei Teshuvos* 222, note 3.

Chapter Seventeen

Baruch She'ptarani—the Bar Mitzvah Berachah

בָּרוּךְ...שֶׁפְּטָרַנִי מֵעָנְשׁוֹ שֶׁל זֶה.

Baruch...she'ptarani me'onsho shel zeh—Blessed...Who has absolved me of the punishment of this one.

A. INTRODUCTION

A father recites the *berachah* of *Baruch she'ptarani* when his son becomes bar mitzvah.[1] Common custom is to recite the *berachah* without including Hashem's name, although there are those who recite it in full. One may answer *Amen* to either version of the *berachah*.[2]

There are a number of interpretations as to the meaning of the *berachah*:

---

1   *Shulchan Aruch* OC 225:2. See *Divrei Halachah* (Rav Weber), p. 466, where it is compared to *Ha'gomel.*

2   *Shulchan Aruch* ad loc.; *Mishnah Berurah* (Dirshu) 225:8:12; *Biur Halachah* 215:4, s.v. *V'assur.* The reason that most people recite the *berachah* without including Hashem's name is because it is not found in the Talmud. The *Gra*, however, argues that since it is mentioned in the midrash, it should be treated as any other *berachah*, similar to the *berachah* of *Ha'nosen l'ya'eif ko'ach* and *Mekadesh es shimcha b'rabim*. See *Kitzur Shulchan Aruch* 61:8 and *Aruch Hashulchan* OC 225:4, who allow one to recite the *berachah* in full. *Halichos Shlomo* 23:40, note 151, relates how Rav Shlomo Zalman Auerbach recited the *berachah* in full, even though he did not recommend that others do so. He also writes that if the parents did not give their son proper *chinuch*, it would simply be inappropriate for them to recite the *berachah* in full. See *Ramat Hashulchan* (Rabbi Ari Enkin), p. 169, for more.

- Until now, the father was responsible for his son's actions. Once the son becomes bar mitzvah, however, he is responsible for his own actions.[3]
- In a somewhat contrasting approach, some explain that until his bar mitzvah, a son may be liable for his father's sins. As such, the father recites the *berachah* to thank Hashem that his son is no longer punished for his sins.[4]

B. WHEN THE *BERACHAH* IS RECITED

The *berachah* is usually recited when the bar mitzvah boy receives an *aliyah* to the Torah for the first time.[5] Some have the custom to wait until the first Shabbos after his bar mitzvah. There is no deadline by which the *berachah* must be recited.[6]

In extenuating circumstances, a father is allowed to recite the *berachah* even if his son isn't present, such as if the father is in the hospital, in jail, or out of town. It should always be recited in the presence of a minyan.[7]

1. Other Relationships

- **Stepson/Adopted Son**: There are different opinions whether a stepfather should recite the *berachah*.[8]
- **Grandson**: A grandfather may recite the *berachah* for his grandson if he does not have a father.[9] A mother, however, does not recite the *berachah*.[10]

---

3   *Mishnah Berurah* 225:7. However, this does not eliminate the father's responsilibty to rebuke (educate) his son after his bar mitzvah when necessary.

4   *Levush* 225:2; *Magen Avraham* 225:5. See *Piskei Teshuvos* 225:28; *Am Mordechai, Berachos* (Rabbi Mordechai Willig), p. 121.

5   *Rama OC* 225:2; *Mishnah Berurah* 225:6. Some recite it when the son is the *shaliach tzibbur* for the first time; see *Piskei Teshuvos* 225:6.

6   *Ketzos Hashulchan* 65:14.

7   *Piskei Teshuvos* 225:6.

8   *Piskei Teshuvos* ad loc., note 29. *Mishneh Halachos* 3:26 rules that a stepfather should not recite it, while *B'Tzeil Hachochmah* 5:3 rules that he should.

9   *Maharsham* 8:33; *Piskei Teshuvos* 225:4. See *Halachos V'Halichos, Bar Mitzvah*, p. 81, for other opinions.

10   *Piskei Teshuvos* 225, note 32; *Pri Megadim EA* 225:5 explains that a mother is never punished for sins of her child. But see *Halachah Berurah* 225:14, who permits a mother to say it.

- **Daughter**: Common custom is that a father does not recite the *berachah* for a daughter. Some authorities do allow this, however, without including Hashem's name, in the presence of family.[11]
- **Twins**: A number of authorities rule that separate *berachos* should be recited for each boy, while others rule that one *berachah* is sufficient for both.[12]

C. BAR MITZVAH *SEUDAH*

It is especially appropriate to prepare a special *seudah* in honor of one's son becoming bar mitzvah.[13] It should ideally take place on the day of his thirteenth birthday, though it may be postponed, if necessary. If it has been postponed, one must be sure to say words of Torah at the *seudah* in order for it to be considered a true *seudas mitzvah*.[14]

It is permitted to combine a *seudas bar mitzvah* with another *simchah*, such as a *sheva berachos*, *hachnasas Sefer Torah*, or Chol Hamoed *seudah*.[15] One may have one *seudah* for twins.[16]

1. Bas Mitzvah *Seudah*

There are different opinions regarding the propriety of having a *seudah* for a bas mitzvah. Some authorities rule that only a small *seudah* should be held with close friends and family.[17] The bas mitzvah girl should recite *She'hecheyanu* while wearing a new dress, and have in mind that the *berachah* serve to cover both the dress and her becoming bas mitzvah.[18]

---

11 See *Piskei Teshuvos* ad loc., note 33; *Yabia Omer* 6:29, 8:29; *Chazon Ovadiah, Berachos,* p. 435.

12 See *Piskei Teshuvos* ad loc., note 34; *Halichos Shlomo* 23:41.

13 *Yam Shel Shlomo, Bava Kama* 7:37. See *Am Mordechai* (Rabbi Mordechai Willig), *Berachos,* p. 122, who compares a bar mitzvah to a wedding (*chuppah*). By the son beginning to be obligated independently to the mitzvah of *talmud Torah*, he is being wedded to the Torah. Perhaps this is why this *berachah* is blessed at the time of the *aliyah l'Torah*.

14 *Shulchan Aruch OC* 225:1.

15 *Piskei Teshuvos* 225:7, notes 57–58; *Minchas Yitzchak* 4:23. One should serve an additional dish in honor of the occasion.

16 *Shevet Halevi* 8:28.

17 *Piskei Teshuvos* 225:8, note 60; *Igros Moshe OC* 2:97 forbids a *seudas bas mitzvah*.

18 *Piskei Teshuvos* 225:8, note 60. See *Ben Ish Chai, Re'eh* 17; *Yabia Omer* 6:29.

D. BIRTHDAYS

There are different approaches among the Sages on how to view a birthday. *Ben Ish Chai* encouraged celebrating a birthday as a sort of personal Yom Tov to thank Hashem for having lived another year to serve Him.[19] Rav Moshe Feinstein did not object to celebrating birthdays, though he didn't think that it was important to do so.[20] In any event, there are a number of significant birthdays that should definitely be recognized, such as when turning sixty,[21] seventy, and perhaps every birthday thereafter.

---

19 *Ben Ish Chai* ad loc. See *Halachic World*, vol. 2, p. 53, where it is related that the Ponovezher Rav once told the Chafetz Chaim that it was his birthday, and the Chafetz Chaim responded by saying that a birthday is a day for davening and asking for things from Hashem. The Lubavitcher Rebbe speaks much about the importance of birthdays. It is quoted in his name that one should be spiritually aroused on one's birthday, and that the "downward flow of Divine Light" is renewed upon a person on that day. One also becomes more complete on one's birthday, receiving some of the completeness of Hashem. One should give *berachos* to others on one's birthday. The Chafetz Chaim once invited his students Rav Elchanan Wasserman and Rav Yosef Kahaneman to celebrate his birthday. He served cake and wine and recited *She'hecheyanu*. See *Journal of Halachah*, vol. 51, p. 77.

20 See *Halachic World*, vol. 2, p. 50 and *Igros Moshe OC* 1:104, 2:30, 4:36. In his "*Laws of Pesach*," Rabbi Blumenkrantz says that one should not use birthday candles, nor blow them out, as doing so is based on a pagan custom. See *Journal of Halachah*, vol. 2, p. 69; see also pp. 64–85 for a full treatment of birthdays.

21 Based on *Mo'ed Katan* 28a, where it says that after sixty one is no longer subject to the punishment of *kares*. See *Yerushalmi, Yevamos* 8:3; *Tzitz Eliezer* 18:33.

Chapter Eighteen

K'rias Shema
al Hamitah—
the Sleep Berachah

A. INTRODUCTION

Sleep is one of the most important parts of life. We use a substantial amount of time in our life for sleep. The *Rambam* speaks about the need to sleep for at least eight hours every night.[1] The Talmud teaches that sleep is one-sixtieth of death.[2] Our Sages instituted a special *berachah* and other *tefillos* that are to be recited before going to sleep.[3] These include the following:

---

[1] *Rambam, Mishneh Torah, Deos* 4:4.

[2] *Berachos* 57b.

[3] *Shulchan Aruch OC* 239:1; *Mishnah Berurah* 239:3. See *Biur Halachah* there. There is much discussion whether *Ha'mapil* is *Birkas Ha'nehenin* or *Birkas Ha'shevach*. If the former, it should be recited as close as possible to going to sleep, while if the latter, this is not as vital. There are those (*Seder Hayom*) who say to recite *Ha'mapil* when you feel tired, comparing it to *Birkas Ha'nehenin* and thus requiring it to be recited as close as possible to the object of pleasure, i.e., the sleep. Others compare it to *Birkas Ha'shevach* like *Elokai Neshamah*, thanking Hashem for the institution of sleep; it is "*minhago shel olam*" that invigorates and refreshes a person after a day of fatigue; *Chayei Adam, Knesses Hagedolah*. It is interesting to note that the Sages instituted two *berachos* on all important matters, a *berachah rishonah* and a *berachah acharonah*. On sleep, *Ha'mapil* is the *berachah rishonah*, and *Elokai Neshamah* is the *berachah acharonah*. Similarly, food gets a *berachah* before eating and a *berachah* afterward. *Levush* points out that on Torah study we also have two *berachos*. The first *berachah* that is recited is a *berachah acharonah* for the previous day's Torah study, and the second *berachah* is the *berachah rishonah* for the coming day's Torah study.

- The *berachah* of *Ha'mapil.*[4]
- The first paragraph of the *Shema*. Some say all three paragraphs of the *Shema*.
- Other readings and supplications, such as *V'Yehi Noam*, *Mah Rabu*, and *Adon Olam*.[5] Some have the custom to add *Vidui*.[6]

B. WHEN BEDTIME PRAYERS SHOULD BE RECITED

Some authorities rule that one may recite the bedtime *Shema* as soon as one begins preparing for sleep, even if one is still fully dressed. One also need not recite the bedtime *Shema* in one's bedroom.[7] Others suggest that it should only be recited immediately before going to sleep. Rav Moshe Feinstien has been quoted to say that it is better to recite it earlier if one will forget it later.[8]

C. ORDER OF THE PRAYERS

There are two customs concerning the order of the bedtime *Shema* prayers and the *Ha'mapil berachah*. Some recite the *Shema* (and other prayers) first and then *Ha'mapil*, arguing that *Ha'mapil* should be recited as close as possible to actually going to sleep.[9] Others recite *Ha'mapil* first and then *Shema* (and other prayers), due to the concern that one might fall asleep quickly before reaching *Ha'mapil*.[10] The *Mishnah Berurah* recommends that people who often fall asleep should recite

---

4   There are those who do not recite this *berachah* because of the possibility that they may have to talk after the *berachah*, thus making it a *berachah l'vatalah* (in vain). See *Chazon Ovadiah, Berachos*, pp. 500–512, for a full discussion on this topic. He quotes from the *Baal Divrei Chaim* that it is better to talk out one hundred times than go to sleep without the *berachah*.

5   See *Halachically Speaking*, vol. 1, p. 135. In *Berachos* 5a, it states: "Whoever recites *k'rias Shema* before going to sleep is considered as if he holds a double-edged sword in his hand to ward off the forces of evil." See also *Shevuos* 15b. There seems to be two aspects to the verses that are recited as part of the bedtime *Shema*: (1) to ward off evil forces, and (2) to recite words of Torah before going to sleep, which strengthens our connection with Hashem. See also *Avnei Yashfe* 4:37; *Piskei Teshuvos* 239, note 32; and *Teshuvos V'Hanhagos* 1:198.

6   It is not said on Shabbos and Yom Tov.

7   *Shulchan Aruch OC* 239:3; *Halichos Shlomo*, p. 170 (13:15).

8   *Masores Moshe*, p. 61.

9   *Kitzur Shulchan Aruch* 71:4; *Mishnah Berurah* 239:2; *Piskei Teshuvos* 239:43.

10   *Rambam, Mishneh Torah, Tefillah* 7:1.

Ha'mapil first.[11] Some authorities rule that all the other prayers should be recited before *Shema* and *Ha'mapil*. It is very appropriate to conclude these prayers with *Adon Olam*.

D. IN WHICH POSITION

One may recite *Ha'mapil* in any position, whether sitting, standing, or lying down in bed. Some authorities recommend that it be said either sitting or standing.[12]

E. HOW LATE MAY *HA'MAPIL* BE RECITED?

One may recite *Ha'mapil* at any time one goes to sleep for the night.[13] There are those (especially some Sephardim) who do not recite *Ha'mapil* if going to sleep after midnight.[14]

F. DAYTIME SLEEP—GOING TO SLEEP EARLY

One does not recite *Ha'mapil* when going to sleep during the day, even if it is one's main sleep, such as those who sleep during the day and work at night. One should still recite *V'Yehi Noam* and the other prayers. Those who go to sleep before nightfall, such as the elderly, children, or those who live in places where nightfall is very late, may recite *Ha'mapil* and the other prayers when going to sleep for the night.[15]

---

11 *Mishnah Berurah* 239:2.

12 *Kitzur Shulchan Aruch* ad loc.; *Aruch Hashulchan OC* 239:6; *Mishnah Berurah* 239:6; *Shaar Hatziyun* 239:10. If one must recite the **entire** *Shema* (three pargraphs) before going to bed, due to having recited *Maariv* early, it should definitely be recited either sitting or standing.

13 *Yechaveh Daas* 4:21; *Avnei Yashfe* 4:37:3.

14 *Kaf Hachaim OC* 239:108; *Teshuvos V'Hanhagos* 1:98, 2:131; *Ohr L'Tzion* 2:15:12. *Ben Ish Chai, Pekudei* 1:12, cites opinions that one should not say *Ha'mapil* with Hashem's name, lest one come to speak before falling asleep. While Rav Ovadiah Yosef recommends reciting a full *berachah* of *Ha'mapil* in general, he suggests that one who goes to sleep after midnight say it without *Shem u'malchus* and concentrating mentally on the name of Hashem; *Chazon Ovadiah*, p. 513.

15 The question is whether these times are called *"z'man shechivah"* for these people. Even though it is not the time that people normally go to sleep, perhaps the *berachah* of *Ha'mapil* is focused on the benefit of sleep and could therefore be recited at these times. See *Chayei Adam* 35:4; *Teshuvos V'Hanhagos* 1:198; *Piskei Teshuvos* 239, note 13. I also heard this from Rav Tzvi Rosen and Rav Yisrael Ber Kaplan.

The reason *Ha'mapil* is not recited for daytime sleep is due to the concern that one may not end up falling asleep. So too, our Sages teach that as a general rule, it is improper to sleep during the day.[16] Indeed, there is some question as to how much value there is to daytime sleep if one's main sleep is at night.[17] One who goes to sleep before dawn, but will likely only fall asleep after dawn, should recite *Ha'mapil* without including Hashem's name.[18]

G. WHEN TRAVELING

One only recites *Ha'mapil* if there is a good chance that one will fall asleep, even if only for a few minutes. Therefore, one who is trying to fall asleep on a plane or a train ride at night may recite *Ha'mapil*.[19] Some authorities only allow doing so if can assume that one will sleep at least thirty to sixty minutes.

H. ONE WHO FORGOT

One who wakes up in the middle of the night and realizes that he fell asleep without reciting *Ha'mapil*, should rub one's hands on a surface to clean them and recite *k'rias Shema* with *Ha'mapil*.[20]

I. INTERRUPTIONS

One should try to avoid all unnecessary talk once one has recited *Ha'mapil*. However, if there are compelling reasons to speak after reciting *Ha'mapil*, one may do so. These might include:

- Saying the *berachah* of *Asher yatzar* after going to the bathroom.[21]
- Saying a *berachah* over food if one needs to eat or drink.
- Saying the *berachah* on lightning or thunder.
- Saying *Kiddush Levanah* or *Sefiras Ha'omer*.[22]

---

16   *Shulchan Aruch* 4:16; *Mishnah Berurah* §36, 231:3.
17   *Chayei Adam* 35:4.
18   *Biur Halachah* 239.
19   *Ohalecha B'Amitecha* 12:1; *Piskei Teshuvos* 239:1:6; *Ishei Yisrael*, p. 351, notes 28–29; *Be'er Moshe* 7:114.
20   *B'Tzeil Hachochmah* 5:166; *Piskei Teshuvos* 239, note 12.
21   See *She'arim Metzuyanim B'Halachah* 71:2 and *Teshuvos V'Hanhagos* 8:8.
22   *Birkas Habayis* 31:2; *Rivevos Ephraim* 6:123; *Piskei Teshuvos* 239:3.

- Reciting *Maariv*.
- Answering an important phone call from one's parents, for one's business, or for *shalom bayis*.
- Telling one's children to go to sleep or to say good night to someone.[23]

In addition:

- One is also permitted to study Torah, read a book, listen to music, or perform any other calming activity that will help one fall asleep.[24]
- One who, for whatever reason, spoke after reciting *Ha'mapil* does not repeat the *berachah*. In such a situation, however, it is praiseworthy to repeat the first paragraph of *Shema*.[25]
- Once one sleeps for even a few minutes, one is no longer bound by the above limitations.
- One who wakes up in the middle of the night does need not repeat *Ha'mapil* or *Shema* before going back to sleep.[26]

J. SPECIAL OCCASIONS AND SITUATIONS

- One who is sick should try to say at least the first paragraph of *Shema* and *Ha'mapil*.[27]
- On the first night of Pesach (and the second night in *chutz la'aretz*), the custom is to only recite *Shema* and *Ha'mapil*, but not any of the other readings. This is because the first night of Pesach is a *Leil Shimurim* (a night of special protection).[28] Some do likewise when sleeping in a sukkah.[29] The special *Ribbono Shel*

---

23   See *Halichos Shlomo* 13:24; *Yechaveh Daas* 4:21; *Ishei Yisrael*, p. 350, note 19. The *Gra* (*OC* 432:2) explains that the *berachah* is on the preparation and desire to go to sleep, not necessarily to actually sleep. This is similar to *bedikas chametz*, in which the mitzvah is simply to search for chametz, not necessarily to find any chametz. On a related note, see *Tosafos*, *Berachos* 11b, s.v. *She'k'var*, as to why there is no *berachah* on sleeping in a *sukkah*.

24   *Tefillah K'Hilchasah* 20:16:17; *Piskei Teshuvos* 239, note 21.

25   *Piskei Teshuvos* 239:3.

26   *Tefillah K'Hilchasah* 20, note 31; *Piskei Teshuvos* 239, note 4.

27   *Rambam, Mishneh Torah, Tefillah* 7:2; *Aruch Hashulchan OC* 239:5; *Ishei Yisrael*, p. 348.

28   *Shulchan Aruch OC* 481:2; *Mishnah Berurah* 481:4; *Piskei Teshuvos* 481:2.

29   *Piskei Teshuvos* 639:20.

Olam vidui and *Tachanun*, which is recited by some, is usually not recited on Shabbos and Yom Tov.

- An *onein* should recite the entire order of the bedtime prayers.[30]

K. TOUCHING/KISSING A MEZUZAH

Some have the custom to touch the mezuzah before going to sleep. Some kiss their hand after doing so.[31]

L. SLEEPING PROCEDURES

- One is advised to go to sleep on one's left side and to later switch to one's right side. Nevertheless, it is not necessary to lose any sleep over it.[32]
- Some have the custom not to sleep alone in a house. Others are not particular about this if there are other houses in the area.[33] So too, some are particular not to sleep alone in a totally dark room unless there is a source of light nearby. Moonlight is acceptable for this purpose.[34]

M. DIFFICULTY FALLING ASLEEP

One who finds it difficult to fall asleep should try one of the following:[35]

- Repeating the first paragraph of *Shema* over and over again
- Repeating *Adon Olam* and the other passages that are recited as part of the bedtime prayers

---

30 *Minchas Shlomo* 91:25:9.
31 *Piskei Teshuvos* 239:4; *Kitzur Shulchan Aruch* 71:4; *Minhag Yisrael Torah* 239:2. Rabbi Ari Enkin noted that the *Kitzur Shulchan Aruch* in chap. 11 writes that the mezuzah should be kissed when entering and exiting one's home. However, in chap. 71, when discussing the custom of touching the mezuzah before going to bed each night, the notion of kissing the mezuzah is mysteriously absent; it merely says that one should place one's hand on the mezuzah before going to bed. Kissing the mezuzah may only be of significance when entering and exiting a room or building, but not when touching it at other times.
32 *Rambam, Mishneh Torah, Deos* 4:5; *Piskei Teshuvos* 239:7; *Kitzur Shulchan Aruch* 71:5; *Mishnah Berurah* 239:6.
33 *Piskei Teshuvos* 239:10.
34 *Mishnah Berurah* 239:9. See *Shabbos* 151b and *Piskei Teshuvos* ad loc.
35 *Shulchan Aruch OC* 239:1; *Mishnah Berurah* 239:7; *Kitzur Shulchan Aruch* 71:4.

- Reciting the verses of "*Torah tzivah lanu Moshe*" and "*Aish tamid tukad al hamizbei'ach lo sichbeh*"
- Thinking about Torah subjects
- Thinking about the waves of the ocean[36]

---

36   *Piskei Teshuvos* 239:5.

Chapter Nineteen

She'hechiyahu— Ha'tov V'Ha'meitiv

A. INTRODUCTION

Among the beautiful *berachos* that a Jew can recite is the *berachah* of *She'hecheyanu*.[1] It shows our appreciation and gratitude to Hashem in three ways:

1. The word *She'hecheyanu* refers to the fact that we are physically alive.
2. The word *v'kiyemanu* refers to the fact that we are spiritually alive.
3. The word *v'higianu* refers to the fact that we have the opportunity to do a mitzvah or to enjoy something new.

We are taught that one should take advantage of any opportunity that arises to recite this special *berachah*.[2]

B. CATEGORIES

There are three different categories of *She'hecheyanu*:

1. For Yamim Tovim and performing new mitzvos. Reciting *She'hecheyanu* in these situations is an **absolute obligation**.[3]

---

1 *Piskei Teshuvos* 225:1. See *Igros Moshe OC* 5:43 about the importance of saying *berachos*, especially short ones. See *Rambam*, end of *Hilchos Berachos*, where he says that we should take advantage of the opportunity to recite *berachos*.

2 See *Igros Moshe OC* 5:43. For a full discussion of the obligation of this *berachah*, see *Shaar Ha'ayin, Iyunim*, pp. 225–33.

3 *Shut Harashba* 1;245; *Shut Shevet Halevi* 4:25; *Rivevos V'Yovlos* 4, p. 257.

2. For new fruit. Reciting *She'hecheyanu* in these situations **has become an obligation.**[4]

3. For new clothes, appliances, and seeing old friends. Reciting *She'hecheyanu* in these situations is **optional but praiseworthy.**[5]

In addition, there is a *berachah* of *"Ha'tov v'ha'meitiv*—He is good and He is good to others," which is usually recited if the joy is shared with more than one person.

Examples:

- Two people who bought something together
- Two people who received a gift together
- Two people drinking different wines together
- Parents of a newborn boy

1. Fulfilling Two Obligations with One *Berachah*

One who must recite *She'hecheyanu* for more than one reason may recite one *berachah* if they all fall under the same category. While many authorities permit reciting one *She'hecheyanu* in one category for items in a different category,[6] some authorities, such as Rav Shlomo Zalman Auerbach, say that one should not recite *She'hecheyanu* for something in Category #1 along with something in Category #2 or #3, but rather recite separate *berachos* (see note).[7]

---

4   *Aruch Hashulchan* 225.

5   Issues falling into Category #1 are based on objective criteria, e.g., a new holiday or a new mitzvah, and one is fully obligated to say *She'hecheyanu* in these instances. Issues falling into Category #2 are based on both subjective (e.g., joy over seeing a new creation) and objective (e.g., new season) criteria. Issues falling into Category #3 are totally dependent on one's personal feeling of *simchah*, and thus the rabbis left the *berachah* as totally optional but praiseworthy. Various authorities are quite lenient regarding this category, since it is not clear what degree of joy is required. See *Piskei Teshuvos* 225, notes 5–8. The *Bach OC* 29 rules that since *She'hecheyanu* is essentially an optional *berachah*, we do not apply the general rules of *safek berachos l'hakel*, and thus one may recite it whenever there is a doubt. Some extend this idea to include all *berachos* of praise, such as *Ha'gomel*.

6   *Shevet Halevi* 4:25; *Ohr L'Tzion* 4:3:4; *Ashrei Ha'ish* 39:1.

7   These are considered to be two different types of *berachos*. The first is *Birkas Ha'zman* (mitzvah), which is based on the enjoyment of the *neshamah*, while the others (Categories #2 and #3) are based on the enjoyment of the body. See *Minchas Shlomo* 1:20 (based on *Kesav Sofer*); *Halichos Shlomo, Mo'adim* 1:16. Thus, according to Rav Shlomo Zalman Auerbach, someone wearing a new garment (Category #3), or eating a new fruit (Category #2), on the first night

Examples where one *berachah* would be sufficient:

- When performing two mitzvos at once, such as when reciting *kiddush* on the night of Sukkos and Pesach, at which time we perform a number of mitzvos at once (Category #1)
- When eating two new fruits (Category #2)
- When purchasing or wearing two new garments (Category #3)
- When eating a new fruit and wearing a new garment (Categories #2 and #3)[8]

2. In Situations of Doubt

When one is in doubt whether to recite *She'hecheyanu*, all authorities agree that one may combine the various categories and thus recite the *berachah*.[9]

For example:

- On the second night of Rosh Hashanah,[10] *She'hecheyanu* is recited for both a new fruit and *kiddush*.
- Reciting *She'hecheyanu* upon fulfilling a mitzvah for the first time, in conjunction with a new fruit or garment.

3. Being *Motzi* Others

Common custom is only to be *motzi* others with *She'hecheyanu* when it is for something in Category #1, such as when reciting *kiddush*, blowing the shofar, or lighting the menorah. Everyone should make their own *berachah* when it is for items in Categories #2 and #3.[11]

---

of Yom Tov (Category #1) should recite two separate *berachos*. The new fruit or garment should ideally not be present when *kiddush* is recited. Alternatively, if they are present, one can have in mind not to include these items with the *She'hecheyanu* of *kiddush*. See also *Ashrei Ha'ish* 62 (*Mishnah Berurah* [*Dirshu*] 600, note 2). However, all agree that one may recite one *berachah* on the second night of Rosh Hashanah.

8   *Minchas Shlomo* 1:20. See also *Igros Moshe OC* 1:87.

9   *Piskei Teshuvos* 225:1.

10   See *Beitzah* 4:5; *Shulchan Aruch OC* 600:2, and *Mishnah Berurah* §2 for more on this.

11   See *Minchas Shlomo* 2:4:33, who explains that with regard to *She'hecheyanu* on mitzvos, everyone has equal (common) joy for the mitzvah, and therefore one person can be *motzi* others. However, on clothes and other such items, the level of enjoyment is subjective (more individualized), and therefore it is better for everyone to recite their own *berachah*. See also *Halichos Shlomo* 23:23.

a. Exception

Although men can often be *motzi* women (and vice versa) when they have similar obligations and have already fulfilled the mitzvah (when necessary), such as for *kiddush*,[12] they may not be able to *motzi* each other if their obligations are different and the man has aready fulfilled the mitzvah. For example, women who hear the shofar from a man who already performed the mitzvah should recite the *berachos* (including *She'hecheyanu*) themselves, rather than have the man recite it for them.[13] In such situations, one woman can be *motzi* the others.

C. *BIRKAS HA'TOV V'HA'MEITIV*

When two people need to recite the *berachah* of *Ha'tov v'ha'meitiv*, such as two people who bought something together, or two people drinking different wines together, or the parents of a newborn boy, one person may recite the *berachah* for both of them.[14]

1. General Rules about *Ha'tov V'Ha'meitiv*

If there is a question or doubt whether to recite the *berachah* of *Ha'tov v'ha'meitiv*, one should try one of the following:

- Recite the *berachah* on something else that certainly requires that *berachah*.
- Ask someone who needs to recite the *berachah* to have you in mind.
- Concentrate on the item, or the possible need for the *berachah*, during the *berachah* of *Ha'tov v'ha'meitiv* in *Birkas Hamazon*.[15]

If there is a question whether to say the *berachah* of *Hatov V'ha'meitiv* or *She'hecheyanu*, one should say *She'hecheyanu*.[16] One who mistakenly said *Ha'tov v'ha'meitiv* instead of *She'hecheyanu* has said a *berachah*

---

12   *Shulchan Aruch OC* 271:2; *Mishnah Berurah* §5; *Shemiras Shabbos K'Hilchasah* 51:9, note 23.

13   *Shulchan Aruch OC* 589:6. In the case of shofar, a man has a full obligation, while a woman has less of an obligation (because it is a time-bound mitzvah), and therefore the rules of *areivus* don't necessarily apply.

14   See *L'Fa'eir U'L'vareich*, p. 114. See also *Halachos of Brochos*, p. 59, note 39.

15   *Mishnah Berurah* 175:2; *L'Fa'eir U'L'varech*, p. 116; *Ohr L'Tzion* 2:14:47.

16   *Mishnah Berurah* 223:21, with *Biur Halachah*, s.v. *Shehi*; *Halachos of Brochos*, p. 64, note 57. So too, if no one else is involved in the pleasure or benefit, it might be a *berachah l'vatalah*.

l'vatalah.[17] However, one who said *She'hecheyanu* instead of *Ha'tov v'ha'meitiv* has discharged one's obligation.[18]

D. WHEN NOT TO RECITE *SHE'HECHEYANU*

There are times during the year when it is questionable whether the *berachah* should be recited.

1. During the Three Weeks and Nine Days

There are different customs regarding reciting *She'hecheyanu* during the Three Weeks and the Nine Days, which is a period of mourning. Some authorities recommend that the *berachah* be postponed until after this period. Other authorities allow one to recite these *berachos* on Shabbos during the Three Weeks, but not during the Nine Days.[19] One who has a great need to buy a new appliance during the Nine Days, such as one whose refrigerator or air conditioner stopped working, should postpone reciting *She'hecheyanu* until after Tishah B'Av.[20] However, if the correct *berachah* to be recited is *Ha'tov v'ha'meitiv* (usually when more than one person benefits),[21] many authorities permit the *berachah* to be recited, even during the Nine Days. So too, it is permitted to recite these *berachos* in the event that they cannot be delayed, such as on the birth of a baby girl, at a *bris milah*, or at a *pidyon ha'ben*.

For this reason, it is better to say the more limited *berachah* of *She'hecheyanu*, which is more relevant for a personal *simchah*, as opposed to *Ha'tov v'hameitv*, which includes others.

17 *Biur Halachah* ad loc. See *L'Fa'eir U'L'varech*, p. 127, which cites the view of Rav Nissim Karelitz that in the case of the birth of a daughter, one may still be *yotzei*.

18 *Biur Halachah* ad loc.; *L'Fa'eir U'L'varech*, p. 120; *Halachos of Brochos* ad loc.

19 *Mishnah Berurah* 551:98; *Dirshu*, notes 55 and 119; *Aruch Hashulchan OC* 551:38. The *Gra* permits reciting *She'hecheyanu* during this entire period. The question on whether *She'hecheyanu* should be recited is dependant on the meaning of "*la'zman ha'zeh*": does it focus specifically on the actual moment of the day (or Shabbos), or the general period of time, i.e., the Three Weeks or Nine Days.

20 See *Igros Moshe OC* 3:80; *Shaarei Teshuvah* 551:10. As far as buying things during the Nine Days, see *Shulchan Aruch OC* 551:2.

21 *Piskei Teshuvos* 551:54; see *Mishnah Berurah (Dirshu)*, note 117; *Kaf Hachaim OC* 175:11; *Igros Moshe OC* 3:80. As far as buying things during this period, see *Shulchan Aruch* ad loc.

2. During the *Sefirah*

Most authorities permit saying *She'hecheyanu* during the *sefirah* period, since there is no clear reason to forbid it. Nevertheless, there are those with the custom not to recite it.[22]

3. Mourner

A mourner is permitted to recite these *berachos* but should try to avoid reciting them in public. As such, a mourner should not light the Chanukah candles in the synagogue on the first night of Chanukah.[23]

---

22   *Mishnah Berurah* 493:2; *Dirshu*, note 4; *Piskei Teshuvos* 493:2.
23   *Mishnah Berurah* 551:98; *Kol Bo*, p. 81.

Chapter Twenty

She'hecheyanu on Holidays

A. INTRODUCTION

The *She'hecheyanu berachah* that is recited on holidays sometimes applies to the actual *simchah* of the holiday, and sometimes also to specific mitzvos of the holiday, as we will see. *Mekor Chaim* points out: "A person is on a trip through life, [and] as he arrives at each new destination, he should thank Hashem for a new opportunity of 'life.'"[1] This shows how the *kavanah* needs to be part of our *berachah* when we recite the *She'hecheyanu*. It is therefore especially important to realize that when one comes to Yom Tov, he should not take life for granted.[2]

B. ROSH HASHANAH

1. Rosh Hashanah Night

She'hecheyanu is recited on the two nights of Rosh Hashanah. Men recite the *She'hecheyanu* in conjunction with *kiddush*, while women usually recite it in conjunction with their lighting of candles.[3] Since there is some question whether *She'hecheyanu* should be recited on the second night on Rosh Hashanah, the custom is to eat a new fruit or wear a new garment so that the *berachah* will cover both the fruit or the garment, as well as the holiday.[4] Women should either be wearing a new garment

---

1 *Mekor Chaim*, p. 167.
2 *Rivevos V'Yovlos* 4, p. 257.
3 *Shulchan Aruch OC* 600:2; *Mishnah Berurah* §2. See also *Mishnah Berurah* 263:23; *Minchas Shlomo* 1:20; *Igros Moshe OC* 4:101. The *Griz* would tell his wife not to recite the *berachah* but to wait until *kiddush* was recited.
4 *Beitzah* 4 refers to the two days of Rosh Hashanah as a *yoma arichta* (one long day), which

or have a new fruit in mind (preferably within sight) when lighting the candles and reciting *She'hecheyanu* on the second night. Nevertheless, *She'hecheyanu* is recited on the second night of Rosh Hashanah even if one does not have a new fruit or garment. There is basis to permit a woman who recited *She'hecheyanu* at candle lighting to answer *Amen* over the *She'hecheyanu* when hearing it during *kiddush*.[5]

2. Rosh Hashanah Day—the Mitzvah of Shofar

She'hecheyanu is recited on both days of Rosh Hashanah, usually by the *baal toke'a*. In many Sephardic communities, *She'hecheyanu* is not recited on the second day.[6] A number of authorities recommend that the *baal toke'a* wear a new garment on the second day of Rosh Hashanah due to the question regarding *She'hecheyanu*, as discussed above.

When the shofar is being blown exclusively for a woman, she should recite the *berachah* and not the *baal toke'a*.

C. YOM KIPPUR

She'hecheyanu should be recited by everyone at the end of *Kol Nidrei*, even though the *chazzan* recites it out loud. However, women who recited it during candle lighting should not repeat it.[7]

D. SUKKOS

She'hecheyanu is recited on the first night of Sukkos and, in *chutz la'aretz*, on the second night as well. (On the second night in *chutz la'aretz*, the order of the *berachos* is reversed from the first day, with *She'hecheyanu* being recited first.[8]) One should have in mind that it is

---

has a number of halachic implications, such as whether to recite *She'hecheyanu* on the second night.

5   See *Har Tzvi OC* 1:154; *Yechaveh Daas* 3:34 considers it an interruption, but *Igros Moshe OC* 2:9 disagrees. See discussion in *Mishnah Berurah (Dirshu)* 600, note 2. Rav Elyashiv would eat a new fruit after *Hamotzi*, but Rav Shlomo Zalman Auerbach would eat the fruit (less than a *shiur*) immediately after *kiddush*.

6   *Shulchan Aruch OC* 600:3; *Mishnah Berurah* 600:6.

7   *Mishnah Berurah* 619:1, 3.

8   On the second night in *chutz la'aretz*, the *berachah* refers only to the holiday and not necessarily on the mitzvah of sukkah. As such, the order of the *berachos* is reversed from the first day, with *She'hecheyanu* being recited first. This is based on the fact that some authorities

for both the holiday and the mitzvah of sitting in the sukkah. The *berachah* of "*Leishev ba'sukkah*" is recited first, followed by *She'hecheyanu*. If the order was mistakenly reversed, one need not repeat the *berachah*.[9]

1. *Arba Minim*

She'hecheyanu is **only** recited on the **first day** of Sukkos, even in *chutz la'aretz*, when performing the mitzvah of the *arba minim*.[10] However, if the first day of Sukkos falls on Shabbos, the mitzvah and the *berachah* are pushed off until the following day.[11]

There are different customs concerning how to hold the lulav at the time of the *berachah*. Many have the custom to hold the esrog with the *pitum* down.[12] There are two customs concerning the position of the esrog at the time of *She'hecheyanu*:

- Some recite the *She'hecheyanu* immediately after the first *berachah* while the esrog is still pointed downward.
- Others recite it only after the esrog is pointed upward.[13]

One who did not recite *She'hecheyanu* when first taking the lulav may do so as long as one is still involved in the mitzvah, such as when reciting *Hallel* or *Hoshanos*.[14] One who has completed these prayers should recite *She'hecheyanu* the next day.[15]

---

rule that the *berachah* of *She'hecheyanu* for the sukkah can be said as soon as one has completed building one's sukkah, although the halachah is not in accordance with that view.

9   *Shulchan Aruch OC* 643:1; *Mishnah Berurah* 643:3.

10   *Shulchan Aruch OC* 662:1. This is in contrast to *hadlakas neiros* and *kiddush*, where *She'hecheyanu* is indeed recited on the second day of Yom Tov. This is because some hold that one who recited *She'hecheyanu* when binding the lulav together on Erev Sukkos does not recite it again when shaking the lulav for the first time. See *Mishnah Berurah* 662:2.

11   *Shulchan Aruch OC* 662:3.

12   This is to allow the *berachah* to be recited before the mitzvah is fulfilled (*over la'asiyasan*). The mitzvah is fulfilled when the esrog is pointed up, which is the way it grows on the tree. See *Shulchan Aruch* for various other ways to fulfill this concept.

13   See *Shulchan Aruch OC* 651:5; *Mishnah Berurah* 651:25; and *Piskei Teshuvos* 651:9, note 47, regarding when to turn over the esrog.

14   *Shulchan Aruch OC* 651; *Mishnah Berurah* §261. As long as one is still shaking or carrying the lulav during these prayers, it is still considered that he is fulfilling the mitzvah.

15   *Mishnah Berurah* 651:26.

2. Shemini Atzeres and Simchas Torah

The Talmud tells us that in many ways Shemini Atzeres is independent of Sukkos,[16] and therefore *She'hecheyanu* is recited as part of *kiddush* (and candle lighting). In *chutz la'aretz*, *She'hecheyanu* is also recited on the second night, which is known as Simchas Torah.[17]

E. CHANUKAH

She'hecheyanu is recited on the first night of Chanukah before lighting the candles. One who forgot to recite *She'hecheyanu* may recite it as long as the candles are still burning.[18] One who forgot to recite it on the first night may recite it on any successive night before lighting the candles.[19] There is a *machlokes* among the authorities concerning one who lights the candles in the synagogue. While Rav Moshe Feinstein rules that one who lit the candles on the first night of Chanukah may recite *She'hecheyanu* when lighting again at home, the *Mishnah Berurah* opines that one should try to make sure that there are other family members present at the lighting to be *yotzei*[20] the mitzvah, for if not, one would not be able to recite the *berachos* of *She'hecheyanu* and *She'asah Nissim* again at home.

F. PURIM

1. Purim Night

She'hecheyanu is recited when reading the megillah. The *baal koreh* is usually the one to recite it on behalf of the congregation. If the *baal koreh* already read or heard the megillah, those listening should recite their own *berachos*.[21] Sephardim, who only recite *She'hecheyanu* on the night of Purim, should have in mind to include all the additional mitzvos of the following day when hearing the *She'hecheyanu* at night.[22]

---

16   *Sukkah* 48a.
17   *Shulchan Aruch OC* 668:1; *Mishnah Berurah* 668:8.
18   *Mishnah Berurah* 676:4.
19   Ibid., § 2.
20   *Shulchan Aruch OC* 671:7; *Mishnah Berurah* §45; *Igros Moshe OC* 1:190; *Piskei Teshuvos* 671:14. It would seem that the same halachah applies to the *berachah* of *She'asah nissim*. For a full discussion on this subject, see *Mishnah Berurah* (*Dirshu*) 671:78.
21   *Shulchan Aruch OC* 692:3.
22   Ibid., §1; *Mishnah Berurah* 692:1; *Kaf Hachaim* 692.

2. Purim Day

There are four mitzvos that must be performed on Purim day:

1. *k'rias megillah*
2. *mishlo'ach manos*
3. *matanos l'evyonim*
4. *seudas Purim*

The standard Ashkenazic practice is to recite *She'hecheyanu* again before the daytime megillah reading and to have in mind all the other mitzvos of the day.[23] As stated above, the common Sephardic practice is not to repeat it in the morning.[24]

G. PESACH

- *She'hecheyanu* is recited on the first night of Pesach (and on the second night in *chutz la'aretz*). One should have the following mitzvos in mind when reciting it:
- The holiday
- Eating matzah
- Reading the Haggadah
- Drinking the four cups of wine[25]

Women should have these mitzvos in mind when lighting the candles or during *kiddush*.

The *berachah* is not recited on the last day(s) of Pesach.

H. SHAVUOS

She'hecheyanu is recited on the first night of Shavuos (and on the second night in *chutz la'aretz*) either when lighting the candles (women) or during *kiddush* (men). One who forgot to recite the *berachah* may do so until the end of Shavuos.[26]

---

23 *Shulchan Aruch OC* 692:1; *Mishnah Berurah* 692:2. It is interesting to note that that the "main" megillah reading is in the morning; see *Mishnah Berurah (Dirshu)* 692, note 6.

24 *Shulchan Aruch OC* 692:1.

25 See *Halichos Shlomo, Pesach* 9, note 151.

26 *Shulchan Aruch OC* 473:1; *Mishnah Berurah* 473:1; *Shaar Hatziyun* 473:5.

I. OTHER TIMES

- At a *pidyon ha'ben*—She'hecheyanu is recited by the father or by the one who was appointed to perform the *pidyon*.[27]
- At a *bris milah*—The *minhag* in Eretz Yisrael is for the father to recite *She'hecheyanu* at his son's *bris*.[28] There is a difference of opinion whether one or two *berachos* are to be said at a *bris* for twins.[29] As such, some authorities suggest that the father wear a new garment and have in mind that the second *She'hecheyanu* should cover both the *bris* and the garment. Others rule that there should be a substantial break between the two *brisos*, if possible.
- In the following situations, authorities discuss reciting the *berachah*:

    1. Upon reaching the age of seventy, and according to some, the age of sixty[30]
    2. Upon completion of writing or buying a *Sefer Torah*[31]
    3. Upon being appointed as a rabbi[32]

Interestingly, there are those who will wear a new garment or eat a new fruit in combination with these occasions to justify reciting a full *berachah*.

---

27 See *Pesachim* 121b; *Shulchan Aruch YD* 305:10.

28 See *Sukkah* 46a; *Tosafos, Bechoros* 49a. Although the *Rambam* and other earlier authorities rule that a father is to recite the *She'hecheyanu* blessing at the *bris* of his son, other authorities disagree and argue that the blessing should be omitted. This is because although the mitzvah of *bris milah* is infrequent, it is, however, a mitzvah that causes pain to the one upon whom it is being performed. The joy in the performance of this mitzvah is therefore somewhat diminished, which indeed calls into question the legitimacy of reciting *She'hecheyanu*. The *Shulchan Aruch* rules that the *She'hecheyanu* blessing is to be recited at a *bris milah* ceremony, and this is the custom in Sephardic communities worldwide, as well as the predominant custom among everyone in Israel. Ashkenazim in the Diaspora generally do not recite *She'hecheyanu* at a *bris* in accordance with the ruling of the *Rama*. See *Aruch Hashulchan YD* 265:27 for more.

29 *Kehillas Yaakov, Berachos* 9; *Halachos of Brochos*, vol. 2, p. 39, note 83.

30 See *Mo'ed Katan* 28a; *Kaf Hachaim OC* 223:29. See also *Halachos of Brochos*, p. 22. Regarding the *She'hecheyanu berachah* on one's seventieth birthday, see *Pri Megadim, MZ* 444:9 and *Chasam Sofer OC* 225; *Ben Ish Chai, Re'eh* 9. For more about birthdays, see above; *Piskei Teshuvos* 223, note 50, and *Peninei Halachah, Berachos*, p. 290.

31 *Piskei Teshuvos* 223:5, note 47; *Peninei Halachah, Berachos*, p. 374; *Harchavos*, p. 288; see discussion question whether the more appropriate *berachah* is *She'hecheyanu* or *Ha'tov v'ha'meitiv*.

32 Ibid.

J. PERFORMING A MITZVAH FOR THE FIRST TIME

There is a difference of opinion as to whether to recite *She'hecheyanu* when performing a mitzvah for the first time. Common custom is not to recite a *berachah*. When possible, some authorities suggest combining the occasion with eating a new fruit or wearing a new garment.[33]

1. Bar Mitzvah/Putting on Tefillin

Common custom is not to recite *She'hecheyanu* when bar mitzvah boys put on tefillin for the first time.[34] However, some boys wear a new suit when putting on tefillin for the first time after their bar mitzvah in order to justify saying a *berachah*. So too, some suggest that a father not should formally give his son tefillin until the day of his bar mitzvah in order to be able to recite *She'hecheyanu* for both the new pair of tefillin (an expensive possession) as well as for performing the mitzvah of tefillin for the first time.[35]

2. Wedding[36]

Regarding the groom, the general *minhag* is not to recite the *berachah* at a wedding. However, some (especially Sephardim and those who have German customs) have the custom to recite *She'hecheyanu* on a new suit or tallis on their wedding day, or to have in mind to include the mitzvah of marriage at the *chuppah* and therefore be able to say the *berachah*.[37]

---

33   See *Shulchan Aruch YD* 28:2. The *Rama* rules that a *berachah* is to be recited, while the *Shach* disagrees. See *Biur Halachah* 22, s.v. *Kana*. The question is whether there needs to be a fixed and specific time for the new mitzvah or if it is sufficient that it is new for the individual person See *Sukkah* 46a; see discussion in *Peninei Halachah, Harchavos*, p. 288. Interesting to note that Rav Avraham Yitzchak Kook told the Gerrer Rebbe to recite *She'hecheyanu* the first time he fulfilled the mitzvah of seperating *terumos u'maasros*.

34   *Igros Moshe YD* 3:14:4.

35   *Minchas Shlomo* 2:4, 33:3; *Halichos Shlomo* 4:19.

36   See *Birkas She'hecheyanu*, p. 286, for a full discussion why the *berachah* of *She'hecheyanu* was not established to be recited at the wedding. See *Aruch Hashulchan* 223:4, *Machazik Berachah* 223:5, *Mekor Chaim*, p. 192.

37   See *Shulchan Aruch OC* 22:1; *Chazon Ovadiah, Berachos*, p. 405.

Regarding the bride, some have the custom to recite *She'hecheyanu* on a new *sheitel* or other new clothes on their wedding day and to have in mind all the mitzvos that a woman begins to perform upon marriage.[38]

Regarding parents of the couple, there is a custom that they should recite *She'hecheyanu* on a new garment and have in mind both the garment and the *simchah* of marrying off a child.[39]

---

38   *Piskei Teshuvos* 222; *Halachos of Brachos* (Bodner), vol. 2, p. 42, note 96; *Kaf Hachaim OC* 223:25; *Chasam Sofer* 55.

39   *Kaf Hachaim OC* 223:25.

Chapter Twenty-One

She'hecheyanu on a New Fruit

A. INTRODUCTION

One who eats any amount[1] of a fruit from a new season[2] and en-joys it[3] should praise Hashem with the *berachah* of *She'hecheyanu*.[4] There is actually a mitzvah to eat a new fruit in order to be able to say *She'hecheyanu*.[5] The *Talmud Yerushalmi* teaches us: "*Asid li'tein din v'cheshsbon*," that one will have to give an accounting for the permitted pleasures that one did not enjoy in this world. Some have the custom to

---

1   *Biur Halachah* 225, s.v. *Pri*; *Shaarei Berachah* 20:9.

2   It makes no difference if it grows in a hothouse or a flowerpot. *Piskei Teshuvos* 225:19.

3   Many authorities rule that if one eats a new fruit but does not truly enjoy it, he does not recite *She'hecheyanu*. See *Mishnah Berurah* 225:10, where he discusses the aspect of the *simchah* over a new fruit. The question is whether it is the personal pleasure of the taste of the "new" fruit or if it is the joy of Hashem producing a new beautiful fruit. See *Mishnah Berurah* (*Dirshu*) §14, which brings *Shevet Halevi* 4:25, who holds that the pleasure element is critical, while *Ashrei Ha'ish* 39:2 (Rav Elyashiv) opines that a *berachah* can be recited even if one does not enjoy the fruit. Rav Shlomo Zalman Auerbach opines that one one must have some enjoyment. See also *Shaarei Berachah* 20, note 5. Today, some authorities rule that *She'hecheyanu* need not be recited on a new fruit due to the doubt whether one is truly *b'simchah* when eating it, and due to the fact that many fruits are available all year long. See *Piskei Teshuvos* 225:66.

4   *Shulchan Aruch OC* 225:3; *Mishnah Berurah* 225:9. The Talmud (*Eruvin* 40) points out that this *berachah* is essentially optional (*reshus*) in nature, though it is a mitzvah to recite it. This is explained to mean that if he does not perform it, he is not punished, but in any case, one should be careful not to miss out. See *Igros Moshe* 5:43:5. *Shaarei Berachah* 20:2 speaks about the importance of saying a *berachah*; see *M'Darchei Ha'ilanos*, p. 137, for a good discussion on this subject. The *Aruch Hashulchan* 225:1 points out that *minhag ha'olam* (*kiblu k'chovah*) is to consider it as an obligation today.

5   *Mishnah Berurah* 225:19; *Aruch Hashulchan OC* 225:5; *Kitzur Shulchan Aruch* 59:19; see *M'Darchei Ha'ilanos*, p. 138.

wait until Shabbos to eat a new fruit in order to show additional honor to Shabbos.[6]

B. WHEN TO RECITE THE *BERACHAH*

Common custom is to recite the *She'hecheyanu* when **eating** a new fruit that is ripe (which one can fully enjoy).[7] It seems that the original custom was to recite it when *seeing* a new fruit for the first time.[8] Some authorities rule that one who is unable to eat a new fruit due to health reasons may recite *She'hecheyanu* when seeing it.[9] A blind person may recite *She'hecheyanu* when eating a new fruit.[10]

C. ENJOYING THE FRUIT

The *She'hecheyanu berachah* is valid even if one discovers that the fruit is sour, spoiled, or not ripe.[11]

One who recited *She'hecheyanu* on a fruit, and then discovers that it is inedible or spoiled, need not recite a new *She'hecheyanu* the next time one eats this fruit.[12]

D. ORDER OF *BERACHOS*

There are various customs concerning the order of the *berachos* that are recited when eating a new fruit. Some authorities rule that *She'hecheyanu* is to be recited before *ha'eitz*,[13] while others (including many Sephardim) rule that *ha'eitz* should be recited before *She'hecheyanu*.[14] There are also those who recite *ha'eitz*, eat a little bit, and then recite the *She'hecheyanu*.[15]

---

6   *Magen Avraham* 225:14; *Piskei Teshuvos* 225:9.

7   *Aruch Hashulchan OC* 225:7; *Igros Moshe OC* 3:13.

8   *Shulchan Aruch OC* 225:3; *Mishnah Berurah* 225:13 says there is more pleasure when seeing it.

9   *Shevet Halevi* 4:25; *Birkas Hashir V'Hashevach*, p. 12, sect. 2; *Yalkut Yosef* 225:1.

10   *Birkas Hashir V'Hashevach* 1:105.

11   *V'Zos Haberachah*, p. 164; *Birkas Hashir V'Hashevach*, section 4, p. 187–88; *Shaarei Berachah* 20, note 17:21.

12   *Birkas Hashir V'Hashevach* ad loc.; *Shaarei Berachah* 20, note 17.

13   *Mishnah Berurah* 225:11; *Kitzur Shulchan Aruch* 59:4; *Chayei Adam* 62:68; *Aruch Hashulchan OC* 225:5. This is because, technically, the obligation begins when one first sees the fruit.

14   *Avnei Nezer* 450; *Halichos Shlomo* 3:13; *Yechaveh Daas* 3:15. This is based on the concept of *tadir v'she'eino tadir, tadir kodem*. *Aruch Hashulchan OC* 225:5 writes that this is the common practice, but he does not personally follow it. See also *Piskei Teshuvos* 225, notes 82–83.

15   *Orchos Rabbeinu*, vol. 1, *hosafos*, p. 12.

1. Forgot to Say *Berachah*

One who forgot to say *She'hecheyanu* before eating a new fruit may recite it as long as one is still in the process of eating it.[16]

2. Many New Fruits

One who has two new fruits, or a new fruit and a new garment, recites one *She'hecheyanu* for both.[17]

3. Precedence

If one has in front of him two fruits, one of the seven species and one regular fruit that requires *She'hecheyanu*, he should first recite *ha'eitz* on the fruit from the seven species and *She'hecheyanu* over the second fruit.[18]

E. DOUBT

One who is in doubt whether one said *She'hecheyanu* on a particular fruit should not say it. This is in accordance with the rule that a *berachah* is not recited in a situation of doubt.[19]

Some *poskim* suggest doing one of the following procedures:

- Listen to another person who has to recite the same *berachah* and have him be *motzi* you with the *berachah* (when possible).[20]
- Say the *berachah* without the using the *shem Hashem* (and the word *Elokeinu*).[21]
- Think and concentrate on the *berachah* mentally (*hirhur*).[22]

---

16 *Shaarei Berachah* 20:7, *Avnei Yashfe* 2:17, *Piskei Teshuvos* 225, note 87; *Ashrei Ha'ish*, p. 261; *Sefer She'hecheyanu*, p. 7.

17 *Shaar Hatziyun* 225:16.

18 *Shaarei Berachah* 12, note 41.

19 *Shaarei Berachah*, p. 448, note 21; *Sefer She'hecheyanu*, p. 534.

20 *Mishnah Berurah* 47:1.

21 *Shulchan Aruch OC, Taz* 621:12; *Eliyahu Rabbah* 621:10; *Shaarei Berachah*, p. 448, note 19; see *Sefer She'hecheyanu*, p. 534; *Rama EH* 34:3) for more discussion.

22 *Kaf Hachaim* 185:5; 209:15; *Aruch Hashulchan OC*185:10: *Yechaveh Daas* 6-10; *Teshuvos V'Hanhagos* 3:77; *Ben Ish Chai, Balak* (year 1:7); see *Sefer She'hecheyanu*, p. 534–46. For a discussion whether the *berachah* can be recited in Aramaic or English, see *Teshuvos V'Hanhagos* 1:639 and *Igros Moshe* 4:40:27 (saying a *berachah* in a foreign language may be a *berachah* in vein).

F. OTHER REQUIREMENTS FOR *SHE'HECHEYANU*

The following conditions should be met before one recites the *She'hecheyanu*:

- The fruit should be ripe.[23]
- The main body of the fruit must be eaten. The *berachah* is not recited when merely eating the peel or the clear juice of the fruit.[24]
- It is clear that the fruit is fresh or clear that it is from a new season. The *berachah* is not recited on dried, preserved, or processed fruits such as jams and olives.[25] However, one is allowed to recite the *berachah* on cooked fruit if it is recognizable that it is from a new season[26] (e.g., rhubarb cooked with other ingredients).
- It is seasonal. Seasonal is defined as a fruit that produces one to two new crops every year,[27] and not a fruit like an esrog or lemon, which are almost always available on their respective trees.
- It must not be available in stores most of the year as a fresh fruit. This excludes fruits that are stocked all year, which grow in hothouses or are imported from other countries. Examples of such fruits and vegetables include potatoes, onions, carrots, and apples. Some rule that one may recite *She'hecheyanu* on fruits that are available all year long if it is clear that the fruit one is eating is from the new season. For example, oranges in Israel at the beginning of the season are green.[28]
- It must be "important" and "special." This excludes carob (*bokser*) because it is primarily fed to animals.[29] One does not

---

23   *Mishnah Berurah* 225:12.
24   Ibid., v. 18; *Kitzur Shulchan Aruch* 59:15; *Shaarei Berachah* 20:9:27; *Piskei Teshuvos* 225:106–7; *Sefer She'hecheyanu*, p. 75; Rav Karelitz opines that even if one drinks a fruit juice, one may still recite the *berachah* on the fruit.
25   *Mishnah Berurah* 225:18.
26   Ibid.; *Shaarei Berachah* 20:8:23; *V'Zos Haberachah*, p. 159.
27   *Shulchan Aruch OC* 225:6; *Mishnah Berurah* 225:16, 18; *Piskei Teshuvos* 225:17–18. One can recite the *berachah* each time. The *minhag* of many Sephardim is to recite it only one time each year; *Kaf Hachaim* 225:42; *Chazon Ovadiah, Berachos*, p. 488.
28   *Mishnah Berurah* 225:16; *V'Zos Haberachah*, p. 161; *Piskei Teshuvos* 225:118.
29   *V'Zos Haberachah* 18:5. It is also noted that one can't tell the difference between old carobs and new carobs.

generally recite the *berachah* on an ancillary food, i.e, a food usually eaten with other foods, e.g., jams, avocado, etc. Thus, when eating an avocado, one may recite *She'hecheyanu* on the food, but when eating avocado spread on bread, one is advised to eat a small amount of avocado before spreading it onto the bread.[30] Similarly, one may recite the *berachah* on fruit drinks that contain recognizable pieces of fruit.[31]

- It may be a fruit that grows in hothouses, as long as it does not grow all year round.[32]

G. AVAILABILITY AT DIFFERENT TIMES AND PLACES

- One may recite *She'hecheyanu* on a new fresh fruit even if it is available in dry, frozen, cooked, or canned form all year long, such as in the case of grapes (raisins), peaches, strawberries, blueberries, and apricots.[33]
- Many authorities allow one to recite *She'hecheyanu* on a fresh fruit that is available in exotic fruit stores all year long, but only available for a very limited time in the mainstream stores and markets.[34]
- One who travels to a new place and eats a fruit they have never tasted before only recites *She'hecheyanu* if it is a seasonal fruit.[35]
- There is a dispute whether one may recite *She'hecheyanu* on a fruit that is available all year long (on the tree) in its country of origin but is only seasonal in countries where it is imported. This is the case with coconuts, which are available for only short periods of time in different countries.[36]

---

30 *Shulchan Aruch OC* 225:3. See *Shaarei Berachah*, p. 504; *V'Zos Haberachah*, p. 165; *Avnei Yashfe* 1:48:1; *Birkas Hashir V'Hashevach* 1:47.

31 *Piskei Teshuvos* 225:16.

32 *Shaarei Berachah* 20:22; *Piskei Teshuvos* 225:19.

33 *Aruch Hashulchan OC* 225:12; *V'Zos Haberachah*, p. 159; *V'Aleihu Lo Yibol*, p. 123.

34 *Mishnah Berurah* 225:18. We look at the "majority" of regular shops, and not at the exclusive exotic shops. See *Shaarei Berachah* 20, note 59; *Piskei Teshuvos* 225, note 111, 132; *V'Zos Haberachah*, p. 160, quotes Rav Elyashiv, who seems to disagree with this opinion.

35 *V'Zos Haberachah*, p. 161.

36 Ibid., §8. Coconuts are found on the tree all year; thus in the places where they grow, they

- One who goes to another country and finds a "new" fruit (from a new season) that one has not eaten in the last thirty days may recite *She'hecheyanu*,[37] such as in the case of one who travels from the Northern Hemisphere to the Southern Hemisphere.

1. Grafted Fruit

There is a dispute among the authorities whether one may recite *She'hecheyanu* on a fruit that is the result of forbidden grafting. However, if the seeds of the fruit tree are from an already crossbred tree (i.e., it is no longer a first-generation fruit, such as with most of our fruit today), or if it was planted by a non-Jew, one may recite the *berachah*.[38] Common custom nowadays is to recite *She'hecheyanu* on all fruit.

2. Similar Fruit with Similar Taste

She'hecheyanu is not recited on a fruit that is of the same species, and has a similar taste, as a fruit that one previously recited *She'hecheyanu*. For example, one who recited *She'hecheyanu* on a pink grapefruit does not recite it again on a yellow one, or on a different type of orange or clementine.

3. Similar Fruit with Different Tastes

However, if the taste of the two fruits is distinctly different, such as in the case of green grapes and purple grapes, or different types of plums, there is basis to recite another *She'hecheyanu*. Ideally, the *Mishnah Berurah* points out that one should take a different new fruit and recite *She'hecheyanu* on it while having in mind to cover the fruit in doubt.[39]

---

are excluded from the *berachah*. However, there are authorities who hold that if in another country, where there is limited access and they are only imported at special seasons, that is enough for it to be considered "new" (quoted in the name of Rav Mordechai Eliyahu, and also heard from Rav Zvi Rosen and other authorities).

37   See *Halichos Shlomo* 23:21 and *Shaarei Berachah* 20, note 59.

38   *Biur Halachah* 225:1, s.v. *Pri*; *Sh'eilas Yaavetz* 1:63. For more on the fruit from grafted trees, see *V'Zos Haberachah*, p. 163; *Teshuvos V'Hanhagos* 1:192; *Shaarei Berachah* 20:32; *Igros Moshe OC* 2:58; *Halichos Sadeh*, Kislev 5771. Note that a nectarine is clearly considered a type of peach, and not a grafted fruit.

39   *Mishnah Berurah* 225:14; *Shaar Hatziyun* 225:18; *Ashrei Ha'ish*, p. 261. But see *Aruch Hashulchan OC* 225:9 and *Chazon Ovadiah, Berachos*, p. 446, who rule that only one *berachah* is recited.

It must be noted that different types of citrus fruits, such as oranges, clementines, and pomellas, are all considered different species.[40]

H. NOTABLE TIMES OF YEAR

- **Tu B'Shevat**: There is a custom to say *She'hecheyanu* on a new fruit on this day.[41] This is because Tu B'Shevat is the New Year for trees, making it a very auspicious day for doing so.
- **The Three Weeks**: There are different opinions on whether to say *She'hecheyanu* on a new fruit during the Three Weeks. It is best to delay eating the fruit until Shabbos, if possible, but preferably not on Shabbos Chazon.[42]
- *Sefiras Ha'omer*: Most authorities allow one to recite *She'hecheyanu* on a new fruit during the *sefirah* period, while others are strict about not doing so.[43]
- **Rosh Hashanah**: Common custom is to recite *She'hecheyanu* on a new fruit or garment on the second night of Rosh Hashanah.[44]
- Many authorities rule that a mourner may recite *She'hecheyanu* on a new fruit.[45]

One may recite *She'hecheyanu* on any of the following fruit in Eretz Yisrael: anona, apricots, blueberries, carambola (star fruit), cherries, chestnuts,[46] clementines, dates, dragon fruit (pitaya), figs, fresh pineapple,[47] grapes, guava, kiwi, loquats, lychee, mango, melon, nectarines,

---

40   *Halichos Shlomo* 23:19; *Shaarei Berachah* 20:14.

41   See *M'Darkei Ha'ilanos* (from p. 147) concerning customs for Tu B'Shevat. Among them is to eat esrog jam and pray for a beautiful esrog for Sukkos. *B'nei Yissaschar*, Shevat 2:2; there is discussion about the propriety of saying the *berachah* on esrog jam. Some contend the *She'hecheyanu* on the *arba minim* is sufficient. Others point out that an esrog is an example of a fruit that is on the tree all year. However, there are some Sephardic authorities who permit reciting a *She'hecheyanu* on eating esrog jam; see *Ashrei Ha'ish* (Rav Elyashiv), p. 260; *Kaf Hachaim* 225:43; *Ben Ish Chai, Re'eh* 11; and *Chazon Ovadiah, Berachos*, p. 131, for discussion.

42   *Shulchan Aruch OC* 551:17; *Mishnah Berurah* 551:98.

43   *Shulchan Aruch OC* 493:2; *Mishnah Berurah* 493:2; *Dirshu* ad loc.; *Halichos Shlomo, Sefiras Ha'omer* 11:53.

44   *OC* 600:2; *Mishnah Berurah* 600:2.

45   *Birkas Hashir V'Hashevach* 1:89; *Yalkut Yosef* 7:154:2.

46   See *Shaarei Berachah*, p. 507, for a full discussion on why we recite *ha'eitz* on chestnuts.

47   See *Shaarei Berachah*, p. 516. It is interesting to note that Hawaiian pineapples have peak

peaches, oranges, papaya, passion fruit, persimmon, plums, pomegran-
ate, quinces, rhubarb, sabras, strawberries, and watermelon.

Note: This list is subject to change based on different geographic realities. So too, some Sephardim recite *She'hecheyanu* on certain vegetables.[48] Questionable fruit include coconut[49] and esrog (jam).[50]

---

season from April to May, and Caribbean pineapples have two seasons: December to February and August to September. Israeli pineapples have one season. However, in any case, some suggest that the taste of fresh pineapple is not very different from canned pineapple and would not deserve a *berachah* (heard from Rav Ganz); others disagree.

48   *V'Zos Haberachah*, p. 160; *Yalkut Yosef*, *Mo'adim* 254.

49   Coconuts are found for limited periods in Israel but are on the trees all year in their place of origin (see earlier discussion).

50   See earlier discussion.

Chapter Twenty-Two

She'hecheyanu on Garments and Other Objects

A. INTRODUCTION

One who acquires or receives a gift of new clothing that brings one a feeling of intense joy recites the *berachah* of *She'hecheyanu*.[1] In addition, many have the custom to add the *berachah* of *Malbish arumim*.[2] Common custom is to recite these *berachos* when one first wears the new garments. Some authorities rule that one who receives clothes as a gift should recite the *berachah* of *Ha'tov v'ha'meitiv*.[3]

B. WHEN TO SAY THE *BERACHAH*

One who did not recite *She'hecheyanu* when the garment was first worn may recite it as long as one still has a feeling of newness and joy for the garment.[4]

---

1   There are various authorities who point out that today the custom is not to recite this *berachah* because people buy clothes much more often than in the past, and the *simchah* is thus diluted. This may also be the reason why the *berachah* of *Malbish arumin* is not so commonly said.

2   *Shulchan Aruch OC* 223:4; *Mishnah Berurah* 18; *V'Zos Haberachah*, p. 167; *Kitzur Shulchan Aruch* 59:8. But see *Kaf Hachaim OC* 223:32, and *Piskei Teshuvos* 223, note 67. Some authorities say that one should recite the *berachah* without including Hashem's name, while others suggest that one have the garment in mind when reciting *Malbish arumim* in *Birchos Ha'shachar*. It seems that it was common practice to recite the full *berachah* in Lithuania and Germany before the war.

3   *Shulchan Aruch OC* 223:5; *Mishnah Berurah* 223:19; *Igros Moshe OC* 3:79; *Kitzur Shulchan Aruch* 59:10.

4   *Mishnah Berurah* 223:15; *Halichos Shlomo* 23:21; *Chazon Ovadiah, Berachos*, p. 402.

C. WHAT TYPE OF GARMENTS—HOW HAPPY MUST A PERSON BE

- A number of authorities rule that in order for clothes to qualify for the *She'hecheyanu berachah*, they must be **chashuv** (special). This refers to clothes that are worn on special occasions, such as on Shabbos or at a wedding. It should also be of the type of clothing that is not bought very often, such as a new suit, dress, hat, or *sheitel*.[5] Others rule that as long as the garment is very nice and **makes one happy**, one may recite *She'hecheyanu* (and the *berachah* of *Malbish Arumim*, if relevant; see further).[6] In any event, one does not recite the *berachos* if the new garment does not bring one joy.[7] It makes no difference how much one paid for the garment; the defining factor is whether or not the garment makes one happy.

- Most authorities rule that the *berachah* may be recited on a garment made of any material, including leather and fur.

- The *berachah* is not recited on garments that are generally not considered special, such as shoes,[8] pajamas,[9] pants,[10] scarves, or sweaters.[11]

- One may even recite the *berachah* on second-hand clothing and hand-me-downs if they bring one much joy[12] and are *chashuv*

---

5   *Mishnah Berurah* 223:23; *V'Zos Haberachah*, p. 166. Garments that (in general) people have in abundance, such as shirts and skirts, may not be considered *chashuv*. In that case, even a poor person would not recite a *berachah*. *Terumas Hadeshen* points out that it is appropriate to say "*la'zman ha'zeh*" upon clothes that people do not buy too often.

6   *Ohr L'Tzion* 2:46:60; *V'Zos Haberachah*, p. 166.

7   *Be'er Heitev* 223:16.

8   Even though nowadays women may consider shoes very special, Rav Chaim Pinchas Scheinberg rules (which I heard personally) that a *berachah* is not recited. It seems that shoes (in general) were not considered "special" but more of a necessity. See also *Aruch Hashulchan OC* 223:6 and *Halichos Shlomo* 23:15. However, see *V'Zos Haberachah*, p. 168, who quotes Rav Elyashiv that a *berachah* may be recited. Some say that a *berachah* is not recited on leather shoes because it involves killing an animal for a non-food purpose.

9   But see *Ohr L'Tzion* 2:46:60, who says one may recite the *beracha* on pajamas.

10   Rav Chaim Kanievsky rules that a *berachah* may be recited.

11   *Shulchan Aruch OC* 223:6.

12   Ibid., §3.

garments.[13] A *berachah* may also be recited on garments that have been extensively repaired or altered to the point that they look brand new.[14]

1. *Tallis Gadol* and Tefillin

One who buys or receives a *tallis gadol* should recite *She'hecheyanu* (or *Ha'tov v'ha'meitiv*, as will be discussed later), but not on a *tallis katan*.[15] Some rule that one should first recite the *berachah* of *L'hisatef ba'tzitzis* and then *She'hecheyanu*, while others say that one should recite *She'hecheyanu* first.[16] In certain communities, there is also a custom for a groom to recite *She'hecheyanu* on his new tallis at his wedding. There are also different customs regarding *She'hecheyanu* on new tefillin.[17]

2. BUYING ON CREDIT

One may recite the *berachos* on garments that one purchased on credit or with postdated checks.[18]

D. *MALBISH ARUMIM* AND *OTER YISRAEL B'SIFARAH*—NEW HAT

- Some have the custom to recite the *berachah* of *Malbish arumim* before the *berachah* of *She'hecheyanu* when wearing new clothes.[19] However, if one was wearing the garment while reciting *Malbish arumim* during *Birchos Ha'shachar*, one need not

---

13   *Mishnah Berurah* 223:22–23.

14   See *Igros Moshe OC* 3:79.

15   See *Shulchan Aruch OC* 22:1; *Igros Moshe OC* 3:80; *Piskei Teshuvos* 22:1. There are those who recite it on a woolen *tallis katan* if it brings one *simchah*.

16   *Mishnah Berurah* 22:3. However, see *Be'er Heitev* 22:2; who says *She'hecheyanu* comes first; *Kitzur Shulchan Aruch* 59:5; *Mishnah Berurah* (*Dirshu*) 22:3; see opinion of Rav Chaim Kanievsky that *She'hecheyanu* should be recited after one puts on the tallis.

17   See *Minchas Shlomo* 2:4:333. Rav Shlomo Zalman Auerbach gave his son tefillin for his bar mitzvah and his son recited *She'hecheyanu* for both the tefillin and for fulfilling the mitzvah for the first time. Tefillin is a valuable item, and therefore *She'hecheyanu* is appropriate (see above).

18   For more on this, see *Tzitz Eliezer* 8:12:19; *Kaf Hachaim OC* 223:18; *Birkas Hashir V'Hashevach* 2:24. Rav Elyashiv applies this to one who only has a fixed job.

19   *Mishnah Berurah* 223:18. This is due to the rule of *tadir v'he'eino tadir tadir kodem*, meaning, something more frequent takes priority. But see *Aruch Hashulchan* 223:6; *Mesoros*

recite it again. Some authorities suggest reciting the *berachah* without including Hashem's name.[20]

- Some authorities rule that the *berachah* of *Oter Yisrael b'sifarah* is to be recited on a new hat. To comply with this view, one should wear the hat when reciting *Birchos Ha'shachar* or say the *berachah* without including Hashem's name.[21]

- It is customary to congratulate someone for a new garment by saying *"Tevaleh v'tischadesh*—Wear it well and get a new one." This is generally not said for a garment made of leather because it involved killing an animal for a non-food purpose. It is explained that although doing so is permissible, it is contrary to the teaching *"V'rachamav al kol maasav*—His mercy is upon all of His creations."[22]

E. LAWS ABOUT NEW ITEMS AND HOUSEHOLD APPLIANCES

Regarding one who purchases items of significant value that brings one much joy:[23]

- If the only one benefitting from the item is the purchaser, *She'hecheyanu* should be recited.

- If other people, such as family members or roommates, will also derive benefit from the item, *Ha'tov v'ha'meitiv* should be recited.[24]

Some communities (especially Sephardim) do not recite these *berachos*, or at times will do so without Hashem's name.[25]

Moshe 2, p. 47; *Kaf Hachaim OC* 223:32; *Be'er Heitev* 223:13; *Ben Ish Chai, Re'eh*, who says that *She'hecheyanu* comes first (so that there should be no *hefsek* after the *berachah*).

20   *Kaf Hachaim OC* 223:33.

21   *Be'er Heitev* 223:13. See also *Kaf Hachaim OC* 223:33 and *Kitzur Shulchan Aruch* 59:8.

22   *Shulchan Aruch OC* 223:6. It should be noted that even though this expression is not said, one may recite *She'hecheyanu* on garments made from animals. See *Sefer Habayis*, p. 271.

23   *Shulchan Aruch OC* 223:5. Some authorities rule that *She'hecheyanu* is only recited on new clothes and on new fruit, presumably because other items do not arouse as much *simchah*. *Ben Ish Chai, Re'eh* 5; *Kaf Hachaim OC* 223:20; *V'Zos Haberachah*, p. 169.

24   *Shulchan Aruch OC* 223:5; *Mishnah Berurah* 223:19; *Shaarei Berachah* 20:22.

25   *Yalkut Yosef* 223:1. See also previous notes.

1. How Many *Berachos* and Who Recites Them

- If the item has one owner, and others will only benefit from the item indirectly, only the owner recites *Hatov V'ha'meitiv*, such as in the case of one who buys a computer or laptop but will allow family members or roommates to use it.
- If there is more than one owner, such as when the item belongs to both husband and wife, one person may recite *Hatov V'ha'meitiv* for both, if both are present. Otherwise, each person should recite his own *berachah*. This is often the case when purchasing a fridge, stove, or car that is jointly owned and jointly used.
- A parent who buys an item for the entire family, such as a new washing machine, should have the entire family in mind when reciting the *berachah*.[26]
- If a wife buys an expensive gift with her husband's money, or children with their parents' money, the *berachah* should be recited by the wife or the children.[27]
- For parents who buy especially attractive clothes for their children, some authorities point out that the parents should recite the *berachah* of *Ha'tov v'ha'meitiv*.[28]

2. Receiving Gifts

According to the *Mishnah Berurah*, one who receives an expensive gift should recite *She'hecheyanu*.[29] However, other authorities rule that *Ha'tov v'hameitv* is recited.[30]

---

26 *Halichos Shlomo* 23:24.
27 See *Shulchan Aruch EH* 90:16; *V'Zos Haberachah*, p. 168 (heard from Rav Zvi Rosen).
28 *Mishnah Berurah* 223:19; *Peninei Halachah*, p. 332.In discussion with various poskim I was told that today many do not follow this procedure.
29 *Shulchan Aruch OC* 223:5; *Mishnah Berurah* 223:21. *Biur Halachah* 223, s.v., *Shehi*, says that it is better to recite *She'hecheyanu*, since it has the ability to also exempt *Ha'tov v'ha'meitiv* (see next note).
30 *Shulchan Aruch* ad loc.; *Mishnah Berurah* ad loc. There is a *machlokes* between the *Talmud Bavli* and *Talmud Yerushalmi* concerning this issue. *Talmud Bavli* (*Berachos*) holds that the receiver recites the *She'hecheyanu*, as he receives actual physical joy from the item, while the *Talmud Yerushalmi* says that since the giver also gets joy (i.e., if the receiver is poor, his joy is that he gave charity, and if the receiver is rich, the giver is happy that the rich man accepted it), it is appropriate to recite *Ha'tov v'ha'meitiv*. See *Kitzur Shulchan Aruch* 59:10; *Igros Moshe EH* 4:84.

Some examples include:

- When a *kallah* receives gifts and jewelry, or a *chassan* receives a gold watch or *becher*
- When a wife receives an expensive piece of jewelry from her husband
- When a newly married couple receives a gift
- When children receive expensive gifts from their parents[31]

3. *Chassan* and *Kallah*

According to many authorities, a *chassan* does not recite a *berachah* when purchasing an engagement ring for his *kallah*, but rather the *kallah* recites *She'hecheyanu* when she receives it.[32] There is also a view that no *berachah* is recited in these instances, as such purchases are simply considered to be a fulfillment of financial obligations between families when a couple becomes engaged.[33]

4. Which Items

Items that warrant reciting *She'hecheyanu* or *Hatov V'ha'meitiv* include:

- Expensive kitchen appliances, such as a fridge or stove
- Furniture, such as a sofa and a bedroom set
- Expensive electrical appliances, such as an air conditioner, stereo, or washing machine[34]
- Others expensive items, such as candlesticks,[35] menorah,[36] a computer, dishes, jewelry,[37] a car, pets,[38] and curtains[39]

---

31   *Mishnah Berurah* 223:19; *Kaf Hachaim* 223:36; *Peninei Halachah*, p. 363.

32   See *Igros Moshe EH* 4:84, who says that a *chassan* should recite *She'hecheyanu* when purchasing an engagement ring, and a *kallah* should recite *Hatov V'ha'meitiv* when receiving it. See also *V'Zos Haberachah*, p. 168.

33   See *V'Zos Haberachah* ad loc. for the opinion of Rav Shlomo Zalman Auerbach.

34   Rav Nissim Karelitz points out that the wife should recite the *berachah*; *Chut Shani*, p. 180.

35   *Biur Halachah* 673:13; *Shaarei Berachah* 20:61; *Halachos of Brochos*, p. 16, note 75. Rav Moshe Feinstein and Rav Elyashiv opine that *Ha'tov v'ha'meitiv* should be recited, while Rav Shlomo Zalman Auerbach and Rav Chaim Kanievsky say that *She'hecheyanu* should be recited. See also *Birkas Hashir V'Hashevach*, p. 53.

36   *Birkas Hashir V'Hashevach* ad loc.

37   But see *Halichos Shlomo* 23:15, who rules that no *berachah* is recited over jewelry.

38   *Nesivos Haberachah*, p. 410.

39   *V'Zos Haberachah*, p. 167.

- Expensive *sifrei kodesh*, such as a new *Shas*;[40] expensive sets of books, i.e., encyclopedia. Some combine the *She'hecheyanu* on such items with a new fruit.

There are grounds to recite *berachos* over the following if they bring one much *simchah*:

- A business car[41]
- Work tools[42]
- Braces[43]
- Glasses[44]

5. Similar Items

One may recite a *berachah* when acquiring a new item even if one has a similar item, such as when buying another air-conditioning unit for one's home.[45]

6. When/How Long

- Common custom is to recite the *berachah* when one begins to use the item.[46]
- Still, one may recite the *berachah* as long as one still has a feeling of excitement about the new item.[47]

---

40 *Mishnah Berurah* 223:13; he quotes different opinions but concludes that there are grounds to permit either opinion ("*ein limchos b'yad ha'mevarech*"). The question is whether to look more at the pleasure of the contents (knowledge) of the *sefer*, though mitzvos were not given for their physical pleasure (*lav l'hanus nitnu*) or to look at its physical qualities, i.e., that they are a nice new possession. *Chayei Adam* 62:5 says that if the person was looking for the *sefer* for a long time, he should recite a *berachah* for the *simchah* of buying it, and not on its use. *Halichos Shlomo* 23:17 permits one to recite the *berachah* on a new *Shas*. When Reb Baruch Ber received *Shut Rav Akiva Eiger*, he recited a *berachah*. *Chazon Ovadiah* points out that there are grounds for both opinions; see more in *Shaarei Berachah* 20–29, note 84.

41 *Igros Moshe OC* 3:80.

42 *Peninei Halachah*, p. 286; *Igros Moshe* 3:80; *Shaarei Berachah* 20:75.

43 *Be'er Moshe* 5:67.

44 *Avnei Yashfe* 5:41; *L'Fa'eir U'L'vareich*, p. 128. Rav Elyashiv and Rav Karelitz opine that a *berachah* can be recited (especially today with exclusive styles of glasses), but Rav Shlomo Zalman Auerbach opines that no *berachah* is recited because of their medicinal character.

45 *Shulchan Aruch OC* 223:3.

46 *Mishnah Berurah* 223:17; *Shaarei Berachah* 20:24.

47 *Mishnah Berurah* 223:15.

7. Other Halachos

- According to most authorities, one may recite the *berachah* even when buying items with a credit card or postdated check.[48]
- One who bought an item and recited the *berachah*, but then discovers that the item is defective, is permitted to recite the *berachah* again when getting a new one.[49]

F. BUYING A HOUSE

- While technically one may recite the *berachah* at the time a house is bought, many have the custom to delay the *berachah* on a new house until after one moves into the house,[50] the furniture is in place, and the mezuzahs are affixed.[51] If one has a family, the *berachah* of *Ha'tov v'ha'meitiv* should be recited.
- Most authorities rule that one may recite the *berachah* even if one has a mortgage,[52] as long as the house is registered in one's name.[53]
- One who rented a home and later bought it can recite the *berachah* at that time.[54]
- A number of authorities rule that a *berachah* is not recited when buying an item for investment purposes or to rent out.[55]
- A *berachah* may be recited when making substantial renovations to one's home that bring one much joy, such as when adding a room or swimming pool.[56]

---

48   *L'Fa'eir U'L'vareich*, p. 128; *V'Zos Haberachah*, p. 168; *Tzitz Eliezer* 12:19.
49   *Shevet Halevi* 8:35:1.
50   *Shulchan Aruch OC* 223:3; *Mishnah Berurah* 223:11; *Birkas Hashir V'Hashevach*, p. 55. See *Midrash Tanchuma, Bereishis* 4 for a source to recite *berachos* on a house, and by extension on all appliances. See discussion in *Sefer She'hecheyanu*, p. 192,
51   *Halichos Shlomo* 23:13, note 54; *Shaarei Berachah* 20:60.
52   See *Tzitz Eliezer* 12:19; *Peninei Halachah, Berachos*, p. 370; *Harchavos, Berachos*, p. 284; *V'Sein Berachah*, p. 12.
53   *Halichos Shlomo* 23:13.
54   Ibid., §14.
55   *Shaarei Berachah* 20:2; *Birkas Hashir V'Hashevach*, p. 454; *Piskei Teshuvos* 223:3.
56   *Mishnah Berurah* 223:12. See also *Shaar Hatziyun* 223:14; *Shaarei Berachah* 20:25; *Avnei Yashfe* 5:41; *Birkas Hashir V'Hashevach*, p. 56; *Rivevos Ephraim* 3:138:1.

1. *Chanukas Ha'bayis*

There is a special custom among many to have a special ceremony and meal (*seudas mitzvah*) upon moving into a new house, especially in Eretz Yisrael.[57]

2. BUILDING A SYNAGOGUE

There is a difference of opinion whether *She'hecheyanu* or *Ha'tov v'ha'meitiv* is to be recited upon the completion of a synagogue.[58] The *Mishnah Berurah* opines that one member of the congregation should recite the *berachah* of *Ha'tov v'ha'meitiv* for all. There are other opinions that since the main purpose of the synagogue is for its spiritual value, and not for any physical benefit or pleasure (*hechsher mitzvah*), no *berachah* is necessary.[59] The *Kaf Hachaim* recommends combining the occasion with wearing a new suit or eating a new fruit and reciting the *berachah* on that.

G. MAKING OR RECEIVING MONEY

One who receives extraordinary amount of money as gift, such as for a wedding or birthday,[60] inheritance,[61] compensation damages, or stipend,[62] may say the appropriate *berachah* if it brings much joy.

The same is true if one finds money, wins the lottery, or makes a large profit in a business or a real-estate deal.[63]

One does not recite the *berachah* upon receiving charity.[64]

---

57   *Ben Ish Chai* 1, *Re'eh* 6; *Kaf Hachaim* 223:17, 19, for full discussion. See *Shaarei Toras Habayis*, pp. 276–81, and *Sefer Habayis*, pp. 273–97.

58   See *Aruch Hashulchan OC* 223:8, who rules that no *berachah* is recited, while *Mishnah Berurah* 223:11 rules that a *berachah* is recited. See also *Shaarei Berachah* 20:22:69; *Peninei Halachah*, p. 371; *Harchavos*, p. 289, for more discussion.

59   *Aruch Hashulchan OC* 223:8.

60   *Shaarei Berachah* 20:76, note 75. See also *Birkas Hashir V'Hashevach*, p. 295, that receiving charity is considered embarrassing.

61   *Mishnah Berurah* 223:9; *Halichos Shlomo* 1:285.

62   *Peninei Halachah*, p. 367; *Harchavos*, p. 286.

63   *Avnei Yashfe* 1:41. See also *Shaarei Berachah* 20:76 and *Peninei Halachah, Berachos*, p. 281, for different opinions.

64   The embarrassment minimizes the joy.

Chapter Twenty-Three

Good News and Bad News

A. INTRODUCTION

One who hears exceptionally good news[1] that brings one much joy may recite a *berachah*, either *She'hecheyanu* or *Ha'tov v'ha'meitiv*, as appropriate.[2] If one is not sure if one is feeling enough joy to warrant a *berachah*, one should recite it without including Hashem's name. It is also proper to say the verse *"Hodu la'Hashem ki tov ki l'olam chasdo,"* and pray for Hashem's continued help in the future.[3]

Examples:

- When one hears that one's wife gave birth to a boy[4]
- When one receives investment returns far exceeding one's expectations
- When one wins a big settlement in court
- When one receives a raise in salary far beyond one's expectations
- When one receives an outstanding position (with financial benefit)
- When one is returned a very expensive item that was lost or stolen
- When one wins a lottery or raffle

---

1   It is interesting to note the language of the Mishnah in *Berachos*: *"Besuros tovos...Ha'tov v'ha'meitiv, al shemu'os ra'os...Dayan ha'emes."* See the *diyuk* of the Gra, who points out the difference between the use of **besurah**—sharing with others good news, and the use of **shemi'ah**—hearing, but without sharing, when it comes to sad things. One should spread good news, but must avoid sharing bad news, unless there is an important reason to do so. See *Shulchan Aruch YD* 404.

2   *Shulchan Aruch OC* 222:1, 4.

3   *Kaf Hachaim OC* 222:9; *Piskei Teshuvos* 222:1.

4   *Shulchan Aruch OC* 223:1. One need not recite the *berachah* again when seeing one's son for the first time. For a girl, however, the *berachah* is only recited when one sees her for the first time. *Mishnah Berurah* 223:2.

- When one passes critical tests (such as serious school examinations or a driving test)
- When one receives an honor of distinction[5]

B. WHICH *BERACHOS*

- If the good news affects only oneself, then *She'hecheyanu* is recited.
- If the good news also directly affects others, one should recite *Ha'tov v'ha'meitiv.*[6]
- If the good news primarily affects others, there is question of whether a *berachah* is to be recited at all.[7] As such, one should say the *berachah* without including Hashem's name.[8] Examples of this include when one's sister gets engaged, when one's son makes a lot of money, when a relative or good friend successfully undergoes a serious operation, and upon hearing that a grandchild was born.[9]
- Whenever one is in doubt if he feels a sufficient amount of joy, he should say the *berachah* without including Hashem's name.

The *berachah* may be recited as long as one still feels intense joy from the news.[10]

C. BAD OR SAD NEWS

- One who hears bad news that causes one much pain should recite the *berachah* of *Dayan ha'emes*,[11] which is a type of *tzidduk*

---

5   *Peninei Halachos, Harchavos*, p. 286. *Mor U'Ketziah* 223 questions this ruling, because one's feeling may be mixed with false pride. Therefore, he recommends making the *berachah* in conjunction with a new fruit or garment. Alternatively, one may recite the *berachah* without including Hashem's name.

6   *Shulchan Aruch OC* 222:1.

7   See *Biur Halachah* 223, s.v. *Yaldah*, but see *Ketzos Hashulchan* 64:10; *Ma'amar Mordechai* 222:1; *Seder Birchos Ha'nehenin* 12:7; *Peninei Halachah, Harchavos*, p. 373.

8   See *Shaarei Berachah* 22:19.

9   However, if one sees a new grandchild, there is basis to recite a full *berachah* (see above).

10   *Mishnah Berurah* 223:3; see *Ketzos Hashulchan* 64:11.

11   *Shulchan Aruch OC* 222:2.

ha'din, showing that we accept Hashem's decrees and decisions in this world.

- Common custom is only to recite the *berachah* in full on the loss of one's closest relatives, which include one's father, mother, brother, sister, son, daughter, and wife. The *berachah* is recited when hearing of their death, or at the funeral before performing *keriah*.

- Although some authorities rule that the complete *berachah* should be recited on the passing of a *talmid chacham*, common custom is to recite the *berachah* without including Hashem's name. The same is true when hearing of the death of any Jew whose passing brings one much pain.[12]

- The *berachah* is also recited, without including Hashem's name,[13] when hearing of a loss of property to oneself or a good friend, for example a house burned down (*chas v'shalom*), the loss of business, and the loss of a job (even if one may find a better job).[14]

- The *berachah* is only recited upon the loss of something that one owned, but not on a potential gain that never materialized.[15]

- The *berachah* may be recited on Shabbos.[16]

- One is considered to be on an especially high spiritual level if one can recite this *berachah* with some level of joy, that one is happily accepting upon oneself Hashem's decree.[17] One should reflect on the fact that all suffering, whether physical or financial, as well as embarrassment,[18] is ultimately for the best and may even be an atonement for one's sins.

---

12   *Mishnah Berurah* 223:8; *Ashrei Ha'ish*, p. 254.
13   See *Biur Halachah* 222 s.v. *Al*.
14   *Berachos* 60a; *Shulchan Aruch OC* 222:4.
15   *Biur Halachah* ad loc.
16   *Piskei Teshuvos* 222:2.
17   *Shulchan Aruch OC* 222:3; *Mishnah Berurah* 222:4.
18   The *Tomer Devorah* teaches that the best suffering in the world is to be embarrassed, since it is not a physical suffering and allows one to do mitzvos. One who is afflicted with an illness is often unable to do mitzvos. For more discussion, see *Pele Yo'etz*, *Yesurim*.

- One should try to empathize when hearing bad news about others. One should say to one who suffered a significant loss, "*Ha'makom yemaleh chesroncha*—May Hashem fill your loss."[19]

One should spread good news as quickly as possible.[20] Bad news, however, should only be spread if there is a constructive purpose in doing so, and even then, in an indirect manner, if possible.[21]

---

19   See *Piskei Teshuvos* 223:4.

20   See *Ohr Hachaim*, *Vayechi* 45:26, but not necessarily in a shocking way; *Kaf Hachaim* OC 222:10.

21   *Pele Yo'etz*, *Besurah*; *Piskei Teshuvos* 222:4, similar to Serach bas Asher, who informed Yaakov that Yosef was still alive in a special singsong: "*Od Yosef chai…*"

Chapter Twenty-Four

Ha'tov V'Ha'meitiv on Additional Wine

A. INTRODUCTION

In certain situations, upon drinking more than one kind of wine at a meal, our Sages have instituted an additional *berachah* of *Ha'tov v'ha'meitiv* to be recited when drinking the second wine.

B. REASONS FOR THE *BERACHAH*

The *Mishnah Berurah* points out reasons for this *berachah*:[1]

- One who drinks such an abundance of wine, which is a symbol of true luxury, is required to give special thanks to Hashem when doing so and to share the wine with others.
- In addition, the *berachah Ha'tov vha'meitiv* is derived from the fourth *berachah* of *Birkas Hamazon*, which is associated with death.[2] Thus it is a reminder that too much wine can have terrible consequences and that we should focus more on spiritual matters.

In general, one who has two different wines in front of him should recite *Ha'gafen* on the superior wine,[3] and then no additional *berachah*

---

1   *Shulchan Aruch OC* 175:1; *Mishnah Berurah* 175:2. See also *Aruch Hashulchan OC* 175:1; *Shaarei Berachah* 18:50.

2   *Berachos* 48b teaches that the fourth *berachah* of *Birkas Hamazon* was instituted in memory of the massacre at Beitar, where two miracles occurred: (1) The Romans finally let the Jews bury the dead; and (2) the dead bodies had not putrefied.

3   In discussion with *poskim*, I have heard from some that the criteria for superiority is the cost factor, while other *poskim* have told me that personal preference (taste) is also a criterion.

is recited upon the second wine.[4] However, there are various situations that would enable one to recite the *berachah* of *Ha'tov v'ha'meitiv*.

C. CONDITIONS

While today there are various wine connoisseurs who can clearly identify superior wines, many people do not differentiate between qualities of wine but rather by their tastes. The *Shulchan Aruch* (175:2) points out that one may recite the *berachah* of *Ha'tov v'ha'meitiv*, even if one is in doubt about the quality of the wine, as long as he knows that it is not an inferior wine.

The primary conditions that are required in order to be able to recite the *berachah* are as follows:

- The additional wine should be (a) either a wine clearly superior to the first wine (as pointed out above, there are conoisseurs who know this); or (b) a wine that he is unsure (in doubt) whether it is clearly superior, but he knows that it is not an inferior wine.[5]
- There are at least two adults drinking together who will drink both wines—even a husband and his wife or a father and his son.[6]
- The second bottle of wine has been brought out in order to enjoy the taste of a different wine, and not because they ran out of the first wine.[7]
- One does not change one's place or make a decision to stop drinking in the interim (*hesach ha'daas*).
- The bottles of wine remain on the table and are available for everyone to drink.[8]

---

4   Indeed, one should always give precedence to superior foods when reciting a *berachah*, i.e., with foods with the same *berachah*, one should always recite the *berachah* on the *chaviv* (more desirable) food first. See *Shulchan Aruch* 211 for more details.

5   See *Shoneh Halachos* 175 2; *Sefer She'hecheyanu*, p. 325, especially note 39, based on *Shulchan Aruch* 175:2; *Birkas Hashem* 4, p. 194.

6   *Shulchan Aruch OC* 175:4. See discussion in *Shaarei Berachah* 18:50. See discussion in *Sefer She'hecheyanu*, p. 320, about whether they both must be drinking the same wines; see also *Magen Avraham* 175:4.

7   *Shulchan Aruch OC* 175:4; *Mishnah Berurah* §3.

8   *Mishnah Berurah* 175:15; *Kitzur Shulchan Aruch* 49:14.

If the above conditions are met, then each person should recite their own *berachah*.[9]

Some authorities add the following *hiddurim* (stringencies):

- Every person must drink at least a *revi'is* of each type of wine.[10]
- The second wine should not be present when *Ha'gafen* is recited over the first wine.[11]

1. Application

Ha'tov v'ha'meitiv may be said on the second wine if:[12]

- After one recited a *berachah* on wine A, a different wine B was brought to the table, and wine B is either equal or superior quality to wine A, but not lower quality.
- There were various wines on the table at the time of the first *berachah*, but (1) there was no clearly superior wine (see above),[13] or (2) even if there was a superior wine, one prefers to use the other wine because of its taste (see further for examples).

Since there are many different conditions and opinions as to when the *berachah* should be recited, one should ask one's rabbi for guidance in this area.[14]

---

9   *Shulchan Aruch OC* 175:5.

10 *Shaarei Berachah* 18:31, note 50.

11 *Mishnah Berurah* 175:14. Rav Nebenzhal recommended this procedure per the recommendation of the *Mishnah Berurah*. For further discussion, see *Sefer She'hecheyanu*, p. 315, note 18. See *Mishnah Berurah* 175:5, 14, where it seems that one can still recite a *berachah*. The opinion of the *Levush* is that one does not recite a *berachah* under these conditions See *Birkas Hashem* 4, p. 208.

12 See *Shoneh Halachos* 175:1–2. There are some authorities who recommend that in order to avoid any questions, arrange to place all the wines that one intends to drink on the table and to recite the *berachah* on the best one (if that can be determined). Alternatively, one should not drink more than one type of wine at each meal, *Kaf Hachaim OC* 175:11.

13 This may apply to many people who are not wine connoiseurs. For discussion on differences between red and white wine, see *Shaarei Berachah*, p. 419.

14 Much of this section is based on *V'Zos Haberachah*, p. 170, and *Libun Haberachah*, p. 435. Many *poskim* discuss the parameters of the *berachah* including *Chayei Adam* 62, *Aruch Hashulchan* 175, and *Mishnah Berurah* 175. See also *Kaf Hachaim OC* 175:11 as to why many people shy away from reciting this *berachah*. See *Halachos of Brochos*, vol. 2, pp. 44–45 and notes, where he discusses how many modern-day *gedolim* assumed that the *berachah* can be recited (with proper knowledge of the conditions). See *Birkas Hashir V'Hashevach* 16:40, who

D. COMMON EXAMPLES

Hatov v'ha'meitiv may be recited in the following situations:

- One who is drinking wine A, and then decides to drink another type of wine (B), which is either superior to the first wine or at least not inferior to it. For example, one made *kiddush* on wine A (or grape juice),[15] and later decides to drink another type of wine, i.e., dry wine or sparkling wine.

- One who has two wines and is not sure which of the two wines is truly superior may recite *Ha'tov v'ha'meitiv* on the second wine. For example, one who had different wines on the table before *kiddush* (one dry and one sweet) may recite *Hatov V'ha'meitiv* on the second wine.[16] (Some authorities recommend removing the second type of wine from the table when reciting *Ha'gafen*, and to bring it to the table later on in order to recite *Ha'tov v'ha'meitiv*.[17])

- One who has two wines (and the second wine may be superior), but prefers to use a sweet wine (or grape juice) for *kiddush* in order not to get intoxicated, or because he likes its taste, recites *Ha'gafen* on the first wine and *Ha'tov v'ha'meitiv* on the second wine.

---

quotes Rav Chaim Kanievsky in saying that when conditions are met, the *berachah* should be said. See *Shoneh Halachos* 175. These sections were written based upon consultation with Rav Avigdor Nebenzhal (Rav Yoel Yehoshua).

15 See *Avnei Yashfe* 1:36. Rav Shlomo Zalman Auerbach (as heard from Rav Nebenzhal), Rav David Feinstein (*V'Dibarta Bam* 54), and other *poskim* permit reciting *Ha'tov v'ha'meitiv* on grape juice. However, see *V'Zos Haberachah*, p. 171, who quotes Rav Elyashiv as disagreeing, because it does not have the characteristic of being *mesamei'ach*.

16 See *Mishnah Berurah* 175:14; *Piskei Teshuvos* 175:1, note 26; *Shulchan Hatahor* 175:4; *Mishnah Berurah (Dirshu)* 175, note 9, for the opinion of Rav Chaim Pinchas Scheinberg.

17 See above.

Chapter Twenty-Five

The Laws of Amen

A. INTRODUCTION

One who hears a *berachah* being recited by a fellow Jew is obligated to answer *Amen*.[1] The source of this law is based on the verse, *"Ki shem Hashem ekra havu godel l'Elokeinu*—Whenever I recite the Name of G-d, give praise to our G-d" (*Devarim* 32:3).[2]

The word *Amen* can mean either, "I affirm/I believe that Hashem is the source of blessing," or "I confirm that this expression should be fulfilled."[3] These are the proper *kavanos* one should have when one reciting *Amen*. The letters of the word *Amen* stand for the words *"Kel melech ne'eman*—the Lord Who is the trustworthy King." The *sefer Yesod V'Shoresh Ha'avodah*[4] explains how a *berachah* that is rounded out with *Amen* fills out the *berachah* and creates the full connection with Hakadosh Baruch Hu.

---

1   See *Shelmas Chaim* 198, that the *Zohar* is particular about one who hears the entire *berachah*, but if he hears only part, responding *Amen* is optional.

2   *Shulchan Aruch OC* 124:6. *Chayei Adam* 6:1. See *Tur* 124 for further explanation. The recitation of *Amen* is based on the practice in the Beis Hamikdash, where one would recite the phrase *"Baruch shem kevod malchuso l'olam va'ed"* after every mention of the (Special) Name of Hashem. See the discussion in *Pischei Halachah* (in English), p. 87, on why it was not permitted to say *Amen* in the Beis Hamikdash (*Berachos* 63a). The word *Amen*, which implies trust and faith, was basically superfluous in the Beis Hamikdash, where Hashem's *Shechinah* was clear to all. See *Meiri, Taanis* 16b, who explains that *Amen* suggests an ending of a *berachah*, while in the Beis Hamikdash a *berachah* had an ongoing effect.

3   For *berachos* of praise, e.g., those over food or mitzvos, the focus should be on the affirmation of the truth of the blessing. When it comes to a *berachah* of prayer, e.g., the middle *berachos* of the *Shemoneh Esreh*, one should intend that the *Amen* be an entreaty to Hashem to fulfill the prayer. (See *Shulchan Aruch OC* 124; *Mishnah Berurah* ad loc. §24–25; *Shulchan Aruch OC* 215, *Mishnah Berurah* ad loc. 8. See also *Shaarei Berachah* 10:29.)

4   Chap. 10.

The Talmud tells us that greater is the power of the one who answers *Amen* than the person who actually recites the *berachah*.[5]

Amen is a word that has a holy connotation and should not be used casually, rather, only when it is used in relationship to Hashem (see examples later).

B. PROPER PRONUNCIATION

One should pronounce every letter of the word *Amen* slowly and properly. It should take the amount of time it takes to say the words "*Kel melech ne'eman*."[6]

C. HOW LOUD

The one who answers *Amen* should not say it louder than the one who recited the *berachah*. We learn this from the *pasuk*, "*Gadlu l'Hashem iti*—Declare the greatness of Hashem with me."[7] The same rule applies to responding to *Barchu* and a *zimun*. However, it is permitted to say it louder if it is in order to inspire others.[8]

D. HOW LONG AFTER THE *BERACHAH*

One should respond *Amen* within two to three seconds (*toch k'dei dibbur*) after the conclusion of the *berachah*. However, it is best to answer immediately. If one is answering *Amen* together with a group, he should finish by the time the majority of people have finished reciting *Amen*.[9]

---

5   *Berachos* 53b. See *Shaarei Teshuvah* 215:2. See explanations by *Rabbeinu Bachya*, *Kad Hakemach* (*Emunah*). *Amen* concretizes the *berachah*; it is compared to the signature attesting to the validity of a document. Some compare it to the second of two witnesses who give credence to the testimony (*eidus*) in a court (*Piskei Halachah* [English], p. 86. See also *Kaf Hachaim* 124:31, who quotes the commentary *Perishah* 124:7). Since we have the principle of *shomei'a k'oneh* (hearing is considered as reciting), it is considered as if the *berachah* was said twice. Rav Avigdor Miller explains the great reward a person receives from answering *Amen* while in the middle of a project; the time in which he interrupted his activities in order to praise G-d, even for a second, is considered a great sacrifice.

6   *Shulchan Aruch OC* 124:8.

7   *Tehillim* 34:4.

8   *Shulchan Aruch OC* 124:12; *Mishnah Berurah* 47.

9   *Shulchan Aruch OC* 124, *Mishnah Berurah* ad loc. 30, 34–35, 42; *Biur Halachah*, s.v. *Miyad*.

If one interrupted even with one word after the *berachah* was said, he can no longer say *Amen*.[10]

E. OTHER INSTANCES OF REPLYING *AMEN*

In addition to reciting *Amen* after hearing a standard *berachah*, it is good practice to respond *Amen* upon hearing any *tefillah* (even without the classic form of a *berachah*),[11] such as after "*Al Yechasreinu*" and all the *Harachaman* requests in *Birkas Hamazon*,[12] *Mi She'beirach*, and *Birkas Kohanim*. The *Magen Avraham* adds that it is appropriate to reply *Amen* to simple salutations, such as "Have a good morning," "*Refuah shelei-mah*—A speedy recovery," being wished *hatzlachah* (success) on a test, or *Birkas Menachamim* ("*HaMakom yenacheim eschem...*")[13] recited in the house of a mourner.

F. WHEN TO ANSWER

Even though it is praiseworthy to answer *Amen* to any *berachah*,[14] if it will interfere or diminish one's concentration in the middle of learning or *tefillos*, one need not answer *Amen*.

If one has remnants of food or something in his mouth (e.g., a piece of gum), he should still say *Amen*.[15]

If one is in a bathroom or dressing room when he hears a *berachah* (as long as he is not exposed to *ervah* and there is no bad smell or dirt), he may say *Amen*.[16]

---

10   *Halichos Shlomo, Tefillah* 22:18; *Libun Haberachah*, p. 103.

11   *Shulchan Aruch OC* 215, *Mishnah Berurah* ad loc. 9; *Mishnah Berurah (Dirshu)* 189, note 2; *Mishnah Berurah (Dirshu)* 124, note 42; *Aruch Hashulchan* 215:1, "One fulfills the mitzvah of '*v'ahavta l'rei'acha k'mocha*,' especially when responding to a *Mi She'beirach*."

12   *Shulchan Aruch OC* 189, *Mishnah Berurah* ad loc. 5.

13   *V'Zos Haberachah*, p. 188.

14   *Shulchan Aruch OC* 167; *Biur Halachah*, s.v. *V'yanu*; *Shaarei Berachah* 10:26, note 72; *Shevet Halevi* 9:43; *Halichos Shlomo, Tefillah* 9:6.

15   *Shut Ohr L'Tzion* 2:46:50. See *Libun Haberachah*, p. 103, which discusses why the principle of "*ein masichin b'seudah*—not talking during a meal" does not apply today.

16   *Shulchan Aruch OC* 84, heard from Rav Yisrael Ber Kaplan.

G. QUESTIONABLE SITUATIONS

Amen is a holy word and should not be said in vain. In the following cases one **should not** say *Amen*:

1. Improper *Berachah*

If one hears a person recite a *berachah l'vatalah* (recited in vain), or a *berachah she'einah tzrichah* (that was not necessary), one does not answer *Amen*.[17]

If one hears a *berachah* he is not obligated to hear and he does not know which *berachah* is being recited, he **should not** recite *Amen* (e.g., he walks into shul and hears everyone saying *Amen*).[18]

If one knows which *berachah* was said, he may say *Amen* even if he does not hear the end of the *berachah* (e.g., he walks into shul and hears the end of a *berachah* or cannot hear all of *berachah*, or the *berachah* was unclear but he knows which *berachah* was said).[19]

2. *Berachah* over a Microphone during a Live Broadcast

If one hears someone recite a *berachah* over a loudspeaker, telephone, or radio (i.e., a live broadcast), various *poskim* permit saying *Amen* at the conclusion of the *berachah*.[20] Other *poskim* question this practice and permit answering only if there is a minyan of people standing close enough to hear the actual voice of the one reciting the *berachah*.[21]

---

17 See *Shulchan Aruch OC* 214:1, and *Piskei Teshuvos* 214:1, for details of what is considered a proper *berachah*: One must say (1) *Baruch*, (2) at least one Name of Hashem, and (3) *Melech ha'olam*.

18 It is considered an *Amen yesomah*, an "orphaned *Amen*," which one is forbidden to say. See *Shulchan Aruch OC* 124:8, *Mishnah Berurah* ad loc. 31; *Biur Halachah*, s.v. *V'zeh eino shomei'a*. See *Peninei Halachah, Harchavos*, p. 169, for a full discussion, especially regarding a *beis knesses* in Alexandria (a huge synagogue where people did not actually hear the *Amen* of the *baal tefillah* but knew which *berachah* was being said).

19 *Shulchan Aruch OC* 124:8, *Mishnah Berurah* ad loc. 31–33; *Biur Halachah*, s.v. *V'yesh*; *Shaarei Berachah* 10:28, note 3.

20 *Igros Moshe OC* 4:91:4; *Yechaveh Daas* 2:68; *Shaarei Berachah* 10:16.

21 See *Minchas Shlomo* 1:9. Fuller discussions can be found in *Libun Haberachah*, pp. 107–9. Also see *Shaarei Berachah*, p. 206, notes 43, 44.

(Concerning whether one can be *yotzei* a *berachah* said this way, see note below.[22]) If it is not a live broadcast, *Amen* should definitely not be said.[23]

3. Questionable *Berachos*

One does not answer *Amen* after hearing the ending of the following *berachos*: *Ha'maavir sheinah* in *Birkos Ha'shachar*, before *"vihi ratzon..."*[24] and *La'asok b'divrei sorah* before *"v'haarev na"* in *Birkas HaTorah*.[25] There are different opinions concerning whether one can answer *Amen* upon hearing the *berachah* of *Al mitzvas tefillin* (recited on *tefillin shel rosh*). *Poskim* recommend that the *berachah* be said in a low voice so people cannot hear. In any case, where one heard the *berachah*, he may still recite *Amen*.[26]

There are various customs concerning the recitation of *Amen* after the *berachos* of *Ahavah Rabbah* and *Ahavas Olam* (before *k'rias Shema*). While some have the custom that the *baal tefillah* recite the end of these *berachos* in a very low voice or that everyone recites it together, others have the custom to say the *Amen* normally.[27]

There are also different customs concerning the answering of *Amen* after the *berachah* of *Ga'al Yisrael*. While some have the custom that

---

22   See *Igros Moshe* OC 4:91, 2:108, who opines that one may be *yotzei* on Havdalah or megillah over the telephone *b'shaas ha'dechak* (when there is no other choice); *Har Tzvi, Mikra'ei Kodesh, Megillah* 11; *Shut Tzitz Eliezer* 8:11; *Peninei Halachah, Harchavos*, p. 175. However, see *Yechaveh Daas* 2:68, who opines that one cannot be *yotzei* but should answer *Amen* like in the *beis knesses* in Alexandria. See *Minchas Shlomo* 1:9 and Rav Elyashiv (*Libun Haberachah*, p. 106), who rule that one should not say *Amen* even under these conditions.

23   *Yalkut Yosef* 215:4; *V'Zos Haberachah*, p. 189.

24   *Shulchan Aruch* OC 41:1.

25   *Shulchan Aruch* OC 47:6, *Mishnah Berurah* ad loc. 11. See the discussion of whether the *berachah* of *La'asok* is a separate *berachah*. See *Ishei Yisrael*, p. 51, note 10, who quotes *Daas Torah* 47:6, who permits saying *Amen* in this case.

26   *Halichos Shlomo, Tefillah* 4:19, note 27; *Shaarei Berachah* 10, note 79.

27   *Shulchan Aruch* OC 61, *Mishnah Berurah* ad loc. 16; *Shulchan Aruch* OC 59, *Mishnah Berurah* ad loc. 4; *Shaarei Teshuvah* 59:5. See *Ishei Yisrael* 17:12. I heard from Rav Zvi Rosen that Rav Aryeh Leib Heiman (rav of the local synagogue in Bayit Vegan) followed the custom of Rav Aharon Kotler and recited *Amen* regularly to these *berachos*. The question is whether these *berachos* are to be considered a special *Birkas Ha'mitzvah* on *k'rias Shema* and thus there should be no interruption.

the *baal tefillah* should conclude the *berachah* in a low voice so that he cannot be heard,[28] others allow finishing it the normal way.[29]

4. Children Reciting *Berachos*

It is very appropriate to train children to recite *Amen* from a very early age.[30]

When teaching children (or even adults when necessary) how to recite *berachos* (but not Chumash or Gemara), one may use the proper Name of Hashem. If possible, try to guide them without repeating each full word.[31] If one hears the *berachos* of children who are learning to make *berachos*, he does not answer *Amen*.[32]

If the children are actually reciting a proper *berachah*:

- If the child is the age of *chinuch*,[33] one recites *Amen* after the *berachah*.
- If the child is very young (below the age of *chinuch*), while many have the custom to still recite a regular *Amen*,[34] other *poskim* are of the opinion that one should avoid saying it. (However, for *chinuch* purposes, he should "fake it.")[35]

---

28   Or to start the beginning of *Shemoneh Esreh* ("*Hashem sefasai...*").

29   *Shulchan Aruch OC* 66:7, *Mishnah Berurah* ad loc. 35–36. See *Mishnah Berurah* (*Dirshu*) §18; *Ishei Yisrael* 17:24, note 64. In *Halichos Shlomo, Tefillah* 7:18, Rav Shlomo Zalman Auerbach held that it is disrespectful to treat a *berachah* in such a way. The question at hand is whether the recitation of *Amen* at this point warrants a violation of the concept of *semichas geulah l'tefillah*.

30   *Shulchan Aruch OC* 124:7; *Sanhedrin* 110b.

31   *Shulchan Aruch OC* 167, *Mishnah Berurah* ad loc. 93. Also, *Shulchan Aruch OC* 215:3. See *Halichos Shlomo, Tefillah* 22:8, when at times he recommends not saying the Names of Hashem correctly, e.g., mumbling the Name.

32   *Shulchan Aruch OC* 215:3, *Mishnah Berurah* ad loc. 3.

33   *Shaarei Berachah* 10:35, note 90. Rav Yehoshua Neuwirth says the age of *chinuch* for this matter is when a child begins saying *berachos* on his own; but see *Yabia Omer* 2:13, which says not to answer *Amen* to a child under the age of five or six.

34   *Shaarei Berachah* 10:35, note 90; *Piskei Teshuvah* 215:8, note 46; *Mishnah Berurah* (*Dirshu*) 124, note 69; *Kaf Hachaim* 124:30. See *Halichos Shlomo, Tefillah*, p. 373, for a story about the consequences of not answering *Amen* to a child's *berachah*.

35   *Shulchan Aruch OC* 215, *Mishnah Berurah* ad loc. 16; *Aruch Hashulchan* 2; *Halichos Shlomo, Tefillah* 22:20. See *Ohr L'Tzion* 14:33, who says to say the verse "*Baruch Hashem l'olam Amen v'Amen.*"

H. HEARING *BERACHOS* FROM...

If one hears an entire *berachah* from a non-Jew, one may answer *Amen*.[36]

Many *poskim* hold that one may recite *Amen* after hearing the *berachah* of a deaf person. Rav Shlomo Zalman Auerbach encouraged teaching children with severe disabilities to say *berachos*, but to try to avoid saying the proper Name of Hashem and answering *Amen* in the full form.[37]

Generally, one may recite *Amen* after the *berachah* of a nonobservant Jew or of one not wearing a *kippah*.[38]

I. *AMEN* AFTER ONE'S OWN *BERACHAH*

Ashkenazic custom is not to answer *Amen* on one's own *berachah*,[39] except after the third *berachah* of *Birkas Hamazon*.[40] Sephardic custom is to recite *Amen* at the conclusion of a set of *berachos*, i.e., *Hallel*, *Yishtabach* in *Shacharis*, and *Hashkiveinu* in *Maariv*.

J. TWO SIMULTANEOUS *BERACHOS*

If one finished saying a *berachah* at the same time as his friend finished saying the same *berachah*, he should not answer *Amen*.[41] However, if they are saying two different *berachos*, he may answer *Amen*.[42]

---

36 *Shaarei Berachah* 10:92 says that we assume his intention is to our G-d. See *Shulchan Aruch OC* 215:2, *Mishnah Berurah* ad loc. 12; *Shaar Hatziyun*, notes 9 and 12. The *Kaf Hachaim* points out that the custom is not to answer *Amen*.

37 See *Halichos Shlomo, Tefillah* 22:8, when at times he recommends not saying the Names of Hashem correctly, e.g., mumbling the Name. See *Shulchan Aruch OC* 124, *Mishnah Berurah* ad loc. 47; see *Shevet Halevi* 10:45; *Shaarei Berachah* 10:9; *Halichos Shlomo, Tefillah*, chap. 22, note 70; *Nishmas Avraham* 5, p. 81.

38 *Shulchan Aruch OC* 215; *Mishnah Berurah* ad loc. 10; see *Mishnah Berurah (Dirshu)*, note 7. See *Biur Halachah*, s.v. *Shelo* and s.v. *Ha'mevarech*; *Igros Moshe OC* 2:50, 3:21 (about *apikorsim*). See *Piskei Teshuvah* 271:9 on whether one can be *yotzei kiddush* on Shabbos from a *mechallel Shabbos* (it's best to say it with him word for word).

39 *Shulchan Aruch OC* 215:1. See reason in *Aruch Hashulchan* 215:4. *Amen* is to strengthen the bounty of *berachah*; it is therefore inappropriate for the person himself to reinforce it (it is *gaivah*, a sign of pride). See *Igros Moshe OC* 5:9:1, that it is disrespectful to add to the exclusive formulas of the rabbis.

40 See *Shulchan Aruch OC* 188:1; *Shulchan Aruch OC* 215, *Mishnah Berurah* ad loc. 4, which distinguish between the first three *berachos*, which are based on Torah concepts, and the fourth, which was a later Rabbinic addition in the days of Rabban Gamliel; see *Rabbeinu Yonah, Berachos* 33b.

41 It looks like he is answering *Amen* to his own *berachah*.

42 See *Shulchan Aruch OC* 51. *Mishnah Berurah* ad loc. 3 points out that if he finishes after

If one hears two *berachos* simultaneously, he may recite two *Amens* or "*Amen v'Amen.*"[43]

K. RECITING "*BARUCH HU U'VARUCH SHEMO*"

It is praiseworthy that when one hears a *berachah*, he should add the words, "*Baruch hu u'varuch shemo*," after the Name of Hashem, to show additional respect to Hashem.[44] The source of this custom is the verse, "*Ki shem Hashem ekra havu godel l'Elokeinu*—Whenever I recite the Name of G-d, give praise to our G-d" (*Devarim* 32:3).[45] Therefore, one should say a *berachah* slowly so that one who hears it can respond with *Baruch hu u'varuch shemo* at the right time, and still have enough time to say *Amen* at the end of the *berachah*.[46]

There are various times when the halachah does not require saying *Baruch Hu u'varuch shemo*. This includes:

- If there is not enough time to be able to answer *Amen* properly
- When one wants to be *yotzei* with a *berachah* of another person, e.g., *kiddush*, shofar (in the case where one said *Baruch Hu u'varuch shemo*, many *poskim* hold that one is still *yotzei* the *berachah*)[47]

Hallel or Yishtabach or "*Shomer Yisrael la'ad*," one may answer *Amen* immediately after the *baal tefillah* finishes (even according to Ashkenazic opinion). See above.

43 *Shulchan Aruch OC* 124, *Mishnah Berurah* 25. He must have proper intention for each *berachah*.

44 *Kaf Hachaim* 5:12. This is to show that Hashem is blessed by Himself and does not need our blessings. *Tur OC* 124, explains, based on the verse in *Mishlei* (10:7), "*Zecher tzaddik livrachah*—The mention of a righteous man is for a blessing," that if one must respond with a praise to the mention of a tzaddik's name, one must surely respond as such to the Name of Hashem.

45 *Shulchan Aruch OC* 124, *Mishnah Berurah* ad loc. 22; *Tur* 124:5. See *Yosef Ometz*, who suggests that each time one hears the Name of Hashem, *Baruch hu u'varuch shemo* should be said. The *Kaf Hachaim* 124:27 points out that there is a *minhag* to say *Baruch hu u'varuch shemo* during *Birkas Kohanim*.

46 *Shulchan Aruch OC* 124, *Mishnah Berurah* ad loc. 22; *Shaar Hatziyun* 24. For this reason, some refrain from reciting *Baruch hu u'varuch shemo* so they can be sure to hear the end of the *berachah* and thus recite *Amen* (see *Shaarei Berachah* 10, note 100). The *Gra* (*Maasei Rav* 43) did not recite *Baruch hu u'varuch shemo* during the repetition of *Shemoneh Esreh*, since the *Amen* must refer back to the entire *berachah*, and reciting *Baruch hu u'varuch shemo* is considered an interruption.

47 *Shulchan Aruch OC* 124, *Mishnah Berurah* ad loc. 21; *Shaarei Berachah* 10, note 101; *Igros Moshe OC* 2:98, but see *Shaarei Teshuvah* 213:1 and *Aruch Hashulchan* 124:10.

- When one is in the middle of various *tefillos* or *berachos*, e.g., in the middle of davening *Shacharis* from *Baruch She'amar* until after the silent *Shemoneh Esreh*, or in *Maariv* from after *Barchu* until after the silent *Shemoneh Esreh*
- When one is in the middle of learning[48]

---

48   See *Kaf Hachaim* 124:25.

Chapter Twenty-Six
The Shem Hashem

A. INTRODUCTION

The Names of G-d are very holy and must be treated with great respect, as the Torah tells us, *"Es Hashem Elokecha tira*—You must fear Hashem, your G-d."[1] It is forbidden to recite the Name of Hashem in vain, even in a foreign language, unless one specifically has in mind to praise Hashem. In many cases, it is also forbidden to erase the Names of Hashem.[2] Similarly, it is forbidden to recite a *berachah* in vain, even if one's intention is to praise Hashem.[3]

B. THE THREE CATEGORIES OF THE NAMES OF HASHEM

1. Category #1: The *Shem Havayah*

The Special Explicit Name, the *Shem Havayah* (also known as the Tetragrammaton), is *yud-hei-vav-hei*. The Name represents the quintessential being of Hashem and His timelessness. The Name is a combination of three Hebrew words: *"Hayah, Hoveh, Yihiyeh*—He was, He is, He will be forever."* Kabbalistic authorities provide deeper and more profound *kavanos*.[4]

In many of our siddurim today, this Name may be written as *yud-yud*, representing the full Name. In any case, it is always pronounced *"Adonai"* (my Master).[5]

---

1   *Temurah* 4a; *Devarim* 12:3 and 4, and 28:58.

2   *Shulchan Aruch OC* 215, *Mishnah Berurah* ad loc. 19 and 20; *Shulchan Aruch OC* 85, *Mishnah Berurah* ad loc. 11.

3   *Shulchan Aruch OC* 215:20. However, see *Chavas Daas, YD* 20 and *Beis Hasafek* 20, who suggest that there is basis for one to be allowed to recite a full *berachah* if it is said as an optional praise of Hashem. See the *L'Fa'eir U'L'varech*, p. 100.

4   *Shaar Hakavanos*, *"Hakdamah She'kodem Hakdamas Beis Haknesses."*

5   See *Rashi, Shemos* 3:15. For a full discussion, see *Pischei Halachah* (English), p. 49, about pronouncing the Tetragrammaton. See *Chayei Adam* 5:27, and *Mishnah Berurah* 5:2.

2. Category #2: Other Names of Hashem

Other Names of Hashem (*einam nimchakim*, not to be erased) include *Adonai* (my Master); *El*, *Elohim* (all forms of these words); *Eheyeh* (if the intention is as a Name of Hashem); and *Shaddai*, *Tzeva'os*, and *Yah*.[6]

3. Category #3: *Kinuim*

Hashem is referred to by other names that are really only descriptions of Him. These include *Rachum* (Merciful One), *Chanun* (Gracious One), *Shalom* and *Emes* (where the intention is to refer to Hashem),[7] and *Yud-Yud*.[8]

C. SPECIAL CONCENTRATION WHILE SAYING HASHEM'S NAMES

Ideally, one should give his fullest concentration and reflect on the meaning of Hashem's Name every time a Name is mentioned (see below, note 11). The *Yesod V'Shoresh Ha'avodah* explains that the entire creation receives sustenance from His holy Name and upon its proper recital, the Heavens shake, similar to when one shakes the trunk of a tree and causes the leaves to rustle.

Each of the Names of Hashem denotes a different aspect of His Divine power:

- The *Shem Havayah* represents the quintessential being of Hashem and His timelessness (as it is a combination of *hayah hoveh v'yihiyeh* [He was, He is, He will be forever]).
- The Name *Adonai* refers to Hashem as the Master and Owner of all creation,[9] Who has everything under His sovereignty.

Note: Since the *Shem Havayah* is pronounced as "*Adonai*," one should reflect on both of the above meanings while saying it. However, more attention should be given to the pronounced form ("*Adonai*") than to the way it is written.[10]

---

6   *Shulchan Aruch OC 215, Mishnah Berurah ad loc. 19; Piskei Teshuvos 215:12.*
7   *Piskei Teshuvos 215:12; see also 154:18.*
8   See *Shulchan Aruch YD 276:10, Rama ad loc.*
9   *Shulchan Aruch OC 5.*
10   *Shulchan Aruch OC 5, Mishnah Berurah ad loc.* 3 cites the opinion of the *Gra* that one should

- The Names *Elohim* and *Eloheinu* signify that Hashem is all-powerful (*El*), omnipotent, and the source of all forces.[11]

D. PRONOUNCING

1. Category #1: The *Shem Havayah*

As mentioned above, we usually pronounce the Tetragrammaton as "*Ad-onai*." It is not only forbidden to pronounce this Name,[12] but even to say the letters consecutively: "*Yud-hei-vav...*"[13] One must say, "*Yud-kei-vav-kei*," or "Letter *yud*, letter *hei*, letter *vav*, letter *hei*." Neither is one permitted to enunciate even the first two letters (one should say, "*yud-kei*").[14]

One should not write this word, except for holy purposes, e.g., writing a *Sefer Torah* or tefillin.

There are different opinions whether one is permitted to say or write "Je-hovah" in English, as this is not the correct transliteration of the *Shem Havayah*.[15]

2. Category #2: Other Names of Hashem

It is generally forbidden to pronounce these Names in the normal way unless one is in the process of praising Hashem for a holy purpose (see

---

mainly concentrate on the pronounced Name (except during *k'rias Shema*, when one should concentrate on both).

11   Ideally one should try to have the special *kavanos* for all the different Names every time a Name is mentioned. However, due to the difficulty of fulfilling this requirement, some authorities suggest that one make a condition at the start of the day that all the proper "intentions" should go into effect when saying the Name (this declaration appears at the beginning of some siddurim). Others say that one of the purposes of saying *Adon Olam* at the beginning of *Shacharis* should be to indicate that all the Names said during the day should have the intention of the prayer of *Adon Olam*.

12   *Sanhedrin* 90a.

13   *Chayei Adam* 5:27. One who pronounces the Ineffable Name will lose his portion to the World to Come (*Sanhedrin* 90a). See *Tosafos, Sukkah* 5a, s.v. *Yud*. See *Maharsha* there.

14   *Chayei Adam* 5:27.

15   On the one hand, it seems to be a different pronunciation, therefore it should have no *kedu-shah* (heard from Rav Tzvi Rosen). However, other *poskim* mention that even if it is not the actual name it may be considered a *kinui* and thus should not be recited or written (heard from Rav Kornfein).

further for examples). Otherwise one should use a different letter so as not to pronounce the full word, e.g., Elokim, Tzevakos, Shakai, etc.

Holy purposes include:

- **Special *tefillos***: One may pronounce the Names while reciting private supplications or thanks.[16]
- **Teaching *berachos***: It is permitted to pronounce the Names while teaching children (or adults when necessary)[17] *berachos*, or when assisting an adult in reciting a *berachah*.[18] When teaching a boy for his bar mitzvah, one may recite the *berachah* in its full form (i.e., without changing Hashem's Name).[19]
- **Studying Gemara and Tanach**: Some opinions permit one to use the proper Names when reading (even parts of) *pesukim*.[20] The more accepted opinion today is that one should never use the actual Names of Hashem.[21]
- ***Derashos***: Ashkenazic rabbis avoid using the Name in *derashos*, while many Sephardic rabbis do recite it.[22]

---

16 See the discussion in *Piskei Teshuvos* 215, note 106. See *Taz OC* 131:10, that one should never say non-standard *tefillos* with the *nusach* "Baruch atah Hashem," but see *Chavas Daas YD* 110, who permits it since it is not a formal *berachah*, but only as a special *tefillah*.

17 *Iggros Moshe OC* 2:56.

18 *Shulchan Aruch OC* 215, *Mishnah Berurah* ad loc. 14; *Piskei Teshuvos* 215:9; but don't answer *Amen* unless it's a real *berachah*. However, *Eishel Avraham* points out that whenever possible it is better to hintw to the child.

19 This is in order to avoid needless public embarrassment to the bar mitzvah if he were to recite the Name incorrectly; *Piskei Halachah* (English), p. 52.

20 *Shulchan Aruch OC* 215, *Mishnah Berurah* ad loc. 14; *Sh'eilas Yaavetz*, no. 81; *Piskei Teshuvos* 215:10; *Yabia Omer* 3:14; *Yechaveh Daas* 3:13; *Shut Tzitz Eliezer* 13:1. It is not proper respect to Hashem when reciting *pesukim*. See *Maharsha, Sanhedrin* 104b for further discussion.

21 *Aruch Hashulchan* 215:2; *Piskei Teshuvos* 215, note 57. See *Igros Moshe OC* 2:56, who points out that if a complete verse is quoted, it is preferable to pronounce the Name; otherwise it is forbidden to recite partial *pesukim*. This may be the reason that teachers refrain from using the Name—because they may stop in the middle many times. See *Piskei Halachah* (Hebrew), p. 21, note 50a, for fuller discussion. See p. 22, note 52, and notes at the end of the *sefer*.

22 *Piskei Teshuvos* 215, note 58.

- *Zemiros* **on Shabbos and Yom Tov**: While many people avoid using the Name in *zemiros*, those who use it should be careful not to repeat it when it does not add any additional praise of Hashem.[23]
- **Greetings**: While there is a halachic basis in responding to a greeting with the expression "*todah la'El,*" if it is done with the intention of praising Hashem, other opinions suggest one should avoid saying it.[24]
- **Swearing**: One should try to avoid any swearing (especially in the Name of G-d). It is a terrible sin to swear in vain.[25]

E. WRITING THE NAMES

The Names should not be written on various objects. Tablecloths, jewelry, rings, or mezuzos that have a Name of Hashem written on them must be treated with holiness and utmost respect.[26] One must not bring such objects into places that are not clean, e.g., the bathroom (without the proper covering, see below).[27]

1. Categories #1 and #2 (*Shem Havayah* and Other Names of Hashem)

It is forbidden to erase these Names. They must be disposed of only by putting them into *genizah*. One should place unnecessary copies or extras of printed matter with these Names into *genizah*.[28] On a chalkboard or a whiteboard, the Name must be put into *genizah*, but on a computer it may be erased.[29]

---

23   See *Piskei Teshuvos* 215, note 110; *Maharsham, Daas Torah* 21:5; *Avnei Yashfe* 3:23; *Halichos Shlomo* 22, note 29, who permit the use of Hashem in *zemiros*.

24   *Mishnah Berurah* 215:19 permits one saying it *derech shevach* (in praise of Hashem). See *Halichos Shlomo* 22:9, who finds merit in people saying "*todah la'El*" or "thank G-d" even if it lacks the sincerity, so long as the Name of Hashem is on their tongues. However, it is better to say "*baruch Hashem.*" See *Piskei Teshuvos* 215, note 107.

25   *Shulchan Aruch YD* 237:1 (even without the Name of G-d). See also *Kitzur Shulchan Aruch* 181:17; *She'arim Metzuyanim B'Halachah* 181:19 for more sources

26   *Poskim* allow it to be written on a *paroches* or a *Sefer Torah*, but one should avoid writing it on the walls of a shul (*Ginzei Hakodesh* 7:17, 26).

27   *She'arim Metzuyanim B'Halachah* 28:10.

28   *Piskei Teshuvos* 154:16, note 105; *She'arim Metzuyanim B'Halachah* 28:11; *YD* 376:9.

29   *Ginzei Hakodesh* 7:22.

2. Category #3: *Kinuim*

Descriptions, including *Rachum, Chanun, Emes,* and *Shalom*[30] (where the intention is to refer to Hashem[31]), *yud-yud*,[32] and the letter *hei*[33] must be given the proper respect. However, if they were written out, one may erase them.[34] But they should not be thrown directly into the garbage or be brought into undignified places (see below).

F. RECORDING AND ERASING ON ELECTRONIC DEVICES

The following halachos apply to treating the Names of Hashem with modern-day devices, such as tapes, disks, MP3s, smartphones, computers, laptops, slides, etc.

1. Recordings

Listening to a cassette, CD, MP3, or videotape that has the *Shem Hashem* pronounced on it is permitted if it is for a meaningful purpose, e.g., to teach a child for his bar mitzvah or when reliving memories of a *simchah* (e.g., wedding, bar mitzvah).[35]

---

30   *Shulchan Aruch YD* 276:13, *Rama.* Some are particular not to write it out fully. However, see *Shach* 16. See *Shulchan Aruch OC* 84, *Mishnah Berurah* ad loc. 6. Some write "Shalom" without the *vav;* see *Mishnah Berurah* (*Dirshu*) 6. Many are lenient today because they usually don't associate the word with Hashem. See *Igros Moshe OC* 4:40.

31   *Piskei Teshuvos* 215:12; see also ibid., 154:18.

32   See *Shulchan Aruch YD* 276:10, *Rama.*

33   See *Igros Moshe YD* 2:138, which says that the letter *hei* is taken from Hashem's Name, in contrast to *dalet*, which is an arbitrary letter.

34   See *Shulchan Aruch OC* 85:2, *Mishnah Berurah* ad loc. 10; *Ginzei Hakodesh* 7:19. See full discussion in notes 16–19. See *Igros Moshe OC* 4:39 for a discussion on recycling.

35   See *Ginzei Hakodesh*, p. 94. Rav Yaakov Kamenetsky would permit only for *talmud Torah*, but Rav Mordechai Karp points out that the *minhag* is to be lenient. See *Piskei Teshuvos* 154:19, note 127. *Igros Moshe YD* 2:173; see *Tzitz Eliezer* 13:1. Among the reasons for the leniency is that the *issur* does not apply to voices that are a product of electronics. Writing and erasing under these circumstances is halachically considered *grama* (an indirect act) and is permitted (all electrical devices are *derech grama* [Rav Yisroel Ber Kaplan]). See *She'arim Metzuyanim B'Halachah* 6:1 for a full discussion.

2. Erasing a Tape or Disc

The *poskim* permit erasing the Names from a tape, but various *poskim* suggest that it be done only when very necessary or by a non-Jew or a minor.[36]

G. WAYS TO AVOID WRITING THE NAMES OF HASHEM

Many *poskim* say that if the Names of Hashem are written with dashes between the letters of the words (e.g., E-l[37]) or with other letters replacing them (e.g., *Elokim*[38]) they do not require *genizah*. However, they recommend that they be thrown out respectfully and not directly into the garbage.[39]

Writing words or names that have the letters of Hashem's Names (e.g., Eliyahu, Yehudah, Shmuel) is totally permitted and there is no holiness to these words.[40] Yet, there are very devout Jews who will not write such words in their entirety.[41] (This is also the basis for the custom of printers that write *tes-vav* or *tes-zayin* instead of *yud-hei* or *yud-vav*.)

In order to avoid using the proper Names of G-d, we usually substitute the word "Hashem" (which literally means "the Name"), which clearly denotes that the speaker is referring to the Name of G-d. One should not use the word "*Adoshem*," which is meaningless and disrespectful.[42]

---

36   *Igros Moshe YD* 1:173; *Piskei Teshuvos* 154:19, notes 127 and 129; see *Ginzei Hakodesh* 7:22, note 1.

37   *Ginzei Hakodesh* 7:14.

38   *Ginzei Hakodesh* 7:6; *Igros Moshe OC* 4:40; *Igros Moshe YD* 2:135; *Aruch Hashulchan YD* 176:24.

39   *Ginzei Hakodesh*, p. 7, note 28; ibid., p. 11. See *Piskei Teshuvos* 154:18, note 120. Rav Yosef Shalom Elyashiv, Rav Chaim Ozer Grodzinski (*Achiezer*), and Rav Shlomo Zalman Auerbach are quoted as being lenient. See *Avnei Nezer YD* 365, who is *machmir*.

40   *Shulchan Aruch YD* 276:13; *Shulchan Aruch OC* 84, *Mishnah Berurah* (*Dirshu*) note 5; *Ginzei Hakodesh* 7:28.

41   See *Halichos Shlomo* 22:34, which says that he personally would not complete the word but would tell others that it is totally permitted.

42   *Taz OC* 621:2; *Piskei Halachah* (English), p. 49, note 62, says it seems strange that no objection has been raised to saying *Elokim*.

H. DESCRIPTIONS IN OTHER LANGUAGES

According to many authorities, many of these rules apply when the word "G-d" is written out even in English or any foreign language.[43] While on the one hand it does not have *kedushah* (sanctity) and it is permitted to erase it, one should not treat it with disrespect.

One should not write or say the Name (e.g., "Thank G-d," "Oh my G-d") unless there is an implied praise of Hashem. Therefore, it may be better to say, "Oh my gosh."

The word "G-d" should not be recited in the bathroom or any undignified place.

It's always a good idea to write "G-d" (with a dash) so it should not come to a disrespectful state.

The *poskim* point out that there is a general leniency concerning materials that have the word "G-d" on or in them,[44] e.g., dollar bills,[45] newspapers, and non-Jewish books.

If one finds a non-Jewish Bible or New Testament (including the Tanach) in a place outside their home (e.g., in a hotel), while some opinions suggest that it be burned (i.e., by putting in a bag and then into the garbage),[46] others suggest that one may just leave it alone.[47] Some *poskim* suggest that if one can separate the various parts, he should put the Tanach part into *genizah*.[48]

---

43 *Shulchan Aruch YD* 276:11; *Shach YD* 179:11; *Shulchan Aruch OC* 85, *Mishnah Berurah* ad loc. 10; *Achiezer* 3:32; *Igros Moshe OC* 2:55; *Ginzei Hakodesh* 7:12, note 24.

44 This is based on a number of factors, which include: (a) it was not written to be preserved, (b) it was not written by Jew, and (c) it was not written for a holy purpose.

45 Most *poskim* allow one to bring dollar bills into the bathroom, but Rav Chaim Kanievsky does not.

46 *Piskei Teshuvos* 154:17, s.v. *Sefer Torah she'kasvu min yisaref*. It is a *bizayon* that it will remain next to such *tumah*.

47 *Emes L'Yaakov* 8:4, note 16; see *Maharam Shik* that this halachah may not apply to printed *sefarim* indirectly (*ko'ach kocho*). Also, printers don't even know what is written in it.

48 *Piskei Teshuvos* 154:17; *Igros Moshe YD* 2:137; *Avnei Yashfe* 1:104.

I. ABBREVIATED NAMES[49]

The following shortened Names should be treated with special respect:

- *Yud-yud* (the combination of two Names of Hashem, the first letter of the *Shem Havayah* [*yud-hei-vav-hei*] and last letter of "*Adonai*"). One may erase this Name only in cases of great necessity.[50] It should only be written in conjunction with holy matters. While this Name does not require *genizah*, one should be careful to discard it in a respectful way (e.g., put it in a bag and then into the garbage).

- The letter *hei* on its own,[51] such as in ב"ה, ברוך ה', בעז"ה, בעזרת ה', אי"ה, אם ירצה ה', and the like (written in English as well). While many *poskim* are lenient in allowing these words to be thrown out, some *poskim* recommend that they be discarded respectfully.

- The following abbreviated names have no *kedushah* and may be discarded in any way: ד', בס"ד, בעזהי"ת, הקב"ה. (Therefore, various *poskim* recommend that those who put a salutation at the beginning of their letter to use בס"ד or בעזהי"ת instead of ב"ה.[52])

J. COMMON ERRORS

If one accidentally said "*Adonai*," he should add the words of a *pasuk* that starts with that word, such as, "*Adonai yimloch l'olam va'ed.*"[53]

If one started saying a *berachah* and realized he should not have said it:

- After saying the word "*Adonai*," he should continue with the words "*lamdeini chukecha*—teach me Your statutes."[54]

- After saying the word "*Elohei*," he should continue with the *pasuk*: "*Elohei Yisrael avinu mei'olam v'ad olam*—the G-d of Israel,

---

49 *Ginzei Hakodesh* 7:5.

50 *Shulchan Aruch YD* 276, *Rama* ad loc. 10; *Shach* 14; *Biur HaGra* 24; *Aruch Hashulchan* 154:28. See *Ginzei Hakodesh*, p. 90, note 22; *Piskei Teshuvos* 154:18, note 121.

51 *Ginzei Hakodesh* 7:6, note 13; *Igros Moshe OC* 4:40. See *Har Tzvi YD* 234; see *Piskei Teshuvos* 3:293.

52 *Piskei Teshuvos* 154, note 123; *Ginzei Hakodesh* 7, notes 7, 11. In ב"ה, the *hei* may refer directly to G-d, but here it is clearer that it instead refers to the word "Hashem" (literally, "the Name").

53 *Kaf Hachaim* 206:44.

54 *Tehillim* 119:12. This is considered as if one said a verse from *Tehillim*.

our Father, from everlasting to everlasting,"[55] and then say, "*Baruch shem kevod malchuso l'olam va'ed.*"

- While saying the word "*Eloheinu*" (or he said more words or has completed the *berachah*), he should say, "*Baruch shem kevod malchuso l'olam va'ed.*"[56]

1. Fixing *Berachos*

One who recited the wrong description in a *berachah* can fix the *berachah* by adding the proper description *toch k'dei dibbur* (within two to three seconds).[57]

For example, if one erroneously said the *berachah* of *Borei pri ha'eitz* instead of the *berachah* of *Borei pri ha'adamah*, in order to fulfill his obligation, he must add the word "*ha'adamah*" *toch k'dei dibbur*.

2. *Berachos* on Spoiled or Spilled Food

If one recites a *berachah* over a food and then finds that it is spoiled or has spilled, as long as there are either other foods that he had intention to eat, or other foods in front of him that require the same *berachah* (that he did not have the intention to exclude), the original *berachah* can still be used for the other foods.[58] If this is not the case, it is considered a *berachah l'vatalah* and he should recite, "*Baruch shem kevod malchuso l'olam va'ed.*"

---

55   *Divrei Hayamim I* 29:10. The *pasuk* starts with words "*Va'yevarech David.*" See *Kaf Hachaim* 206:44; *Kitzur Shulchan Aruch* 6:4; *Tzelach, Berachos* 39.

56   *Shulchan Aruch OC* 206:6. See *Chayei Adam* 5:1 that what the person said becomes one big praise and renders the pronouncement of Hashem's Name meaningful; it now serves as the subject to which the praise attaches itself. In addition, it demonstrates the desire of the person who uttered the *Shem l'vatalah* to treat Hashem's Name with honor and respect. See *Piskei Halachah* (English), p. 50, note 63. *Aruch Hashulchan* 206:16 points out that since he was disrespectful to the Name, he needs to newly perform *kabbalas ol malchus* (the reacceptance of Hashem's yoke), i.e., to compensate for the disrespectful use. *V'Zos Haberachah*, p. 184, points out that if one said "*Adonai Eloheinu,*" he should continue with the words from the *pasuk*: "*Adonai Eloheinu atah anisam*" (*Tehillim* 99:8). For further discussion, see *Rambam, Mishneh Torah, Shevuos* 12:11; *Piskei Teshuvos* 206:24, note 107; *Shaarei Berachah* 10:14, note 37. There are opinions that saying "*Baruch shem...*" helps even if it is not said immediately after the end of the *berachah*.

57   *Shulchan Aruch OC* 209:2, *Mishnah Berurah* ad loc. 5.

58   *Shulchan Aruch OC* 206:6; *Biur Halachah*, s.v. *Rak*. See *V'Zos Haberachah*, pp. 11, 206, and 330; *Shaarei Berachah* 13:46.

For example, one recited a *berachah* on a cup of water, which then fell or was knocked over. He may use the *berachah* for other foods that require the same *berachah* (e.g., water from a water cooler, candies) if they were in **his presence** at the time he recited the *berachah*. However, he may not use the *berachah* for water that was in the fridge or from the faucet or a water fountain, or for any other items that were not in his presence at the time of the *berachah*, unless he had **in mind** to drink the water from these places.

It is questionable whether one can transfer the *berachah* to another food on the table that requires a different *berachah*.[59] One should therefore immediately recite, "*Baruch shem kevod malchuso l'olam va'ed*" in such a case.

3. One Who Realized He Had Already Recited the *Berachah*

If one recited a *berachah* and then realized that he'd already made a *berachah* on that food, he must recite, "*Baruch shem kevod malchuso l'olam va'ed*."[60] He cannot transfer the *berachah* to other foods.

4. *Berachos* Recited by Mistake

For example:

- After reciting the *berachah*, he finds out that the food is not kosher,[61] or realizes it's a fast day:[62] He should not eat the food, but instead say, "*Baruch shem kevod malchuso l'olam va'ed*."

- He said the *berachah* on a dairy product after recently eating meat: While various opinions forbid tasting the dairy food and recommending one to say, "*Baruch shem kevod malchuso l'olam va'ed*,"[63] other opinions permit eating it (especially if one has

---

59   *V'Zos Haberachah* 206:14 seems that he cannot transfer, but see *Piskei Teshuvos* 109, note 9, based on *Chayei Adam* 5:14, for further discussion.

60   See *V'Zos Haberachah* 206:14 (the *berachah* must relate to a particular food).

61   *Shulchan Aruch OC* 196:1, *Mishnah Berurah* ad loc. 3–4.

62   *She'arim Metzuyanim B'Halachah* 6:3; *Shaarei Berachah* 13:20; *V'Zos Haberachah* 206b. See *Piskei Halachah* (Hebrew), p. 27, for further discussion; see *Yabia Omer YD* 5, who permits eating a small amount. See *Shulchan Aruch OC*, 567:1, *Rama*; *Biur HaGra* 550:4, for a discussion on the character of a fast day.

63   See *V'Zos Haberachah*, p. 206a.

recited a *berachah acharonah* and at least one hour has passed since eating the meat).[64]

- He said the *berachah* before reciting Havdalah: One may eat a small amount of the food.[65]

- He recited a *berachah* over meat during the Nine Days following Rosh Chodesh Av: He should eat a small amount of the food.[66]

K. DOUBTS ABOUT *BERACHOS*

If one is in doubt whether he recited a *berachah*, the general rule in most cases is that "when in doubt, do without."[67] Note that in this case it is still appropriate to say a shortened form of a *berachah*, "*Baruch atah...*" without *Shem u'malchus*.[68] Alternatively, if there is someone who is making the same *berachah*, this person should be *motzi* him.

L. UNNECESSARY *BERACHOS*

It is forbidden to cause the recital of a *berachah* unnecessarily, i.e., a *berachah she'einah tzerichah*.[69] For example, one who is about to eat a meal with bread should recite the *berachah* with the intention to exempt the various foods to be eaten during the meal, and not recite additional *berachos* on individual foods.

---

64   See ibid.; *Yechaveh Daas* 4:41; *Shaarei Berachah* 13:20, note 52, for further discussion.

65   *Shulchan Aruch OC* 271:5, *Rama*; *Mishnah Berurah* 271:26. See *V'Zos Haberachah*, p. 206, and *Yechaveh Daas* 4:41, for a discussion concerning the difference between when the food itself is forbidden (forbidden food, milk and meat) in contrast where it is a timing issue, e.g., eating before Havdalah.

66   *Sdei Chemed* 5, p. 290; *She'arim Metzuyanim B'Halachah* 6:3; *Shaarei Berachah* 13:20; *V'Zos Haberachah*, p. 206.

67   *Shulchan Aruch OC* 215:20; *She'arim Metzuyanim B'Halachah* 21. The exception to this rule would be a man who is totally satiated after eating a bread meal and is unsure whether he recited *Birkas Hamazon*. In that case, he would need to repeat it, since these *berachos* are of Torah status; *Shulchan Aruch OC* 184:4. There is also a question concerning *Birkas HaTorah*. See the discussion in *Shulchan Aruch OC* 47, *Mishnah Berurah* ad loc. 1. Ideally, one should recite *Ahavah Rabbah* with the intention to fulfill the requirement and study some Torah after saying the *Shemoneh Esreh*; *Mishnah Berurah* 47:15.

68   *Minchas Yitzchak*, vol. 4, 12:9; *V'Zos Haberachah*, p. 185.

69   *Shulchan Aruch OC* 215, *Mishnah Berurah* ad loc. 18.

However, the following are a number of exceptions to this rule:

- Drinking wine during the meal[70]
- Eating foods that are not commonly eaten as part of a main meal, e.g., nuts, candies, chocolates, apple on Rosh Hashanah, etc.
- Eating **dessert** (according to some *poskim*)[71]

1. *Berachos* That Are Not Considered Unnecessary

In various cases, one may be allowed to recite additional *berachos* before *Ha'motzi*. For example:

- On Shabbos, some people have a custom to eat certain foods immediately after *kiddush* before *Ha'motzi*.[72]
- Following a fast, people often want to drink something before starting their proper meal.[73]

M. UNDIGNIFIED PLACES

The following matters are forbidden when one is in a bathroom or shower. However, in a dressing room or swimming pool, there are grounds to be lenient (as long as everyone there is dressed properly):[74]

- Saying any Names of Hashem, any words of Torah, or greeting a person with the word *Shalom* is forbidden.[75] Even thinking Torah thoughts should not be done.
- There are various opinions concerning what one may think about in these places. Some *poskim* are of the opinion that one may contemplate Hashem and His amazing acts of creation (*nifla'os haBorei*).[76] Others are of the opinion that one should only

---

70   *Shulchan Aruch OC* 174:1.

71   For a full discussion of this subject, see *Piskei Teshuvos* 177:3 and *V'Zos Haberachah*, pp. 71–78.

72   See *Halachos of Brochos*, p. 340, where he quotes the opinions of Rav Shlomo Zalman Auerbach, Rav Elyashiv, and *Aruch Hashulchan* 176.

73   See *Shulchan Aruch OC* 176, *Mishnah Berurah* ad loc. 2.

74   *Shulchan Aruch OC* 84, *Mishnah Berurah* ad loc. 3. See *Piskei Teshuvos* 84:2 and 3. Thinking about words of Torah and *paskening* a *sh'eilah* is also fine in these places.

75   *Shulchan Aruch OC* 85:2, *Mishnah Berurah* ad loc. 8, says that even thinking words of Torah is forbidden.

76   *Piskei Teshuvos* 85:3; *Shulchan Aruch OC* 85, *Mishnah Berurah (Dirshu)*, note 3, quotes *Nefesh*

think about more neutral things, such as one's business, house, expenses, history, news, and ethics.[77]

- Modern Hebrew may be spoken in these places.[78]
- Singing (humming) melodies in the shower without Torah words is permitted. Listening to songs with Torah words should be avoided.

Hachaim 4:27, who seems to indicate that one can think about his own *middos* anywhere: *"Hu rashai lelech b'zos ha'machshavah gam b'mkomos ha'metunafim."* See *Shulchan Aruch OC* 85, *Mishnah Berurah* ad loc. 5, that one may think about how "small" he is.

77   *Tzitz Eliezer* 13:1; *Halichos Shlomo* 20:23.

78   *Shulchan Aruch OC* 85, *Mishnah Berurah* ad loc. 9; *Shut Shelmas Chaim* 107; *Mishnah Berurah (Dirshu)* 85:2, note 6.

In honor of our dear son

Eli Elias

אליהו יצחק בן דוב בער אליאש נ"י

and

לעילוי נשמת

ר' **אליהו** בן אברהם שלמה אליאש ז"ל

ר' יעקב **יצחק** בן משה יחזקאל הארן ז"ל

ר' משה מניס בן יעקב יצחק הארן ז"ל

DEVORAH AND DOV ELIAS

In memory of his parents

Morris and Regina Neuman

DR. LARRY NEUMAN

In memory of

Dr. Irwin and Lola Resnick
Felix and Helen Graulich

MR. AND MRS. IRWIN GRAULICH

In memory of

Mordechai Zev
ben Masood and Tamar
Bitton

Their humble and pure love lit up the path of everyone
they touched. They loved their family and friends dearly
and brought joy and love to so many souls.

This sefer is dedicated in honor
of the many Jews looking
for the right path back home.

YESH FOUNDATION

MOSAICA PRESS
BOOK PUBLISHERS

Elegant, Meaningful & Bold

info@MosaicaPress.com
www.MosaicaPress.com

The Mosaica Press team of
acclaimed editors and designers
is attracting some of the most
compelling thinkers and teachers
in the Jewish community today.
Our books are available around
the world.

HARAV YAACOV HABER
RABBI DORON KORNBLUTH